Kalmia

Mountain Laurel and Related Species

Kalmia

Mountain Laurel and Related Species

Richard A. Jaynes

Timber Press
Portland, Oregon

ISBN 0-88192-367-2

Printed in Hong Kong

TIMBER PRESS, INC.
The Haseltine Building
133 S.W. Second Avenue, Suite 450
Portland, Oregon 97204, U.S.A.

Library of Congress Cataloging-in-Publication Data

Jaynes, Richard A., 1935-
    Kalmia: mountain laurel and related species/Richard A. Jaynes.
    –[3rd ed.]
    p.   cm.
    Includes biographical references (p.   ) and index.
    ISBN 0-88192-367-2
    1. Kalmia–North America. 2. Mountain laurel–North America.
    3. Botany–North America. I. Title
SB413.K3J38 1997
635.9'3362–dc20   96-18759
                                                                  CIP

To Bruce Briggs

Experimenter, Leader, Nurseryman, Plantsman,
Visionary

Contents

Color plates follow page 128

Preface

This book reflects the passion I have had for most of my adult life to learn about, acquire, grow, and breed new *Kalmia*. As I look back on 35 years of involvement with the genus, it is clear that significant progress has been made in elevating these plants, especially mountain laurel, *Kalmia latifolia*, from primarily a roadside and woodland attraction to a major feature in our gardens that is available in assorted forms and colors. In part, then, this book is an account of the domestication of mountain laurel in the sense of "taming" the wild plant and making use of it in our domestic surroundings. It has been my fortunate circumstance to be at the center of much of this work and, indeed, even to have been paid by the state of Connecticut for some of it while working for more than 25 years as a plant breeder at the Connecticut Agricultural Experiment Station in New Haven. The progress made represents the efforts of many people; certainly my own work has benefited from the cooperation and good will of too many others to enumerate without running the risk of leaving several out. Sadly, some are no longer with us and others have scattered far and wide. Many of these people are mentioned in the text, but all deserve my heartfelt thanks. Often they have been my source of inspiration and know-how and many times the physical hands to do the job.

From summertime employment to full-time breeder and horticulturist at the Connecticut Agricultural Station, I was involved with chestnut (*Castanea*) research for over 30 years. It was enjoyable, but at times oh, so frustrating, because the actual development of a disease-resistant, timber-quality chestnut tree was always years away. With the kalmias I have had the opportunity to be involved with many areas of research and development and then actually see practical results follow. To learn how to make crosses, to follow through a series of four or five generations of plants, to select and name a cultivar—and then to see it become accepted and distributed in nurseries and garden centers—has been very satisfying. The one area of disappointment to me is the scarcity of people involved in growing, breeding, and selecting new *Kalmia* cultivars. To this end I have listed in the appendix areas in which further research and development is needed, some of which could certainly be pursued by amateurs. It is notable that most of the progress in developing current *Kalmia* selections has come not from high technology and sophisticated scientific know-how, but from basic horticultural information and breeding principles spelled out by Gregor Mendel over 100 years ago.

Some readers may find sections of the book a bit technical. To you, I apologize; do not hesitate to skim the more complicated sections and come back to them later. For more information on botany, propagation, and horticulture, seek out one or more of the current college texts at a local library or book store. My intended audience includes amateurs, horticulturists, nursery people, growers, teachers, and scientists. Inherent in this approach is the danger of being too technical for some, too basic for others and, of course, occasionally just too obtuse for anyone.

This is the third edition of my book on *Kalmia*, and I thank Timber Press for the opportunity to finally do it right! Why a third rewrite? The second edition went out of print, and there was really too much new information to just revise bits and pieces of it. Of course, the native species and the principles and practices of breeding have not changed much. The number of cultivars has increased dramatically, however, and substantially more information is available on virtually all the cultivars. Commercial propagation and container growing have moved from promising ventures to reality, and growth-promoting substances allow growers to produce buds on younger and smaller plants. New techniques of producing plants with extra sets of chromosomes (polyploids) will likely result in improved cultivars and new opportunities in breeding kalmias. Also, substantial changes in controlling weeds, pests, and diseases as well as more information on landscaping and growing the plants have been incorporated in this revision. A simple note, such as the recommendation to incorporate coarse organic material in the soil on marginal *Kalmia* sites, could be invaluable information for those who have struggled to grow these plants. Other newly treated subjects include burls, which are characteristic, notable structures of *Kalmia latifolia*, except on those plants produced in tissue culture; and allelopathy of sheep laurel (*K. angustifolia*)—this species has been found to be a major impediment to natural regeneration of conifers across large areas of North America. So, to discuss these topics and to update many others, we have a new book.

There is no *Kalmia* society, but many kindred spirits will be found in the American Rhododendron Society (P. O. Box 1380, Gloucester, Virginia 23061, U.S.A.). It is my wish that more of these members can be convinced to direct some of their efforts to *Kalmia*. Here is a whole society devoted to companion plants for *Kalmia*! I have even had a few members tell me that if they had to choose which plants to keep in their garden, the mountain laurel would stay.

Kalmia never has been, nor ever will be an easy plant to work with ("no pain, no gain"), yet the native plants are prevalent and vigorous over a broad range in North America. And, of course, the genus includes one of the most beautiful evergreen flowering shrubs that grows in temperate climates. These plants indeed deserve our continued attention.

This book should encourage others to pursue further improvements in the hybridizing, selection, propagation, and culture of mountain laurel as well as the other laurel species. Much is yet to be learned about the inheritance of specific traits, better means to successfully complete crosses between species, and down the road, even the introduction of genetic material from related organisms. One step at a time, a red flower here and a tolerance to heavy soil there, will lead to ever-better cultivars—perhaps to some not yet imagined.

Part I
Characteristics and Culture of Laurel Species and Cultivars

CHAPTER 1

In Pursuit of the Perfect Laurel

In the beginning of June,… then the flowers of the laurel may be found, rivalling in their delicacy of color and perfect symmetry of form any of the more showy blossoms of cultivation. It seems as if the climax of all that is dainty and lovely had been reached in this beautiful American wild flower. (Britton 1913)

Mountain laurel—flowering, evergreen, and hardy—has been looked on by some to be the perfect shrub. The late Donald Jones, famous for his part in developing hybrid corn (*Zea mays*) and making it a major world crop, once said to a colleague, "Wouldn't you like to have been the geneticist who developed laurel?" Of course it already existed, but as an attentive graduate student of Jones's at the time, I was inspired by his comment to set off thinking about what might be accomplished by hybridizing *Kalmia*. I later found that, for all its merits, mountain laurel (*Kalmia latifolia*) is neither uniform nor perfect. Indeed, all the kalmias exhibit wide variation and thus offer excellent opportunity for selection and manipulation, although the most important garden plant in the genus is *Kalmia latifolia*. Virtually all the fancy garden plants in this genus selected for flower color, foliage type, and plant growth habit have come from this one species rather than from hybridizing several species, as has been done with *Rhododendron*. The other kalmias are attractive, variable, and have a place in the garden, but they are smaller in stature and, at least to date, have not received the same intensity of selection and breeding as mountain laurel.

Some dramatic selections of mountain laurel have been around for years, but there is still considerable ignorance about these plants. For me, of course, part of the fun has been searching out the unusual and obscure plants, bringing them together, hybridizing, selecting, and then publicizing the merits of these fascinating plants.

With rare exceptions, the named cultivars (cultivated varieties) started out as seedlings, whether they were found in the wild, in a nursery, or among the offspring grown from a controlled cross-pollination. If we only know one parent (the seed parent), the selection process is not nearly as efficient as when we know both the seed and the pollen parent. However, if we choose the right parent plants and know something about the inheritance of particular traits, then we can begin to plan and predict the development of new attractive cultivars. This will be explained in more detail in Chapters 13–16.

My search for better laurel has been filled with its own adventures and rewards. To sample the natural variations of *Kalmia*, I canvassed botanical gardens, nursery people, and home gardeners, inquiring about unusual and distinctive kinds. Slowly I began to accumulate selections and information on the limits of variation.

One of my first memorable encounters was with a man in Connecticut who managed a whole mountainside of native mountain laurel that was open to the public during the nearby town's annual June festival. I asked him if he had ever noticed any plants with unusual flowers or foliage. Of course he had, but he solemnly assured me that, in spite of these variations, all mountain laurel was really the same. Any differences, he said, were due to varying amounts of minerals, such as copper and iron, in the soil. Fortunately, for me, his interesting theory turned out to be false.

The assumption that mountain laurel had quite immutable characteristics was not unique to the Connecticut country squire. I still have a 1961 letter from a then-reputable state botanist known for his work on the native flora stating that "in my experience *Kalmia latifolia* is one of the least variable shrubs. If I have ever seen any variations in flower color, etc., they did not attract my attention." Even the professionals sometimes overlook the obvious.

Having worked with woody plants before, I anticipated the need for patience in propagating and breeding the plants. But I did not anticipate that, in several cases, the real test would be in obtaining the material in the first place. Some people, perhaps with good reason, are very reluctant to share an unusual plant. For example, after learning of a unique mountain laurel clone in 1963 I wrote to sources asking for a few cuttings to use for grafting. The ensuing correspondence makes quite a file. It was not until I had exchanged numerous letters about the plant with three different persons—over a decade!—that cuttings were finally obtained. Most amazing, I was dealing with a "public" garden. Happily, such stories are the exception, not the rule.

The quest for live, native plants of the miniature and willow-leaved mountain laurel (forms *myrtifolia* and *angustata*, respectively) has been, without doubt, the longest saga. In May 1962 the late Professor J. T. Baldwin, Jr., of William and Mary College in Virginia, wrote to me that a Henry M. Wright, in Highlands, North Carolina, had collected some interesting native plants, including at least one unusual *Kalmia* variant. He added that there was no point in writing to Mr. Wright, for he would not reply. Indeed, even if I visited he might not be willing to show me the plants.

Sure enough, Wright did not reply to letters. I thought it might just be the inertia of a good southerner not anxious to respond to a "damned Yankee." I considered sending a copy of my birth certificate which places my origins on the bayous of the Mississippi River in Louisiana, but only later did I learn that Mr. Wright was a carpenter of New England origins. Like a true New Englander, he enjoyed his privacy.

Over the years, I would almost forget about the reclusive Mr. Wright, and then a reference to him and his plants would turn up yet again. In 1969 Professor Fay Hyland at North Carolina State University, Raleigh, described in a letter two unusual mountain laurel plants that Mr. Wright had collected in the wild. Indeed, someone from the University had even obtained live material, but like a true botanist, he or she had pressed the cuttings between paper, dried them, and then put them in the herbarium collection. In the early 1970s horticulturist and graduate student Russell Southall, also at Raleigh, did taxonomic research on *Kalmia* and he did his best to get live material from Wright, but to no avail.

In 1976 Clarence Towe, an accomplished plantsman of Walhalla, South Carolina, read of my difficulties in obtaining these two unusual mountain laurel forms growing in the southern Appalachian mountains, and he jumped on the trail. He contacted Mr. Wright's niece and inveigled an invitation to Wright's garden through her. Clarence made several visits, and by 1979, through his efforts, I finally had cuttings of the miniature and willow-leaved plants that Henry Wright had collected in the wild perhaps 50 years earlier. (Clarence's description of the late Mr. Wright and his garden of unusual native plants was well documented in an article that appeared in the *Journal, American Rhododendron Society* (Towe 1985).)

I had the opportunity to visit Henry Wright's old homestead with Clarence in the summer of 1994 and was disappointed. It was one of those cases in which my mouth watered in anticipation of seeing the garden, and my eyes watered when I actually saw it. The overstory trees had become so large and dense that the resulting shade caused the decline and death of many understory *Kalmia* and other shrubs.

Failure to obtain a plant is not the only frustration facing the plant breeder—sometimes the people cooperate but the plants do not. Ralph Smith found in New York a sectored mountain laurel with green and white leaves, but the first few scions he sent me failed to take upon grafting. Two years later, when I requested more material for another try, it was too late; the plant had died. This was a hard-learned lesson on the need to propagate immediately any unusual, potentially valuable plants to ensure their preservation.

A stable, attractive mountain laurel with variegated leaves has yet to be commercially propagated, but the plants are out there, scattered far and wide. Certainly anyone who has grown large numbers of seedlings has probably seen variegated seedlings or plants with a variegated branch. To date, however, such plants have been unstable or unattractive, prone to sunburn, or are too new to have proven merit. A further complication may arise in their propagation. As *Hosta* enthusiasts know, variegated plants often are unstable, especially when micropropagated—but more on that later.

Plain luck also plays its part in acquiring unusual plants. Robert Bird of the Bristol Nursery in Bristol, Connecticut, tells this amusing story about a fabulous laurel of theirs that had a broad band of burgundy pigment in the open flower. In the fall the Bristol Nursery did some landscaping for a woman in town. When the laurel plantings began to flower the following June, she called to complain that the flowers on one of the plants were abnormal. A nurseryman was sent to examine the plant. Within minutes of his arrival he obligingly replaced it with a "normal" one. The abnormal, broad-banded one, among the most attractive ever found up to that time, was displayed proudly for years in front of Bristol Mums, formerly Bristol Nursery. This 'Bristol' plant played an important role in my breeding work and is in the parentage of several cultivars, including 'Bullseye', 'Galaxy', 'Hearts Desire', 'Kaleidoscope', and 'Keepsake'.

In addition to seeking unusual laurels, I searched for representative seeds or seedlings of the different species from numerous locations within their native ranges. On one trip to Peaked Hill Pond, near Thornton, New Hampshire, I arrived late in the day and camped (in the loosest sense of the word) in nearby White Mountain National Forest. It was one of the worst nights I have ever spent: I had only a sleeping bag, no tent, and no netting, and the tiny "no-see-ums" (little biting flies) greeted me in swarms. To sleep with my head in the bag meant suffocation; to sleep with it out meant torture. So shortly after 3:00 AM I gave up and went for a walk in the moonlight. At dawn I drove to Thornton and started the 2.5-mile (4-kilometer) trek from the road into the laurel stand. By sunup I had reached the laurels and had collected a few small plants, seeds, flowers, and cuttings; by 7:30 I was back at the local restaurant for breakfast. The sun was well up by 9:00 when I got back to the laurels to take pictures. The setting was truly idyllic, with beaver pond, laurel in bloom, a sugar bush (*Acer saccharum*) nearby, wildflowers beneath the trees, and bird songs—well worth one night with the no-see-ums.

A few years later I learned to my disappointment that this northern strain of mountain laurel—which I assumed would be very hardy—was, in fact, very weak. Compared with every other source tested, it did poorly in both sun and shade. A likely explanation is that the laurel at Peaked Hill Pond is an isolated population and may have suffered from inbreeding depression.

To collect laurel specimens from along Connecticut state highways and on state lands I obtained a special permit from the state government. But because of the state law that forbids collecting laurel and the public stigma attached to it, I felt self-conscious digging up plants along the roads in full view of passersby. I stuck to it, though, and one summer I searched for the pinkest and the whitest laurels in the state. In response to my guilty feelings, my assistant had developed the ability to dig and load a 3-foot (1-meter) plant in less than one minute. As we approached a previously identified plant, he would hop out of the truck, shovel in hand, as we rolled to a stop. By the time I could turn the truck around, he would be waiting to bring the plant aboard. The only plants I remember not surviving this snatching technique were those that came out of deep shade and ones that were not pruned heavily on transplanting.

I hasten to point out that these methods were employed for just a few plants and only for one or two years in the early 1960s; it is not a technique condoned now. Indeed, rather than collecting whole plants, now we usually just take cuttings or pollen, or make crosses on the plants in the wild and collect the seeds later.

I encourage any and all who have the opportunity to search for unusual forms of laurel, whether in the wild, nursery, or garden. You will at once be amazed by all the subtle variations and, in time, discouraged by the difficulty in discovering one of outstanding horticultural merit. But it is through the eyes of many, one plant at a time, that superior new plants are discovered.

As a known laurel fanatic, I sometimes receive news of striking and remarkable plants as a total surprise. For example, in 1972 Henry Fuller of the American Rock Garden Society notified me that evidently there were some purple-flowered mountain laurel near Willimantic, Connecticut. Henry was skeptical, he said, because the report had come from an economics professor and not a biologist. I wrote to John Goodrich, a friend of the professor and who had first-hand knowledge of the laurel, fully expecting to find it was nothing more than a native stand of sheep laurel (*Kalmia angustifolia*). But to my surprise my letter was answered immediately, and John's response contained color transparencies of the unusual, banded flowers. On a visit to the native stand in June, I discovered at least 20 of the banded plants. The best was used in crosses, and the most heavily pigmented one was named 'Goodrich' as a tribute to the man who discovered it. By making crosses of these plants in the woods and taking pollen to use on plants in our test garden, we never had to disturb any of these plants in their natural setting, except for a few cuttings taken from the 'Goodrich' for propagation. Incidentally, we still have trouble describing the color of the band on banded flowers, using terms such as burgundy, cinnamon, purple, maroon, and so forth.

News of other laurels has come to me from even farther away. In 1975 I received a letter from Marjorie and Hollis Rogers of Greensboro, North Carolina. They had enclosed a photograph of a completely unknown mountain laurel. Here was a new flower type of the genus, found in the wild more than 700 miles (1100 km) away. Through the Rogers' wonderful cooperation, within weeks I had cuttings for grafts, pollen for crosses, and seeds for planting. The result was a newly named cultivar, 'Shooting Star', and the parent of other new cultivars with this flower form. It was very satisfying to be able to send a couple of these 'Shooting Star' hybrids to the Rogers 20 years later. In 1996 Marjorie and Hollis called to report that the original 'Shooting Star' was still thriving. Because the plant is unique and one of a kind, they claim it to be one of the rarest native plants in the world. To ensure that it not be molested they have disclosed its exact location to only four people.

Closer to home, Dan Cappel, a high school biology teacher from Wilton, Connecticut, discovered a plant that was still in bud on Independence Day, July 4, about two weeks later than normal mountain laurel. Further observation revealed that in most years the flowers remained in bud for a few weeks, as if trying to open, and then collapsed. The plant appears to be completely sterile, with no good pollen and no seed production. When such a unique plant is found, another similar one often turns up. Henry Wright collected one years ago, and in 1980 Clarence Towe "rediscovered" it in Henry's yard and sent me cuttings. Clarence's name for it—'Tightwad'—is appropriate, for the flowers just refuse to open up. More recently, information on at least four other plants similar to 'Tightwad' has come to light: one with deep pink buds came from Douglas MacLise of Guilford, Connecticut; a second was found by Denton Shriver in Sullivan County, New York; a third was found by Tom Dilatush, of Robbinsville, New Jersey, at Dolly Sods, Virginia; and a fourth by Jon Weirether, Orrtanna, Pennsylvania.

Other selections are out there in the wild to be discovered or developed. No one had found a good double-flowered (or hose-in-hose) mountain laurel, but Clarence Towe found a plant in which 25 percent of the flowers have a double corolla, with the anthers converted to petals. His plant could be the start of a new breeding line. "At the least, it tells us that double flowers are possible with *Kalmia*," or so I wrote in the previous edition of this book in 1988. Surprise! In 1992 I learned from Ian Donovan, an active member of the Massachusetts Rhododendron Society, that a nice double-flowered mountain laurel does exist—but where else than on the opposite side of the world from its native range, in a New Zealand garden. It has been given the name 'Madeline' and, barring disaster, will eventually be available to gardeners everywhere (see Chapter 3 for description and photo). These continuing discoveries of new laurel variants convince me that other significant mutations are still to be found, and as each distinct form is discovered, breeding possibilities increase.

Prior to 1975 it was difficult to predict how selections of mountain laurel would be propagated in the future. As a plant breeder, it concerned me that I might be producing museum pieces of limited value because of difficulties in propagation. Fortunately, propagation of mountain laurels in laboratories, through a process of vegetative reproduction commonly referred to as "tissue culture" or "micropropagation", has since come into its own (details in Chapter 5). So, for the first time ever, numerous commercial nurseries are committing themselves to growing named selections. The increasing market is in turn spurring the naming of more fancy selections.

Traditional means of propagation will not disappear, however. Some of the desirable *Kalmia* forms can and will be reproduced from seeds by controlling the pollen and the seed parent. And, of course, it is from seeds of selected parents that new generations of even better cultivars will come about. Some of the easy-to-root selections will be propagated by cuttings. Grafting, though requiring much labor, will fill the need for immediate multiplication of one-of-a-kind plants and where only small numbers of plants are required.

The following is an example comparing the traditional method of rooting stem cuttings with the newer and advantageous method of tissue culture propagation of mountain laurel. In June 1965 I selected a pink-flowered plant from a commercial nursery to use in crosses. By 1971 I had learned and demonstrated that cuttings of this plant rooted well, and limited quantities of cuttings were made available to Connecticut nurseries. By 1974 two nurseries were impressed enough with their success in growing this plant that it was named 'Pink Surprise'. It was not until five years later, however, that one of the nurseries had enough material of sufficient size to begin selling plants. (The other nursery never did get into commercial production.) So, 14 years after a flowering plant was selected, one nursery was in production on only a limited scale.

On the other side of the coin, however, in the spring of 1981 I mailed three to four cuttings each of four unnamed, promising selections to Knight Hollow Nursery. By fall the selections had been isolated in culture, and shoots were beginning to be produced. I had to decide if they could be distributed and, if so, if they were to be released under numbers or names. (Test numbers are often used to identify crosses or accessions before they are named, as is indicated for several of the selections referred to in Chapter 3.) With some concern because of minimal testing, they were named 'Carousel', 'Elf', 'Freckles', and 'Sarah'. Thousands of small plants of these new cultivars were sold commercially within two years of putting them in tissue culture, and all four cultivars are still in commercial production.

This ability to get a new plant into the marketplace seven times more quickly than before is exciting and is a boon to plant breeding, selection, and release. Although there are some problems and limitations with tissue culture, as is discussed in Chapter 5, new technologies are seldom applied without some setbacks along the way. Because of the successes of tissue culture production, the prime problem for the grower is no longer how to get plants of a fancy cultivar started, but how best to grow a good-looking plant fast and economically. Progress continues, and though nobody said it would be easy, growers are succeeding.

Indeed, they are succeeding better than I ever imagined. Who would have thought in 1961, when I began studying *Kalmia*, that we would now have numerous nurseries, each producing thousands of container-grown, named selections of mountain laurel. I, and those administrators at the Connecticut Agricultural Experiment Station who supported the *Kalmia* research, certainly hoped that it would become an important crop. How wonderful it is to see it happening. No one person, institution, or event caused it to take place. A lot of pieces have fallen—well maybe been nudged or even pushed—together. Those responsible, like Richard Bir, Bruce Briggs, John Eichelser, Ludwig Hoffman, Edmund Mezitt, and Clarence Towe, are people who liked the plant and thought that more could and should be done with it. Every nursery grower of *Kalmia* hopes to make a profit, but we all find that growing mountain laurel well commercially takes a personal commitment that goes beyond simple time and money.

Sometimes plant growers do not get paid with money for their plants. Bartering, an age-old concept, took on new meaning for my wife, Sarah, and me years ago. Gene Kline, a vocational high school teacher, supreme cabinet maker, landscaper, and native plant specialist from Georgia, was keen on obtaining some of the new laurel hybrids. In the 1960s he and Alabama nurseryman Tom Dodd, Jr., went plant exploring in the southeastern United States and were instrumental in getting plant material of southern laurel species to me. I reciprocated with a few plants, and then Sarah and I had occasion to visit Gene and his wife. Well, Sarah could not stop raving over Gene's hand-crafted walnut and cherry furniture—especially his grandfather clocks. Lo and behold, a year or so later I got a call from Gene asking if Sarah was still interested in a clock. Gene is soft spoken and has a southern accent; embarrassingly, I had to ask him to repeat himself two or three times before I understood what he was getting at. Well, he was coming up to New England and was suggesting that he could bring the cherry clock that Sarah had admired in exchange for some laurel and other plants I was growing. Now I may have been slow on the pickup, but a good deal was quickly recognized. Although it was 25 years ago, I can remember each of us trying to make sure that the other was satisfied with the exchange. He concluded that he could easily construct another clock cabinet, an unlikely prospect for me, but I could certainly grow more plants.

Every plant breeder worries about the one or ones that might get away—hybrid seedlings culled, given, or sold that turn out to be superior plants. The breeder is a bit like a poker player; one knows what is in one's hand but can only guess at what is in the deck. To see some new cards (plants), one may have to discard what one has to make room for the new. The following is an account of one that got away, was rescued, and then came back to join a look-alike sister plant.

In the early fall of 1990 Joan Yogg, from Wellesley, Massachusetts, stopped by to talk about obtaining a select group of laurel plants for a woodland garden exhibit that the Wellesley Garden Club was entering in the Boston Flower Show in March. We picked out several named cultivars, and she asked that five "normal" light pink laurels also be included. She came to pick them up later in the fall and, along with lots of other plants, transported them to a nurseryman in New Hampshire who had experience in forcing plants for flower shows. His timing was superb, as were the efforts of the garden club members, for they won three awards for their woodland garden featuring laurels. One of the awards was the Ames Award for the most outstanding plant in the show. Joan called and asked the identity of this special plant, which she could not match with any of the named cultivars. I had no idea myself. Then I remembered I had included at least one offspring from a controlled cross where both parents had interesting markings in the flower, but these special "normal" plants had not flowered previously. I scheduled a quick trip to the flower show. The mystery plant was obviously one of these hybrid seedlings, which had been forced to perfection, and it caught the attention of the judges. They noted especially the markings like "peppermint candy" within the flower. Coincidentally, eight months earlier we had selected a flowering plant from the same cross, started to propagate it in tissue culture, and had even tentatively applied the name 'Peppermint'. We were planning to grow the propagated offspring for a few years before introducing it, but the judges and the Wellesley Garden Club inadvertently hurried us along. The members graciously returned the award-winning plant, which is now in the landscape and test garden of Broken Arrow Nursery. In exchange, we gave them some other selections, and then sent back to the Club some of the first propagations of 'Peppermint'.

What's in a Name?

The level of appreciation for the native mountain laurel is indicated by the number of eastern United States communities that have incorporated laurel in their name. I thank Richard Miller and the *National Five-Digit ZIP Code and Post Office Directory* for identifying the following 25 localities. Most, but certainly not all, are within the range of mountain laurel.

Laurel, Delaware	Laurel Dale, West Virginia
Laurel, Florida	Laurel Fork, Virginia
Laurel, Indiana	Laurel Garden, Pennsylvania
Laurel, Iowa	Laurel Heights, Texas
Laurel, Maryland	Laurel Hill, Florida
Laurel, Mississippi	Laurel Hill, North Carolina
Laurel, Montana	Laurel Park, North Carolina
Laurel, Nebraska	Laurel Springs, New Jersey
Laurel, New York	Laurel Springs, North Carolina
Laurel, Washington	Laurelton, Pennsylvania
Laurel Bloomery, Tennessee	Laurelville, Ohio
Laurel Canyon, California	Wolf Laurel, North Carolina
Laurel Creek, Kentucky	

The quintessential of all of these has to be Laurel Bloomery, Tennessee—surely a small, rustic, charming, and quiet town in the state's northeastern mountains.

The origin of the genus name *Kalmia* is discussed in the next chapter. The common name is derived from the resemblance of the American plant's foliage to that of the laurel of antiquity, *Laurus nobilis*, or sweet bay. The branches of the latter, native to the Mediterranean and celebrated in ancient literature, symbolized victory or accomplishment, and the leaves are used for flavor in cooking.

Many other plants also include laurel in their common names, as the following, incomplete list indicates:

Alexandrian laurel—*Calophyllum inophyllum, Danae racemosa*
Australian laurel—*Pittosporum tobira*
bay laurel—*Laurus nobilis*
black laurel—*Gordonia lasianthus*
California laurel—*Umbellularia californica*
Canary Island laurel—*Laurus azorica*
cherry laurel—*Prunus caroliniana, Prunus laurocerasus*
Chilean laurel—*Laurelia serrata*
Chinese laurel—*Antidesma bunius*
drooping laurel—*Leucothoe fontanesiana*
Ecuador laurel—*Cordia alliodora*
English laurel—*Prunus laurocerasus*
great laurel—*Rhododendron maximum*
ground laurel—*Epigea repens*
Himalaya laurel—*Aucuba*
Indian laurel—*Calophyllum inophyllum, Ficus retusa*, and *Termialia alata*
Japanese laurel—*Aucuba japonica*
laurel—*Cordia alliodora, Laurus nobilis* of antiquity
laurel-leaved greenbrier—*Smilax laurifolia*
laurel oak—*Quercus laurifolia*
laurel willow—*Salix pentandra*
madrone laurel—*Arbutus menziesii*
Portugal laurel—*Prunus lusitanica*
purple laurel—*Rhododendron catawbiense*
red-twig laurel—*Leucothoe recurva*
Sierra laurel—*Leucothoe davisiae*
spurge laurel—*Daphne laureola*
swamp laurel—*Magnolia virginiana*
Tasmanian laurel—*Anopterus glandulosus*
tropic laurel—*Ficus benjamina*
variegated laurel—*Codiaeum*
weeping laurel—*Ficus benjamina*
white laurel—*Rhododendron maximum*

This is important testimony to the universal value of Latinized scientific names for helping us to understand exactly to which plant we are referring.

Kalmia Away from the Native Range

Information on the growing of mountain laurel or other *Kalmia* outside of the United States is sketchy and sometimes contradictory. The situation in Great Britain is a notable example (Plates 1, 2, and 3). Mountain laurel is not widely grown there, yet several of the earliest color selections of mountain laurel (*Kalmia latifolia*) and sheep laurel (*K. angustifolia*) were not available in the United States and could only be obtained from Great Britain. Indeed, 'Splendens' and 'Clementine Churchill' (Plate 4), two of the first named mountain laurel cultivars, are of British origin. Furthermore, mountain laurel was once used as a pot plant in England, and seedlings produced there were imported in large numbers by nurseries in the eastern United States.

The bog laurels (*Kalmia microphylla* and *K. polifolia*) do quite well in Scotland. Mountain laurel is also grown to a limited extent in Belgium, the Czech Republic, France, Germany, the Netherlands, and Poland. Indeed, some popular articles on mountain laurel have appeared in German gardening magazines, and there is evidence of university students in Germany taking up the study of *Kalmia*. In my limited travels to gardens in England and the Netherlands, I found some of the best mountain laurel plants in the Gimborn Arboretum, the Netherlands. Significantly, the arboretum also had the best looking mountain andromeda, *Pieris floribunda*, another plant that has stringent requirements for aerated, well-drained soils.

In the northwestern United States and southwestern Canada, mountain laurel can be grown very well. Several cultivars have been selected and grown commercially in this region, and several significant tissue culture laboratories there initiate and produce small plants. As one goes north of Vancouver City, however, the cooler summers may limit growth. Further south, in Washington and Oregon, the summer growing season is usually quite warm and the plants can be grown well, but sometimes less-than-ideal soil drainage must be contended with.

Gardeners in Japan have successfully grown mountain laurel for many years, including seedlings selected for pink, red-budded, or banded flowers (Plates 5 and 6). Named cultivars from micropropagation laboratories are now becoming available in Japan, as well as in New Zealand and Australia. Other horticulturists have suggested that once Japanese gardeners become aware of the great variety in foliage and flower forms of mountain laurel now available, there will be a surge of interest in the plant. Korea is another country where these plants should succeed, but they have not been widely tested there. Ferris Miller of Seoul, South Korea, reports that he has several cultivars that do well in his coastal location (Plate 7), although the plants are often slow growing. It makes sense that when so many Asian plants do well in the United States, where *Kalmia* is native, *Kalmia* might reciprocate and do well in parts of Asia.

J. P. Rumbal, of the large New Zealand nursery firm of Duncan and Davies, says that *Kalmia latifolia* is highly regarded as an ornamental there. In the New Plymouth district it grows well in acidic, free-draining, volcanic-loam soils where annual rainfall is 50 to 60 inches (125 to 150 centimeters). Soils are light and summer shade is essential and mulching with humus material is beneficial. Mountain laurel does not do well in the warmer, drier areas with heavier clay soils. The situation in Australia is somewhat similar in that plants do best in Tasmania and the moister areas of southern Victoria (Plate 8). Summer heat and parching winds are limiting factors in much of Australia.

The potential for success of kalmias in South America is a matter of speculation. The plants should grow well in some of the temperate climate areas, such as parts of Argentina. Information on the success or failure of plants in such areas is hard to come by, if indeed significant attempts have even been made. As time goes on, however, we learn more. Surely there will be disappointments, but what's equally true is that there will be surprises as to how well kalmias can perform in locations distant to their native habitat.

CHAPTER 2

Laurels in the Wild

John E. Ebinger, Professor Emeritus, Botany Department,
Eastern Illinois University

Among the dwarfer evergreens there are few that rank higher in merit than the kalmias. There are altogether seven species known, but of these only three appear to be in cultivation, all of which are valuable as garden shrubs. The genus is purely an American one, extending from arctic regions in the north to as far as Cuba in the south. The tallest growing... is commonly known as mountain laurel, and is one of the chief favorites among the many plants suggested for the national flower of the United States. (Bean 1897)

The laurels, a small group of interesting and beautiful shrubs, are still relatively unknown to many gardeners and plant people. These plants, which have adorned yards and gardens in the eastern United States since colonial times and were used by the Native Americans before that, deserve rediscovery, for improved horticultural forms have gone virtually unnoticed and unused. Botanists recognize seven species of laurel and group them in the genus *Kalmia*. All are native to North America. Mountain laurel, *Kalmia latifolia*, is the best known species and is considered by many to be the most beautiful flowering shrub in North America. This explains why it is highly prized as an ornamental.

References to mountain laurel are found in early colonial literature. Possibly the "rose-trees" referred to in Henry Hudson's log of his 1609 trip to Cape Cod were this species. Captain John Smith observed the occurrence of laurel as an understory shrub in Virginia in 1624. By the early 1700s a few species of the genus had been described and illustrated in some of the botanical works of colonial America. The first color print was published by Mark Catesby in 1743.

One of the first detailed accounts of laurels is found in the journal of Peter Kalm. This Swedish botanist, a student of Carolus Linnaeus, was sent to the New World in 1748 by the Swedish Academy of Science. His mission was to obtain seeds of plants hardy enough to thrive on Swedish soil and, in particular, to discover dye plants, new food and fodder crops, and hardy mulberry trees to develop a silk industry. During his three years in America Kalm's explorations extended through Pennsylvania, New York, and New Jersey and into southern Canada. He ventured as far west as Niagara Falls and was the first to describe the falls in English from first-hand observations. Although primarily a naturalist who made numerous observations of plants and animals, Kalm also made many valuable observations of the colonists themselves. Thus his journal, written after his return to Europe, is an interesting account of life in colonial times: how the people lived, what they ate and drank, how they dressed, the native plants they used, and what they learned from the native populations in America. In this journal he describes in detail the poisonous properties of the "laurel trees." He also discusses the characteristics, economic importance, habitat requirements, and general distribution of mountain laurel and sheep laurel.

Upon his return to Europe, Kalm gave his collection of about 380 species of plants to Carolus Linnaeus, the Swedish naturalist and taxonomist. It was from this material that Linnaeus published a dissertation in which he proposed the generic name *Kalmia* to honor the collector. In this publication both mountain laurel, *Kalmia latifolia*, and sheep laurel, *K. angustifolia*, were named and distinguished from other related genera and species. Linnaeus included both in his *Species Plantarum* (1753), making the names official. Of the 700 species of North American plants described by Linnaeus in the *Species Plantarum*, Kalm was mentioned as the collector of many, with at least 60 new species founded upon specimens he collected.

The use of laurels as ornamentals in colonial gardens was well established when Peter Kalm was in America; in fact, some species were already being used as ornamentals in Europe. Twelve years before his visit, living specimens of both mountain laurel and sheep laurel had been sent to Peter Collinson, a London merchant, by American naturalist John Bartram. Other reports in 1740 tell of mountain laurel flowering in England. A third species, the eastern bog laurel, *Kalmia polifolia*, made its way to England by 1767. As a result of these beginnings, numerous European horticultural forms have been developed, some of which have in turn found their way back to America.

The genus *Kalmia* is a member of the heath family, Ericaceae, which occurs mainly throughout most of the temperate zone, with some species found in the mountains of the tropics and others in subarctic regions. It includes a great variety of plants, most of them shrubs and subshrubs, some herbs, others fairly tall trees, and a few trailing vines. The family contains about 3500 species; the largest genera are the true heaths (*Erica*), the rhododendrons and azaleas (*Rhododendron*), the wintergreens (*Gaultheria*), and the blueberries and cranberries (*Vaccinium*).

Economically the family is important primarily for its many ornamental species; among the most popular are the azaleas and rhododendrons. The evergreen mountain laurel and rhododendron species are popular greens in the floral industry, especially at Christmastime, and of course blueberries and cranberries are an ever-popular source of food.

Botanical Characteristics of Laurel

The laurels are a purely North American genus, occurring from Alaska south to the mountains of California and Utah, east through Canada to the Atlantic Ocean, and south through the eastern United States to Florida and Cuba. All the species are low to medium-sized shrubs or rarely small trees, usually with leathery, evergreen, entire margined, mostly short-petioled leaves that are alternate, opposite, or whorled (Figure 2-1 D). In some species the flowers are solitary in the axils of the leaves, while in others they are in terminal or axillary clusters. The flowers are relatively large, varying from 0.25 to 1 in (6 to 25 mm) in width. The calyx is five-parted and is usually persistent in fruit. The shallow, five-lobed petals are fused into a saucer-shaped corolla with a short narrow tube. Each has 10 small pouches holding the anthers. The 10 stamens have slender filaments and anthers that open by apical slits. The five-celled ovary is superior (above the calyx), and the fruit consists of a globose capsule holding numerous small seeds.

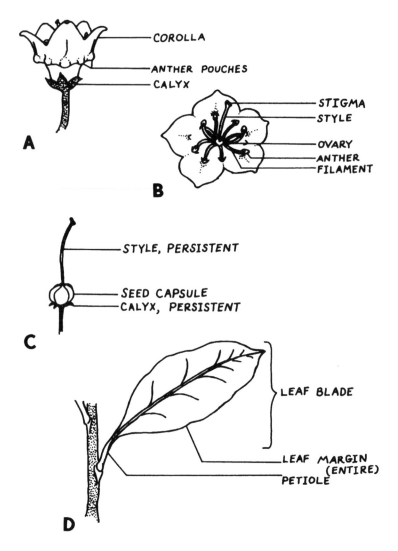

Figure 2-1. *Kalmia* flower, capsule, and leaf diagrams: (A) flower in profile; (B) view from above; (C) developed seed capsule before splitting to release seeds; (D) leaf attached to stem. Drawing by Rita Sorensen-Leonard.

The most distinctive feature of the genus *Kalmia* is the pollen-discharge mechanism. Near the middle of the corolla are 10 pouches forming small lobes on each ridge of the flower bud (Figure 2-1 A and B). Just before the bud opens, the elongating filaments push the anthers upward into these pouches. As the corolla opens, the elastic filaments bend backward under tension, and the anthers are held in the pouches and carried down and outward. When the flower is disturbed by a large insect, one or more of the anthers is released. When this occurs, the tension of the elastic filament is strong enough to throw the pollen 3 to 6 in (7.5 to 15 cm) from the flower. Many early botanists thought this mechanism insured self-pollination because the pollen was thrown toward the stigmas of the flower. American botanist and horticulturist Dr. William J. Beal was probably the first person to report that cross-pollination was necessary for pollination in the laurel species and was the first to describe the way in which cross-pollination occurred. He observed that a bumblebee searching around the base of the flower would release the stamens with its proboscis, thereby projecting the pollen onto the underside of the bee's body. This pollen was then rubbed onto the stigmas of subsequently visited flowers.

Although insects are necessary for pollination, the flowers of laurel do not readily attract insects. In fact, casual observations might lead to the conclusion that no insect pollination occurs. Furthermore, little nectar is secreted at the base of the corolla tube, and none can be found in many flowers, apparently accounting for the comparatively small number of insect visitors. Closer observation reveals, however, that insects are, in fact, usually necessary for pollination in laurels. This can be verified by preventing insects' access to the flower clusters. In flowers thus isolated, none of the stamens is released from the pouches and no seed is produced. Also, most species of laurel are self-incompatible, producing almost no seeds when self-pollination occurs. On the rare occasion when self-pollination does occur, the seedlings show inbreeding depression and are small and slow growing. In fact, measured by height growth, the vigor of outcrossed seedlings is usually twice that of inbred seedlings. Rarely have mountain laurel populations been reported to regularly self-pollinate, but inbreeding depression is still high. These populations may have developed the ability to self-fertilize and set seed as a result of inadequate pollinators (Rathcke and Real 1993).

Compared with other insect-pollinated plants, few species of insects have been observed pollinating laurel. In one study, a population of sheep laurel in an abandoned Maine pasture was observed for three weeks to determine the agents of pollination. Fourteen species of insects were identified as having the ability to spring the stamens while foraging for nectar. Of these, the bumblebee, *Bombus ternarius*, and the mining bee, *Andrena vicina*, were the most common visitors. Other insects observed occasionally visiting the flowers included smaller bees of the superfamily Apoides, three butterflies, one hawkmoth, and one beetle. During the study no honeybees, *Apis*, were observed even though an apiary was located only one-third mile (0.5 km) away. Present information suggests that under normal conditions honeybees rarely visit the laurels.

Bumblebees are by far the most important pollinating agent, because these large insects easily spring the stamens while foraging for nectar. As the bees alight on the flowers, their ventral parts touch the projecting stigma. In most instances, however, the stamens are not released when the bee lands but are sprung by the insect's legs (which get caught under the filaments) or by the insect's proboscis as it searches for the nectar. The proboscis is inserted near the base of the flower between the filaments and the corolla tube and, in a single circular motion, probes completely around the base of the ovary. This liberates all the stamens, projecting the pollen onto the underside of the insect. After being sprung, the stamens remain erect and in contact with the style for two to three hours; then the filaments bend backward and the anthers rest on the corolla.

In most flowering plants the pollen grains are produced in tetrads (groups of four) as a result of meiosis, and these four cells develop into separate and distinct pollen grains. In the genus *Kalmia* as well as many other members of the family Ericaceae, however, these four cells remain united at maturity and are released from the anther as a single unit. These four-celled, compound pollen grains are released as a fine powder in some species of *Kalmia* and in others as a sticky net formed by the presence of fine, noncellular, tacky threads that hold the tetrads together. These threads are derived either from small quantities of protoplasm excluded from the tetrads during development or from the breakdown of elements in the tetrad's outer wall. They have been observed in mountain laurel (*Kalmia latifolia*), sandhill laurel (*K. hirsuta*), and the little-known *K. ericoides*, which grows only in Cuba. The function of these threads is not entirely understood, but they may facilitate pollination in the relatively large upright flowers found in these species.

The Fossil Record

Four extinct species of *Kalmia* have been described, but their fossil remains are extremely fragmentary. As a result, it is difficult to form definite conclusions concerning their relationship to present-day members of the genus. Three fossil species are known only from leaf impressions, and except for size, shape, and probable coriaceous (leathery) texture, there is little reason to consider them members of this genus. They vary in age from Upper Cretaceous to Miocene and were found in various locations throughout North America. The fourth species, *Kalmia saxonica*, from the Lower Miocene period of Europe, may represent a member of this genus or of a closely related genus of the Ericaceae. The remains of this species consist of pieces of leaf cuticle with some upper epidermis attached. The structure and arrangement of the cells and the type of glandular hair bases are similar to that found in present-day laurel. Similar cuticle remains have been placed in the form genus *Kalmiophyllum*.

One present-day species is suspected as having existed relatively recently from scant fossil evidence. Fossils of the eastern bog laurel, *Kalmia polifolia*, were first reported from interglacial deposits at Point Grey near Vancouver, British Columbia. The leaf impressions are the same shape and size as those of living bog laurel. This species was later reported from Pleistocene lake deposits of the upper Connecticut River valley in northern New Hampshire. These fossils are post-glacial in age and appear to be representative of the flora that migrated northward in the wake of the retreating Wisconsin ice sheet. The other fossils in the same deposits indicate a habitat and climate similar to that presently prevalent in the area. Positive identification of these leaf impressions as bog laurel is impossible because of the similarity of the leaves of many Ericaceae.

The Species of Laurel

The genus *Kalmia* is regarded as a relatively primitive (in an evolutionary sense) member of the Ericaceae. It is placed in the tribe Rhododendreae and appears to have close affinities to the alpine azalea, *Loiseleuria procumbens*, and the sand myrtle, *Leiophyllum buxifolium*.

As presently recognized, the genus *Kalmia* consists of seven species. For the most part they are quite distinctive, and identifying them presents no problems. A description of each of these species follows with their general range, habitat, and economic importance. Descriptions are also included of the varieties and forms sometimes encountered in the wild. The following provides a useful botanical key.

Botanical Key to Species of Laurel

a. Leaves opposite
  b. Midrib of leaves lacking stalked glands; seeds less than one-sixteenth inch (1.5 mm) long
    Kalmia microphylla, western laurel
  b. Midrib of leaves with stalked glands; seeds more than one-sixteenth inch (1.5 mm) long
    Kalmia polifolia, eastern bog laurel
a. Leaves alternate or in whorls
  c. Leaves mostly more than three-quarters inch (19 mm) wide; inflorescence terminal; much branched
    Kalmia latifolia, mountain laurel
  c. Leaves mostly less than three-quarters inch (19 mm) wide; flowers solitary or in racemes in the axils of the leaves
    d. Leaves more than five-eighths inch (15 mm) long; flowers in racemes
      e. Leaves in whorls of three, evergreen
        Kalmia angustifolia, sheep laurel
      e. Leaves alternate, deciduous
        Kalmia cuneata, white wicky
    d. Leaves less than five-eighths inch (15 mm) long; flowers usually solitary in the axils of the leaves
      f. Leaves broad, flat, margins only slightly rolled under
        Kalmia hirsuta, sandhill laurel
      f. Leaves narrow, margins strongly rolled under
        Kalmia ericoides, Cuban laurel

Kalmia microphylla, Western Laurel

A short, low-growing alpine shrub, *Kalmia microphylla* is sparsely branched, has slightly two-edged branchlets, and grows up to 24 in (60 cm) tall; it rarely exceeds 6 in (15 cm) in height, but in bogs at lower elevations it may reach a height of 24 in (60 cm). The leaves are opposite, leathery, flat, evergreen, ovate to oval, short petioled, and 0.25 to 1.5 in (6 to 38 mm) long. The midrib of the leaf lacks glandular hairs, and the leaf margins are not revolute (rolled under). The inflorescence is a few-flowered terminal raceme (simple arrangement of stalked flowers on an elongated stem). The flowers on slender stalks grow to 1 in (2.5 cm) in length. Flowering occurs in late spring or early summer. The individual flowers are rose-purple to pink and 0.25 to 0.75 in (6 to 19 mm) across. The fruit is a globose capsule; the seeds have short projections on each end.

The western laurel is the only species of the genus found west of the Rocky Mountains in North America. Its range extends from central California north to Alaska and east to the extreme northwest corner of Manitoba (Figure 2-2).

The species contains two varieties: *Kalmia microphylla* var. *microphylla*, the western alpine laurel, and *K. microphylla* var. *occidentalis*, the western swamp laurel. The two varieties are distinct in habit and general appearance. The western alpine laurel rarely exceeds 6 in (15 cm) in height and has small oval leaves usually less than 0.5 in (12 mm) long. Its flowers are relatively small. The western swamp laurel, in contrast, is a larger plant, growing up to 24 in (60 cm) tall, with lanceolate leaves 0.5 to 1.5 in (12 to 38 mm) long and slightly larger flowers.

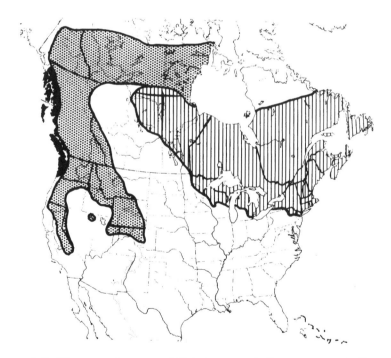

Figure 2-2. The natural range of *Kalmia microphylla* var. *microphylla*, western alpine laurel (dotted area); *Kalmia microphylla* var. *occidentalis*, western swamp laurel (black area); and *Kalmia polifolia*, eastern bog laurel (vertical shading). Range map by John Ebinger.

Kalmia microphylla var. *microphylla*, Western Alpine Laurel

The western alpine laurel, also commonly known as the alpine laurel or the small-leaved kalmia, is found in alpine meadows, bogs, and other open, wet areas where it usually forms dense mats. It is distributed throughout the mountainous regions of western North America, from central California, Nevada, Utah, and Colorado north through the Rocky Mountains to the Yukon and the Northwest Territories (Figure 2-2). There are reports of its occurrence north of the Arctic Circle.

Plant and leaf size in western alpine laurel are controlled to some extent by the environment. In the typical alpine plant the leaves are extremely small, usually less than 0.5 in (12 mm) long. The entire plant may be less than 3 in (7.5 cm) tall (Plate 9). At lower elevations the leaves average about 0.75 in (19 mm) in length and the plants 6 in (15 cm) in height. Larger individuals are rarely found.

Kalmia microphylla var. *occidentalis*, Western Swamp Laurel

Sometimes called the western bog laurel, western swamp laurel (*Kalmia microphylla* var. *occidentalis*) is found in marshes, bogs, and wet, open areas at low elevations in the coastal regions and on the islands of southern Alaska, British Columbia, Washington, and northwestern Oregon. A white-flowered western swamp laurel, form *alba*, has also been described.

Kalmia polifolia, Eastern Bog Laurel

Common names for *Kalmia polifolia* include bog laurel, swamp laurel, pale laurel, and gold withy. This low, sparsely branched, straggling shrub grows less than 3 ft (1 m) tall with leathery, linear to oblong, evergreen, opposite, short-petioled leaves that are 0.5 to 1.5 in (12 to 38 mm) long (Figure 2-3; also see Plate 1). The midrib of the leaf is covered with small, purple, glandular hairs, and the leaf margins are usually revolute. The inflorescence is a few-flowered terminal raceme, with the flowers on slender stalks about 1 in (2.5 cm) long. Flowering is early in the growing season. The individual flowers are usually rose-purple and 0.5 to 0.75 in (12 to 19 mm) across. The fruit is a globose capsule, and the small seeds have projections on each end.

The eastern bog laurel is found in swamps and other wet places, usually forming a border around ponds and lakes. In bogs its roots form dense mats that extend out over the water. Also found at higher elevations in the mountains of the northeastern United States and Canada, this species is the most widely distributed member of the genus (Figure 2-2). It ranges from northeastern Alberta across Canada to the Atlantic coast and south into the United States. In the Great Lakes region this species extends as far south as northern Illinois and on the east coast as far south as central New Jersey. Its entire range is, however, hard to determine with certainty. The two reports of its occurrence in the Arctic Circle now appear to have been based on specimens of the western laurel, *Kalmia microphylla*. *Kalmia polifolia* is naturalized in Scotland.

The eastern bog laurel (*Kalmia polifolia*) and the western laurel (*K. microphylla*) are similar and are often considered together as one highly variable species. Genetic studies now confirm, however, that they should be considered separate species. The chromosome numbers are different and the hybrids between the species are sterile. When considered as separate species, the plant and leaf size are used to make the distinction. The

eastern bog laurel is larger by at least 1 ft (30 cm). Its leaves are 0.5 to 1.5 in (12 to 38 mm) long, and the leaf margins are strongly revolute. Western laurel, in contrast, is most often a mere 6 in (15 cm) tall, and its leaves are less than 0.5 in (12 mm) long and have nonrevolute margins. Usually these characteristics are enough to distinguish the two species. The most reliable characteristic, however, that separates the eastern bog laurel from the western is the presence of purple glandular hairs on the leaf midrib of the former. Another easy way to distinguish is to compare the seeds. Those of the eastern bog laurel are about twice as long as those of the western.

Figure 2-3. Drawing of a *Kalmia polifolia* plant from Nova Scotia. Such plants are typically more compact than plants from further south in the range, 5.5 in (14 cm) from top to bottom. Drawing by Rita Sorensen-Leonard.

A white-flowered form of the eastern bog laurel, *Kalmia polifolia* f. *leucantha*, has been found growing along with the typical rose-purple flowered form in a bog in Newfoundland.

Kalmia latifolia, Mountain Laurel

In addition to the most familiar mountain laurel, other common names for *Kalmia latifolia* include broad-leaved laurel, calico-bush, spoonwood, ivy, mountain ivy, big-leaved ivy, laurel-leaves, and calmoun (Plates 10–15). The leaves of this many-branched shrub are alternate, flat, leathery, elliptic, dark green above, light green to reddish below, petioled, 2 to 5 in (5 to 12 cm) long and less than 2 in (5 cm) wide. Flowering is usually in late spring or early summer after new shoot growth has begun. The inflorescence consists of a terminal compound corymb (convex flower cluster with the outer flowers opening first) with glandular and mostly sticky stalks (Figure 2-4) and numerous flowers. The calyx is green to reddish and usually has stalked glandular hairs; the corolla, up to 1 in (2.5 cm) across, is usually light pink with purple spots around each anther pocket. The fruit is a depressed globose capsule with numerous light brown seeds with short projections on each end.

Figure 2-4. Glandular, sticky hairs on the flower stalk, calyx, and corolla of *Kalmia latifolia*. They are effective in preventing crawling insects from reaching the pollen and nectar.

Figure 2-5. The natural range of *Kalmia latifolia*, mountain laurel, is indicated by the shaded area. Plants from the southern and northern portions of the range appear the same, but plants from the south do not harden off and overwinter well in the north. Range map by John Ebinger.

Mountain laurel commonly forms dense thickets in rocky and sandy forests throughout most of its range, particularly where there are openings in the canopy. It is also found in pastures and open fields and often forms thickets at the edges of roads. This species is restricted to the eastern United States and occurs from southern Maine west through southern New York to central Ohio, south to southern Mississippi, Alabama, and Georgia, and northwestern Florida (Figure 2-5). There are some reports of mountain laurel being native to Canada, but there is no conclusive supporting evidence. These reports possibly were based on cultivated plants or on large-leaved specimens of the more northern sheep laurel, *Kalmia angustifolia*.

Mountain laurel is usually a tall, spreading shrub and throughout most of its range rarely exceeds a height of 12 ft (3.75 m). Yet in the fertile Blue Ridge valleys and in the Allegheny Mountains of the southeastern United States, members of this species may attain the size of a small tree. In 1877 American botanist Asa Gray observed a number of large individuals growing at the bottom of a dell, in back of Caesar's Head on the extreme western border of South Carolina. One of the trunks, at a point 1 ft (30 cm) above ground, measured nearly 50 in (125 cm) in circumference. One of the largest native specimens is located in the North Carolina Arboretum of the University of North Carolina, Asheville (Figure 2-6). The circumference at breast height is nearly 5 ft (1.5 m), spread is 28 ft (8.5 m), and its height is 25 ft (7.5 m).

Figure 2-6. The largest known *Kalmia latifolia,* growing at the North Carolina Arboretum of the University of North Carolina, Asheville. As is often the case with such large plants, they are located on the edge and just above a wet area where they receive adequate moisture and have protection against ground fires.

Like most members of the family Ericaceae, *Kalmia latifolia* is dependent on a mycorrhizal fungus associated with its roots. This symbiotic relationship ensures adequate absorption of water and minerals by the plant, particularly in acid soils. Some members of the family are so dependent on this association that they have lost the ability to make their own food. This condition is well known in the non-green Indian pipe, *Monotropa uniflora,* and a number of its relatives.

Economically the mountain laurel is the most important member of the genus *Kalmia.* The species is sold as an ornamental, particularly in the eastern but also the northwestern United States. The foliage is also used for floral displays and Christmas decorations, continuing a tradition started in 18th-century colonial times. Appalachian mountaineers, and likely Native Americans, produced a yellow dye from the foliage of mountain laurel. Suggestions were made early in 1913 that the species be protected against indiscriminate collecting. In 1924 it was estimated that one thousand tons of mountain laurel foliage was used annually in New York City alone. The estimate for the United States exceeded ten thousand tons. No figures are presently available for decorative use of mountain laurel.

The wood of mountain laurel was occasionally used to make small items such as pipes, where it was a substitute for brier. Peter Kalm wrote in his journal that this strong wood was fashioned into weaver's shuttles, pulleys, and trowels in mid-18th-century America. American Indians used the wood for small dishes and spoons, which probably accounts for the common name spoonwood. Today the wood of mountain laurel is rarely used except for tool handles and novelties. The wood weighs 48 pounds per cubic foot (about 22 kilograms per 100 cubic centimeters), which is about the same as apple (*Malus*) wood and a bit lighter than hickory (*Carya*).

As an understory shrub, mountain laurel effectively prevents water runoff and soil erosion. Studies in the southern Appalachian Mountains have shown that excessive cutting of dense laurel stands greatly increases the amount of water runoff. Since dense thickets of mountain laurel also prevent the natural regeneration of timber trees, the thickets must be cleared to encourage natural regeneration or to plant desirable tree species. Clumps and thickets of mountain laurel are, of course, a haven for wildlife, providing year-round cover and protection for large and small animals alike.

Because of the many variations in flower color, leaf shape and size, plant size, and pubescence, several variants and forms of mountain laurel have been named. A number of these are within the normal range of variation of the population, even if at the extremes, and should be treated as cultivars. At least five, however, are true genetic variants that are distinguished from the normal populations by one or several linked characters and are designated botanical forms.

Kalmia latifolia f. *angustata*, Willow-Leaved Mountain Laurel

First reported in 1945 in Cape May County, New Jersey, *Kalmia latifolia* f. *angustata* is a rare foliage form that exhibits very narrow, willow-shaped leaves less than 0.5 in (12 mm) wide (Figure 2-7 A). Another reference suggests that a plant of this form may have been discovered as early as 1833.

Kalmia latifolia f. *myrtifolia*, Miniature Mountain Laurel

Also called dwarf mountain laurel, miniature mountain laurel (form *myrtifolia*) is a mountain laurel form that has been under cultivation since 1840 and is occasionally found in small gardens. It is a miniature or semi-dwarf mountain laurel, compact, slow growing, and rarely exceeding a height of 3 to 4 ft (1 to 1.2 m). The leaves are generally smaller than those of typical mountain laurel, averaging 0.5 to 1.5 in (12 to 38 mm) long and about 0.5 in (12 mm) wide (Figure 2-7 B), and by appropriate crosses can be obtained true-to-type from seed. Flower size and the length of the stem internodes are one-third to one-half that of normal mountain laurel.

Kalmia latifolia f. *obtusata*, Hedge Mountain Laurel

Kalmia latifolia f. *obtusata* was first found near Pomfret, Connecticut, in 1903. This rare foliage form has oval leaves, usually 1 to 2.5 in (25 to 65 mm) long and up to 1.5 in (38 mm) wide (Figure 2-7 C). Most specimens are slow growing and form compact plants.

Figure 2-7. Three foliage forms of *Kalmia latifolia*: (A) form *angustata* or willow-leaved, having strap-shaped leaves; (B) form *myrtifolia* or miniature, with small leaves; and (C) form *obtusata* or hedge, with oval leaves. All three photos are taken from above and at the same magnification

Kalmia latifolia f. *fuscata*, Banded Mountain Laurel

The banded mountain laurel, also called the crowned mountain laurel, is a form with interesting flower color that has been reported from many localities in the northeastern United States since 1868 or before. Its white to pink flowers have a heavily pigmented, usually continuous, brownish purple or cinnamon band on the inside of the corolla at the level of the anther pockets (Plate 16; Figure 2-8). This band breaks up into brownish dots toward the base and the margin of the corolla. Because the banding shows through the bud, the corolla often has a muddy appearance. Variation exists in the size, shape, and color of the band, and an interrupted band has been observed in some individuals.

A   B

Figure 2-8. Two types of banded mountain laurel, *Kalmia latifolia* f. *fuscata*: (A) narrow-banded selection; (B) the pigmented "band" fills the inside of the corolla.

Kalmia latifolia f. *polypetala*, Feather Petal Mountain Laurel

Discovered on Mount Toby, near South Deerfield, Massachusetts, the *polypetala* form of *Kalmia latifolia* has also been found growing wild in North Carolina and has been known since 1871. The corolla is deeply divided into five narrow to broad petals (Plate 17). In some individuals the extremely narrow and threadlike petals are caused by a rolling of the petal margin. Normally the petals are broader, and a few specimens have been found with flowers like apple (*Malus*) blossoms. Other variations are mere extensions of the polypetala type or may be distinct forms. One lacks petals altogether, apetala (Plates 18 and 134), and a cultivar in which the corolla is reduced in size and deeply lobed was named 'Bettina' by the late T. R. Dudley, formerly of the U.S. National Arboretum.

Kalmia angustifolia, Sheep Laurel

Sheep laurel, *Kalmia angustifolia*, is a many-branched shrub that may grow 6 ft (2 m) tall, although heights of 3 ft (1 m) or less are more common. Branchlets are reddish brown. The leaves in whorls of three are somewhat leathery, evergreen, flat, mostly oblong, and 1 to 2.5 in (25 to 65 mm) long. The leaves and stems are slightly hairy and have stalked glandular hairs on their surfaces. The flowers are borne in numerous small clusters

from the axils of the previous year's leaves. The blooming period is generally June (earlier in the south and later in the north), about the same time as
mountain laurel. The calyx is usually green with red tips or red throughout,
and the corolla is less than 0.5 in (12 mm) across and reddish purple to
pink (Plates 19 and 20). The fruit is composed of a depressed globose capsule with numerous small, yellowish seeds that have two short wings.

The sheep laurel is common in northeastern and eastern North
America (Figure 2-9). John K. Small, an American botanist who studied the
flora of the southeastern United States, classified *Kalmia angustifolia* as two
separate species in 1914, and more recently R. M. Southall and J. W.
Hardin (1974) also treated sheep laurel as two species. Most botanists,
however, consider the sheep laurel complex as being one species with two
fairly distinct varieties. The genetic and morphological similarities make it
more realistic to follow this latter view. Therefore, we treat this species as
two varieties of sheep laurel: the northern sheep laurel, *K. angustifolia* var.
angustifolia, and the southern sheep laurel, *K. angustifolia* var. *caroliniana*.
The two varieties are similar in habit and general appearance but are easily
distinguished by differences in leaf and calyx pubescence. In the northern
sheep laurel the calyx is densely glandular pubescent (small hairs), and the
leaves are glabrous (hairless). The southern sheep laurel has no glandular
hairs on the calyx, and the leaves are densely pubescent beneath with a mat
of extremely short hairs.

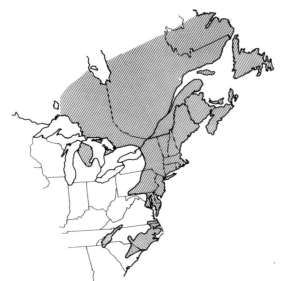

Figure 2-9. The natural
range of *Kalmia angustifolia*
var. *angustifolia*, northern
sheep laurel (vertical shading), and *Kalmia angustifolia*
var. *caroliniana*, southern
sheep laurel (dotted area).
With such a broad range
and disjunct distribution,
considerable variation
exists with the species.
Range map by John
Ebinger.

Kalmia angustifolia var. *angustifolia*, Northern Sheep Laurel

Common names for *Kalmia angustifolia* var. *angustifolia* include lamb-kill, sheepkill, wicky, narrow-leaved kalmia, dwarf laurel, and pig laurel, in addition to the most familiar northern sheep laurel. It occurs in bogs, swamps, and other wet places, forming dense thickets around ponds and lakes, and in open woods, as a weed in pastures, and in the moist openings of pine savannas. In the northern part of its range, sheep laurel sometimes forms large, dense heaths and can be an impediment to forest tree regeneration (see Chapter 12). It is distributed from the northeastern part of the Michigan peninsula and the eastern half of Ontario east through Quebec, the Maritime provinces, and Newfoundland; north to the Attawapiskat River (Kenora District) in Ontario, and to Goose Bay and Cartwright in Labrador; and south in the eastern United States through New England and eastern New York, eastern Pennsylvania and Maryland, to the coast in New Jersey and Delaware and the southeastern tip of Virginia (Figure 2-9).

Most of the subspecific categories proposed for the northern sheep laurel are for variations and extremes in flower color, variation in size and habit, and variation in leaf shape and color. In general, the differences in flower color represent natural variation within populations, and selections should be treated as cultivars (Plates 21 and 22). The variation in leaf shape and color and, in part, variation in plant height should be treated the same way. Low-growing plants are generally selections from more northern or high-altitude sources, or the result of inbreeding depression.

A white-flowered form of the northern sheep laurel, *Kalmia angustifolia* var. *angustifolia* f. *candida*, was first reported from Newfoundland in 1915 and has now been observed in a few other locations in Canada and the northeastern United States. The presence of pigment in sheep laurel is controlled by a single dominant gene, and the true-breeding recessive is white flowered. These white-flowered individuals also have green stems, unlike the normal wild types which have reddish stems (Plates 21 and 23).

Kalmia angustifolia var. *caroliniana*, Southern Sheep Laurel

Kalmia angustifolia var. *caroliniana* is a variety of sheep laurel common in North Carolina. It occurs in open woods and shrubby bogs in the mountains, in sandy woods, pocosins (marsh or swamp), savannas, and bogs on the coastal plain. Sporadic occurrence has been reported on the coastal plains of South Carolina and southern Virginia and in a few locations in the mountains of eastern Tennessee and two mountain bogs in the Blue Ridge Mountains of northeastern Georgia (Figure 2-9).

A white-flowered form of the southern sheep laurel also exists. It is similar genetically to the white-flowered form of the northern sheep laurel in that the true-breeding recessive is white flowered. The only known plants of this form came from Garden in the Woods, New England Wildflower Society, Framingham, Massachusetts. No wild individuals have been observed, and the origin of the nursery material is unknown.

Kalmia cuneata, White Wicky

One of the rarest shrubs in North America, white wicky (*Kalmia cuneata*) is a many-branched, erect shrub that may grow to 5 ft (1.5 m) tall. The leaves are alternate, deciduous, thin and flat, petioled, oblanceolate (lance-shaped but broadest near the apex), and 1 to 2.5 in (25 to 65 mm) long. Stalked glandular hairs are scattered over most parts of the plant. The flowers are borne in clusters of three to ten in the upper axils of the previous year's growth. Flowering occurs in late spring shortly after mountain laurel and sheep laurel bloom. The corolla is 0.5 to 0.75 in (12 to 19 mm) across and creamy white with a red band within. The fruit is a depressed globose capsule on a recurved stalk. The light brown seeds are small.

White wicky is a distinctive species (Plates 24 and 25). It could be confused only with the sheep laurel (*Kalmia angustifolia*), since their general habit and leaf size are similar. White wicky, however, is the only deciduous member of the genus. It is found exclusively in wet thickets and shrub bogs (the pocosin ecotone) in eight counties of southeastern North Carolina and

Figure 2-10. The natural range of *Kalmia cuneata*, white wicky (dotted area), and *Kalmia hirsuta*, sandhill laurel (vertical shading). Despite limited geographic distribution, there exists within each of these species considerable variation for plant form and flower color. Range map by John Ebinger.

adjacent South Carolina (Figure 2-10). These sites are marshy upland areas of the coastal plain, very close to the Piedmont.

Kalmia hirsuta, Sandhill Laurel

Sometimes called calico-bush, sandhill laurel (*Kalmia hirsuta*) is a low, lightly branched shrub less than 24 in (60 cm) tall and has alternate, commonly short-petioled, elliptic to ovate leaves less than 0.5 in (12 mm) long with margins only slightly revolute. The leaves and stems are covered with short, densely packed hairs as well as scattered, long coarse hairs and stalked glandular hairs (Plate 26). The flowers are usually solitary in the axils of the leaves of new growth (Plate 27). The blooming period is extended, often from early summer until fall. The calyx is green, leaflike, and tardily deciduous in fruit. The corolla is about 0.5 in (12 mm) across and light pink, with red markings around the anther pockets and a red ring near its base. The fruit is a subglobose capsule covered with glandular hairs and containing numerous light brown seeds.

The sandhill laurel has a relatively limited distribution, occurring along the coastal plain in the southeastern United States (Figure 2-10). It has been observed from extreme southern Alabama and northern Florida north through Georgia to the southeastern tip of South Carolina. Usually found in low, sandy pine savannas, sandhills, dunes, and flat, relatively open pine woods, this low-growing plant forms clumps among the understory. It does extremely well in sunny areas and is found in pine woods in openings resulting from logging or burning. Fire appears to be important in the ecology of this species since seed dormancy is most effectively broken by

Figure 2-11. The banded pattern typical of the *Kalmia latifolia* form *fuscata*, but in this case seen on the flower of *Kalmia hirsuta*. Photo by Benjamin MacFarland.

treating the seed under humid conditions at temperatures between 140 and 195°F (60 to 90°C). This adaptation to high temperatures may have evolved in response to recurring ground fires in its environment.

Horticultural variants of sandhill laurel have not been described in the literature, but Tom Dodd, Jr., of Semmes, Alabama, observed a colony of sandhill laurel with hose-in-hose (double-cupped) flowers while on a field trip in southeastern Georgia. This trait would be of great ornamental value in cultivated laurels. Sandhill laurels with a banded or *fuscata*-type flower have also been observed (Figure 2-11).

Kalmia ericoides, Cuban Laurel

Sparsely branched, *Kalmia ericoides* is an erect to spreading shrub, sometimes reaching a height of 3 ft (1 m). The leaves are alternate, persistent, thick, leathery, subsessile (virtually no petiole), linear, and about 0.5 in (12 mm) long with strongly revolute margins. Most of the plant is covered with densely packed short hairs, scattered long coarse hairs, and well-developed stalked glandular hairs. The flowers are solitary in the axils of the leaves near the ends of the branches, forming tight terminal clusters. The calyx is green, leaflike, and tardily deciduous in fruit. The corolla is about 0.5 in (12 mm) across and light pink, with red markings around the anther pockets and a red ring near the base. The fruit is a subglobose capsule covered with glandular hairs and containing numerous reddish brown seeds.

Kalmia ericoides is endemic to the savannas and pine barrens of western Cuba. Although it has a very limited distribution, the variation that exists in leaf pubescence and in the compactness of the inflorescence has led to the division of this species into three species by some botanists, while others consider it a single, highly variable species. It now appears that the compactness of the inflorescence is not a completely reliable characteristic. The variation in leaf pubescence, however, is relatively stable; two varieties probably exist in this complex. *Kalmia ericoides* var. *ericoides* has foliage that is nearly glabrous (hairless) on the upper surface, whereas the foliage of variety *aggregata* is pubescent.

The Cuban laurel appears to be most closely related to the sandhill laurel (*Kalmia hirsuta*) of the southeastern United States. Both have relatively small leaves (about 0.5 in [12 mm] long) covered with long coarse hairs and stalked glandular hairs. Their flowers are borne singly in the axils of the leaves, and the calyx is leafy and tardily deciduous in fruit. The two are easily separated, however, since the leaves of the Cuban laurel are thick and leathery with strongly revolute margins, whereas in the sandhill laurel the leaves are thin and lack a strongly revolute margin. Also, the flowers are scattered along the stem in the sandhill laurel, but those of the Cuban laurel are found toward the end of the stem, giving the appearance of a terminal cluster.

CHAPTER 3

Laurel Cultivars

Kalmia latifolia. This is the most showy species, and is one of the most ornamental of our indigenous plants.... The flowers vary from pure white to deep pink, and thus constitute the varieties of some nursery catalogues.

Kalmia angustifolia. It is... very pretty, and improves greatly on acquaintance. The foliage is... not ornamental. The flowers vary from pale pink to deepest red. The plant is too pretty to be neglected, and were it less common would be highly esteemed. Planted on the border of a rhododendron-bed, it increases rapidly by suckers, and never fails to flower freely. (Rand 1876)

All known named selections of *Kalmia* are dealt with in this chapter. Most, of course, are selections of mountain laurel, *Kalmia latifolia*.

The naming and description of selected plants for a horticulturally important and variable species like mountain laurel is a constantly evolving process. Not only are new cultivars named each year, but our knowledge of existing ones increases. Typically, a newly named mountain laurel cultivar only has limited testing. Before release, the original plant is observed for several years at one location and new propagations are made, but they often are not widely distributed until the plant is named and introduced. Thus a new cultivar may be known to have a spectacular flower and distinct growth habit, but its response over a broad range of growing sites is unknown. There is no fast and easy way to accumulate this information.

Ultimately we want selections that are "good doers" over a range of environmental conditions. I may be confident that a new selection will do well here in Connecticut where it was developed, but whether it will be an equal success in other areas where mountain laurel is grown, such as the southern United States, the Pacific Northwest, England, or New Zealand, has to be determined. Most of the cultivars released from Massachusetts and Connecticut are hardy to U.S. Department of Agriculture hardiness zone 5, but unless we have a couple of exceptionally cold winters, it is hard to even guess which selections are most likely to survive in zone 4.

Test sites at scattered geographic locations, where numerous cultivars are compared in a single planting, are invaluable for obtaining information on hardiness, growth rate, flower color, insect and disease resistance, and much more. Likewise, every time a nursery person propagates a cultivar or a customer purchases a plant, the database of experience enlarges. So in time, and only after the plant breeder and nursery owner decide it is a unique and attractive plant that can be economically grown do we learn whether a new selection is accepted in the marketplace. Occasionally, plants that do well in the landscape may be difficult for the commercial grower; conversely, a plant may be great in the commercial grower's hands but has serious faults in the landscape.

It is only recently that a few formal test plantings were instituted (Plate 28).

Highstead Arboretum, Redding, Connecticut, Gregory Waters, Director

North Carolina State University, Fletcher, Dr. Richard Bir, Mountain Horticultural Crops Research and Extension Station

University of Connecticut, Storrs, Dr. Mark Brand, Plant Science Department

University of Maine, Orono, Dr. Paul Cappiello, Plant, Soil and Environmental Sciences

At each of these locations, two or more plants of each of the available cultivars were established. Valuable information on hardiness, growth rate, leafspot resistance, and other traits will be forthcoming—part of the arsenal of information useful to determine the cultivars that are most heat tolerant, cold tolerant, disease resistant, and just plain superior. Other test sites in the United States, such as in the Great Lakes area, the deep South, and the

Northwest, would be valuable additions to those already established along the East Coast.

The plant breeder or selector releasing a new variety can have pretty good intuition about the future success of a plant, though he or she is often blinded by personal prejudices. Plants that are outstanding in one location often prove to be the best over a wide geographic area. The popularity and adaptability of the rhododendrons 'PJM' and 'Scintillation' are examples of this, as is the *Pieris* hybrid 'Brouwer's Beauty'. A contrasting example is the mountain laurel 'Goodrich'. Although selected from the wild, 'Goodrich' has proven to be a "poor doer" at all United States locations tried—in the Northeast, Northwest, and South.

In principle we should be using a standard color chart and standard color names to describe the flower color of these plants, but alas, this is not being done. It would, however, be a fine task for a horticultural student looking for a special project. Color can be measured by sophisticated instruments called spectrophotometers, and the measurements could be correlated with cellular pigments.

Patents and Breeder Fees

To date no *Kalmia* cultivars have been patented. I have been tempted to patent one or more, but plant patents can be a snare and delusion. Aside from the high initial expense of filing for a patent, royalty fees can have a negative effect on propagation and sales. Nursery people will favor other selections where no royalty fee to produce the plants is imposed. Furthermore, the patent holder has the responsibility of enforcing the patent, and if propagators pay U.S. $0.25 to 2.00 fee per plant, then they expect the patent holder to advertise and promote sales.

Alternatively, some individuals, arboreta, universities, and others have worked out less-formal agreements with growers wherein they agree to pay a fee for plants produced. The amount per plant (U.S. $0.15 to 0.35) is usually less than a patent royalty. The agreements do not have the same legal status as a patent, but they can be just as effective. In either case the breeder or "releaser" has to rely on the good faith and cooperation of growers. Fortunately, nursery people and especially propagators are an honorable group of people.

I have released several cultivars under a breeder fee arrangement (see list at the end of this chapter). Most of these plants are produced in micropropagation (tissue culture) laboratories. By prior arrangement, these propagators have agreed to pay me U.S. $0.15 for each plant they sell of the newly selected cultivars. I rely on their honesty and in turn they count on me to make new releases available to them. For *Kalmia*, then, breeder fees seem to work as well as patents, with less paperwork for the person releasing and introducing the new plant. Also, because the fees are low, there is less resistance by propagators to produce and promote the plants.

Cultivars

The *International Code of Nomenclature for Cultivated Plants* (Trehane 1995) provides the rules for naming cultivated varieties (cultivars) of plants, and the Council of the International Society of Horticultural Science designates International Registration Authorities. For *Kalmia*, I have been the designated National Authority since 1977 and the International Registration Authority since 1978. What these fancy titles really mean is that I have agreed to try to keep track of and coordinate the naming of new cultivars. One of the first steps was to publish in 1983 a checklist of all cultivated laurels then known (Jaynes 1983). Before then no checklist or register of cultivated names had been published for the genus. Anyone introducing a new *Kalmia* should notify me so a duplicate or inappropriate name is not used. It also aids in keeping checklists, like the following one, current.

The first horticultural varieties of *Kalmia latifolia* were described in the 1800s and, with few exceptions, most cultivated kalmias are of this species. The selection and propagation of *K. latifolia* has for most of its history been sporadic. Since the early 1960s, however, the breeding of *K. latifolia*, combined with the more recently acquired ability to propagate selections in sterile (tissue) culture, has resulted in the release of many new cultivars. There were 26 valid cultivars recognized in the 1983 list, 48 in 1988, and nearly 80 in this one, and certainly more will be released in the future.

The purpose of the following list is to inform, reduce confusion, encourage consistency of nomenclature within the group, and aid in the correct identification of plants. Dr. Tony Webster of the East Malling Research Station, England, stated that as many as 50 to 60 percent of woody ornamental cultivars were being sold under the wrong name in the United Kingdom (Bent 1994). The figure seems high, especially for a country of gardeners, but it points out that accurate identification is a significant problem. The species and form names (botanical nomenclature) used here are based on Ebinger's taxonomic work (1974); see also Chapter 2 of this book for further descriptions of species, varieties, and forms.

Format:

1. Regardless of rank, all names (botanical varieties, botanical forms, and cultivars) are listed in alphabetical order under each species.

2. The earliest published reference for a name and description of a plant in cultivation is indicated in parentheses. See the bibliography and the list of sources of *Kalmia* in Appendix C for more information on many of these sources.

3. Descriptive information from published as well as unpublished sources is included.

4. a) Cultivar names are shown with the conventional single quotes.

    b) Invalid cultivar names are so indicated and shown without single quotes.

    c) Botanical names are in italic type. I have taken the liberty in this chapter of not repeating the species name (*Kalmia latifolia*) every time a form name like *fuscata* is used.

    d) Many of the cultivars have characteristics that are typical of one or more botanical forms and this is indicated parenthetically in the descriptions. For instance, 'Elf' is a miniature or semidwarf laurel whose growth is typical of the form *myrtifolia*, and 'Minuet' is a miniature and has banded flowers, typical of the forms *myrtifolia* and *fuscata*, respectively. These cultivars were not found in the wild, however, but are derived from controlled crosses. Therefore, to a botanist they are not true botanical forms.

5. An estimate of height and width after 10 years in a "normal" landscape environment is given at the end of each description. Obviously plants will grow faster or slower depending on soil conditions, care, length of growing season, and exposure to sun or shade, among other factors.

6. If a breeder fee or royalty payment is requested by the originator, that is stated along with the amount and the originator's name.

Notable and characteristic differences in leaf shape, petiole length, and leaf thickness are present among the cultivars. Size is also important but may vary greatly, depending on growing conditions and whether the shoot was vegetative or flowering. At the risk of oversimplification, I have included an outline of a "typical" leaf for most of the cultivars. Bear in mind that leaves of mountain laurel vary greatly within a particular plant, but variation between plants is greater. Leaves were chosen from the midpoint of a flush of growth, four to seven leaves back from the tip, and one leaf was taken from each of three or more shoots. The print is of one such leaf. Thickness of the leaves was also measured, but there was a great deal of variation based on where the plants grew. For instance, well-grown container plants usually had thicker leaves than those of field-grown plants of the same cultivar. More study is thus required before a reliable listing of average leaf thickness can be reported. (Note: leaf outlines are reproduced at 50 percent.)

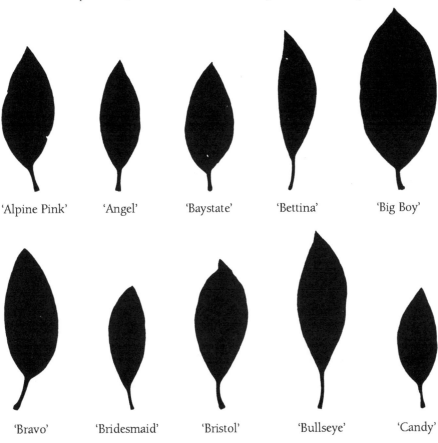

'Alpine Pink'   'Angel'   'Baystate'   'Bettina'   'Big Boy'

'Bravo'   'Bridesmaid'   'Bristol'   'Bullseye'   'Candy'

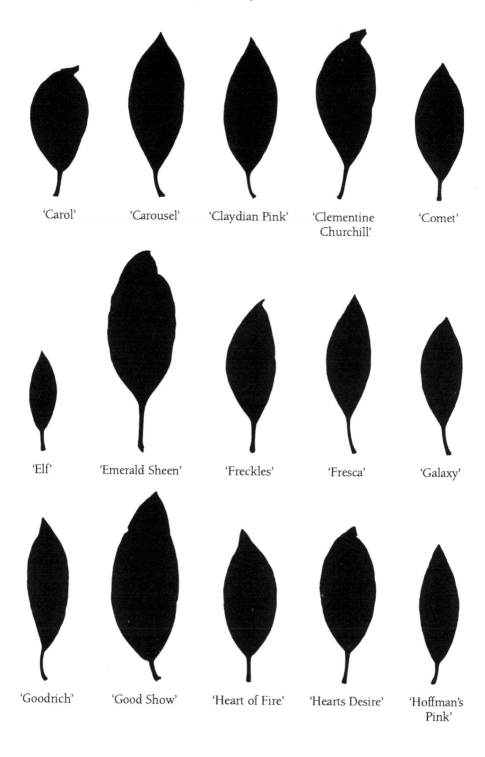

'Carol'   'Carousel'   'Claydian Pink'   'Clementine   'Comet'
                                                       Churchill'

'Elf'   'Emerald Sheen'   'Freckles'   'Fresca'   'Galaxy'

'Goodrich'   'Good Show'   'Heart of Fire'   'Hearts Desire'   'Hoffman's
                                                                         Pink'

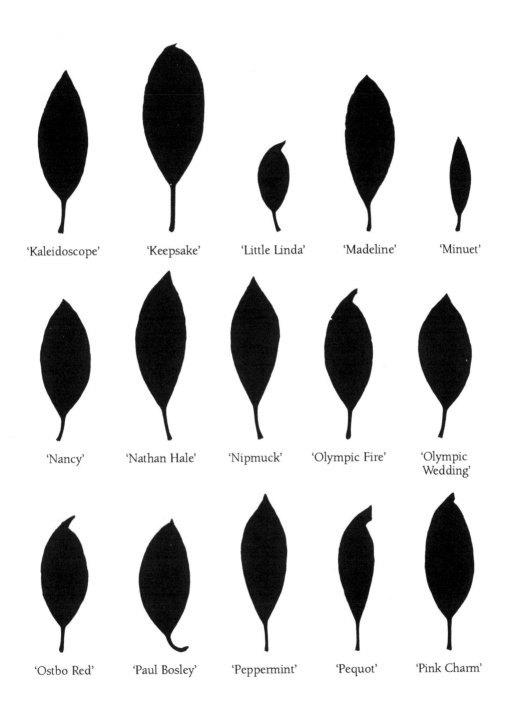

'Kaleidoscope'   'Keepsake'   'Little Linda'   'Madeline'   'Minuet'

'Nancy'   'Nathan Hale'   'Nipmuck'   'Olympic Fire'   'Olympic Wedding'

'Ostbo Red'   'Paul Bosley'   'Peppermint'   'Pequot'   'Pink Charm'

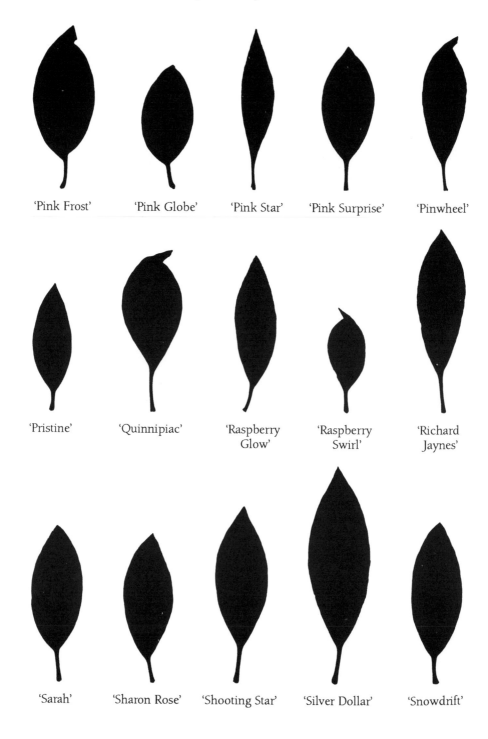

'Pink Frost'   'Pink Globe'   'Pink Star'   'Pink Surprise'   'Pinwheel'

'Pristine'   'Quinnipiac'   'Raspberry Glow'   'Raspberry Swirl'   'Richard Jaynes'

'Sarah'   'Sharon Rose'   'Shooting Star'   'Silver Dollar'   'Snowdrift'

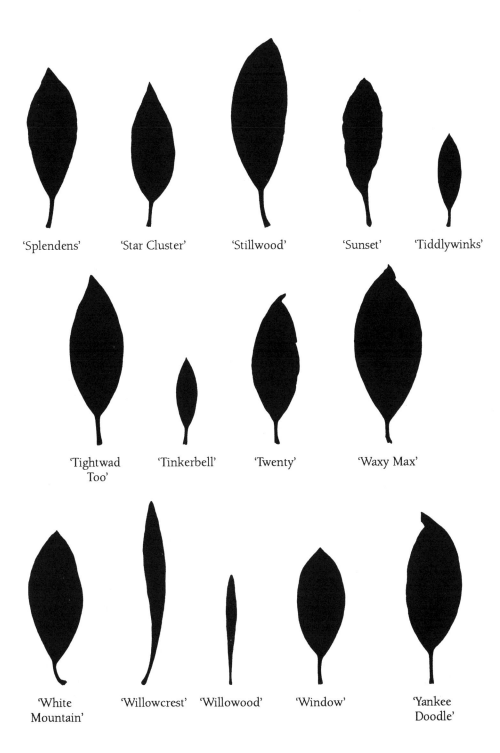

'Splendens'   'Star Cluster'   'Stillwood'   'Sunset'   'Tiddlywinks'

'Tightwad
Too'   'Tinkerbell'   'Twenty'   'Waxy Max'

'White
Mountain'   'Willowcrest'   'Willowood'   'Window'   'Yankee
Doodle'

Kalmia latifolia Linnaeus, Mountain Laurel

Alba. This is an invalid cultivar name applied to plants with white or near-white flowers.

'Alpine Pink' (Briggs Nursery, Olympia, Washington, 1982 catalog, color photo). Plate 29. John Eichelser selected and originally released this cultivar as J-12. Flowers are a rich, dark pink in bud and medium pink when open, the inside center of the open corolla near white. Foliage is a glossy light green, heavy textured, broad, and leafspot resistant. Unfortunately, the last flush of growth often turns yellow, especially under good growing conditions. Petioles and stems of new growth are moderately pigmented purplish red. Growth habit is dense and broad. 3.5 ft high × 4.0 ft wide (1.1 × 1.2 m)

f. *angustata* Rehd. (*Journal of the Arnold Arboretum*, 1945). A botanical form rarely found in nature, the form *angustata* has unusual foliage under the control of a single recessive gene (*w*). It is characterized by narrowly oblanceolate to linear leaves that are 1.5 to 3.2 in (4 to 8 cm) long and 0.2 to 0.4 in (5 to 10 mm) wide. Its common name is willow-leaved laurel. 'Willowcrest' and 'Willowood' are cultivars with this characteristic.

'Angel' (Clark's Greenhouse and Nursery, Salem, Connecticut, 1988 price list). Gerald Verkade selected 'Angel' from open-pollinated seedlings of 'Stillwood'. Flowers are white, although some years there may be a light pink blush on the buds. The leafspot-resistant foliage is a bright yellowish green with relatively flat leaf blades; new stems and petioles are greenish yellow. Plant growth is upright. Foliage density is reported excellent by one grower and poor by another. 4.5 ft high × 3.5 ft wide (1.4 × 1.1 m)

Apetala. This is an invalid cultivar name because this Latinized name was not used prior to 1959. However, it is appropriately descriptive of those plants having no corolla (Plates 18 and 134). Ebinger (1974) groups apetala plants with the form *polypetala*. My original plant came from the late Will Curtis of Garden in the Woods, Framingham, Massachusetts. The origin before that is unknown. The apetalous trait is under the control of a single recessive gene (*ap*). See also f. *polypetala*.

'Bay State' (Briggs Nursery, Olympia, Washington, 1989–1990 liner list). Plate 30. This plant was selected by Elinor Clarke of Ashfield, Massachusetts (aka the Bay State), from seed grown by John Smart, who probably obtained the seed from plants at Weston Nurseries, Hopkinton,

Massachusetts. David Leach of North Madison, Ohio, received a plant from Mrs. Clarke and named and introduced it in 1987 through Briggs Nursery. This selection falls within the broad group called red-buds. The distinctive trait of 'Bay State' is the red to salmon-pink flowers, also described as coral-colored, that are devoid of any blue admixture. The plant buds well when young. Although 'Bay State' was not noted originally for remarkable foliage or growth habit, container-grown plants have thick, lustrous, dark green foliage that is leafspot resistant and a dense growth habit. 4.0 ft high × 4.0 ft wide (1.2 × 1.2 m)

'Bettina' (T. R. Dudley, *American Horticultural Magazine*, October 1967). Plate 133. Selected by Sylvester March in the 1950s at the U.S. National Arboretum, Washington, D.C., 'Bettina' was named by T. R. Dudley, also of the National Arboretum, for his wife. The corolla is reduced (f. *polypetala*) and deep purplish pink when grown in full sun, faintly pigmented in shade. The small flowers persist longer than those of the common species. Anther filaments and style are of normal length. Flower form is under the control of a single recessive gene (*be*). The leaf blade is somewhat narrow, but otherwise foliage is typical for the species. 3.5 ft high × 3.0 ft wide (1.1 × 0.9 m)

'Big Boy' (Wright's Nursery, Canby, Oregon, 1991 catalog). This was a seedling of 'Sharon Rose', selected in about 1986 by Arthur A. Wright. Flowers are normal in size, pink in bud, and soft pink when open. The leaves are large, slightly wavy, thick, and dark green, and stems are heavy; growth is slow, compact, and upright. These growth traits make this sturdy plant look as much like a *Rhododendron* as a *Kalmia*. Wright says the plant does best in light shade. 4.0 ft high × 4.0 ft wide (1.2 × 1.2 m)

'Bravo' (Richard A. Jaynes, *Kalmia: The Laurel Book II*, 1988). Selected before 1973 by the late Edmund Mezitt, Weston Nurseries, this third- or fourth-generation pink selection was propagated by grafting and sold under this name for several years at Weston Nurseries' garden center, but was not listed in their catalog. Both flower buds and open blossoms are dark pink. The leaves are large, rounded, and glossy; new growth has purplish red stems. 4.0 ft high × 4.0 ft wide (1.2 × 1.2 m)

'Bridesmaid' (Richard A. Jaynes, 1988). Plate 31. Selected by me around 1973 at the Connecticut Agricultural Experiment Station, New Haven, it was commercially propagated and introduced by Bolton Technologies,

Bolton, Connecticut, in 1986. The flower is a rich, deep pink in bud and typically bicolor when open, with the outer two-thirds of the corolla deep pink and the center nearly white. The edge of the corolla rolls back as the flower ages. Leaves are lustrous, dark green, broad, and heavily textured. The plant buds well when young and buds every year—almost to a fault. Without deadheading, the excessive flowering comes at the expense of vegetative growth. It does well in shade. The habit is somewhat spreading and semicompact, and the foliage is resistant to leafspot. It is from a 1968 controlled cross (965) of a deep pink (293) and a red-bud selection (299). 3.0 ft high × 3.5 ft wide (0.9 × 1.1 m)

'Brilliant' (R. Hay and P. M. Synge, *The Color Dictionary of Flowers and Plants for Home and Garden*, Crown Publishers, New York, 1969, color photo). 'Brilliant' has been described as one of the finest forms, with deep pink flowers that are crimson in bud. This may not be a valid cultivar, however. It was apparently grown in Great Britain, but information on origin, original description, and propagation is lacking.

'Bristol' (Richard A. Jaynes, described here). Plate 32. This plant has a broad cinnamon-maroon band in the corolla (f. *fuscata*). It was discovered by employees of Bristol Nurseries, Connecticut, in about 1960 among plants in a landscape planting. The original plant survived at the nursery until it succumbed to mistreatment in transplanting in 1994. Because it was one of the first plants discovered with such a broad band and because it is in the parentage of several of my releases ('Bullseye', 'Hearts Desire', 'Kaleidoscope', 'Keepsake'), I am naming it. 'Bristol' has not been commercially propagated; it is difficult to root, so we have propagated it largely by grafting. The foliage and growth habit are typical of the species. 4.0 ft high × 4.0 ft wide (1.2 × 1.2 m)

'Bullseye' (Richard A. Jaynes, *International Plant Propagators' Society, Proceedings*, 1982). Plates 33 and 34. Commercially introduced by Knight Hollow Nursery, Madison, Wisconsin, in 1983. The flowers have a broad purplish cinnamon band of pigmentation on the inside of the corolla with a white center and white edge (f. *fuscata*)—hence the name 'Bullseye'. It does not produce flower buds well when young, but it does respond to some of the new growth regulators like Bonzi (see Chapter 7). Stems of new growth and petioles are purplish red on the sun side, and leaf edges are wavy and have intermediate leafspot resistance. 'Bullseye' is a rapid grower in the nursery and new growth is often a bronze-red. It is from a cross (1144) of a red-bud selection (137) and the broad-banded plant 'Bristol'. 4.5 ft high × 4.5 ft wide (1.4 × 1.4 m)

CAES 137 (Briggs Nursery, Olympia, Washington, 1982 catalog). An invalid cultivar name, this is a test number of a selection I made in 1962 for the Connecticut Agricultural Experiment Station at Weston Nurseries. It is a red-bud selection, less intense in color than similarly named cultivars, and is a parent of 'Bullseye', 'Carousel', 'Nipmuck', and 'Quinnipiac'.

Calico. This is an invalid cultivar name for one or more f. *fuscata* plants propagated around 1970 by La Bars Rhododendron Nursery, Stroudsburg, Pennsylvania. See Kalico Kal, also an invalid name.

'Candy' (Briggs Nursery, Olympia, Washington, 1985 catalog). This plant flowered in about 1970 and was selected and named in 1972 by Edmund Mezitt, Weston Nurseries. A third- or fourth-generation pink selection, it was propagated and sold under the name 'Candy' for several years at Weston Nurseries but was not listed in their catalog. The flower buds and the open corolla are dark pink. Foliage is blue-green on vigorous plants but has a dusty gray-green appearance on plants with low fertility. Petioles and new stems are purplish red, but late-season flushes of growth are often yellow. Leaves are broad, heavy, and ovate in shape and highly resistant to leafspot. 'Candy' is an upright grower and buds well. 3.5 ft high × 3.0 ft wide (1.1 × 0.9 m)

'Carol' (Richard A. Jaynes, *Connecticut Agricultural Experiment Station Mimeo List*, 1984). Plate 35. Named for Carol Clarke, who worked with me at the Agricultural Experiment Station, this cultivar was selected in 1975 and commercially propagated in 1986 by Bolton Technologies. The bright, intense red buds contrast well with the near white of newly opened corollas. The open flowers become deeper pink as they age. Under certain growing conditions, such as shade and/or warm nights, the flower buds may only be a rich pink. This is a compact-growing plant with dense, broad, lustrous, glossy foliage that is leafspot resistant. Leaf blades appear thick and are often twisted and wavy, and somewhat cupped in cross section. Stems of recent growth and petioles are moderately purplish red. 'Carol' may not perform well under stress and low fertility. It originated from a 1969 controlled cross (1049) I made of a deep pink (116l) female, and a red-bud (776c). 3.5 ft high × 3.5 ft wide (1.1 × 1.1 m)

'Carousel' (Richard A. Jaynes, *International Plant Propagators' Society, Proceedings*, 1982). Plate 36. 'Carousel' has an intricate pattern of bright, purplish cinnamon pigmentation on the inside of the corolla (f. *fuscata*). Resulting from a controlled cross (1153) of a red-bud selection (CAES 137) and a 'Goodrich'-like banded plant, its flower is similar to that of 'Goodrich' but with brighter pigment and showing more white. It is a rapid grower and has a fairly dense habit if pruned often in the nursery. Foliage is dark green, glossy, and leafspot resistant. Cuttings are relatively easy to root. Petioles and current-season stems are moderately pigmented purplish red. 4.0 ft high × 4.0 ft wide (1.2 × 1.2 m)

'Claydian Pink' (Clay's Nurseries and Laboratories, Langley, British Columbia, 1983 price list). This seedling was selected by Les Clay in about 1978 for its good, dark green, glossy foliage; dense, upright habit; medium pink flower buds; and blush pink-to-white flowers. It appears to be resistant to leafspot. It is a good choice for those desiring an upright selection with handsome foliage and light pink flowers like the native. 4.5 ft high × 3.5 ft wide (1.4 × 1.1 m)

'Clementine Churchill' (A. G. Soames, Award of Merit, *Journal of the Royal Horticultural Society*, 1952). Plates 4 and 37. This cultivar originated at Sheffield Park, Sussex, England. Outside the corolla is Tyrian rose; inside, rose-red (rose-madder). The foliage is dark green, dense, and leafspot resistant. Leaves vary greatly in size and include many that are broad and large; most are cupped in cross section and have a bit of a twist. This is a proven selection in Great Britain and it deserves to be commercially tested in the United States. 3.5 ft high × 4.0 ft wide (1.1 × 1.2 m)

'Comet' (Broken Arrow Nursery, Hamden, Connecticut, 1994–95 price list). Plate 38. Flowers of this selection are like those of 'Shooting Star'— white, deeply lobed, and open wide—but they reflex less and the flowers are larger. The original 'Shooting Star' was an outstanding discovery by Marjorie and Hollis Rogers of Greensboro, North Carolina, in 1972. No *Kalmia* with these strongly lobed flowers had been known previously. Unfortunately, as a garden plant 'Shooting Star' leaves something to be desired, with a habit that is upright, open, and a bit ungainly and foliage that tends to blemish, and hardiness in the north (zone 5) is questionable. I have made many crosses with 'Shooting Star' to obtain a hardy, compact, dense-foliaged plant. 'Comet' is a third-generation selection that promises to be a significant improvement. One of its great-grandparents is 'Stillwood', which was selected for white flowers and hardiness from a native stand in New Hampshire. The plant habit of 'Comet' is rounded, and the foliage is glossy, rich green, and leafspot resistant; leaf blades are relatively flat in cross section. There is a breeder fee of U.S. $0.15 for each plant propagated and sold (Jaynes). 3.5 ft high × 3.5 ft wide (1.1 × 1.1 m)

Den Window. See 'Window'

Dexter Pink (Greer Gardens, Eugene, Oregon, 1981 catalog). This is an invalid cultivar name applied to a strain of pink-flowered seedlings grown from seedlings of plants originally selected from the Charles Dexter Estate, Sandwich, Massachusetts. They were named Dexter Pink by John Eichelser of Melrose Nursery, Olympia, Washington, to distinguish these plants from the clonally propagated 'Ostbo Red' he was growing. More recently, a plant has been propagated in tissue culture and sold under this name by B & B Laboratories, Mount Vernon, Washington (1986 catalog).

'Elf' (Richard A. Jaynes, *International Plant Propagators' Society, Proceedings*, 1982). Plate 39. Commercially introduced by Briggs Nursery in 1982, this is a miniature or semidwarf mountain laurel (f. *myrtifolia*) characterized by reduced leaf size, slower growth, and leaves more closely spaced along stems. Young plants are capable of vigorous growth, however; unless pruned heavily when young, plants may become leggy and appear stiffly branched. Form and rate of growth vary greatly with cultural conditions. Older and more slowly grown plants develop considerable charm and grace. The short petioles and stems of new growth are purplish red on the sun side. Foliage is medium to dark green and leafspot resistant. Flowers are typical of the wild type, light pink in bud and near white when open. Cuttings root somewhat easier than most, and the plant buds well. This plant has been good commercially. It is from a cross (1-76) I made, while employed at the Connecticut Agricultural Experiment Station, by caging six miniature plants with a bumblebee (see Chapter 15). 3.0 ft high × 3.0 ft wide (0.9 × 0.9 m)

'Eloise Butler' (Richard A. Jaynes, described here). The original plant of this selection grows on the grounds of the Eloise Butler Wildflower Garden and Bird Sanctuary in Minneapolis, Minnesota, and is named for the founder and person who brought the plant to the sanctuary from Massachusetts. 'Eloise Butler' is notable because it has withstood the

Minnesota climate (zone 4; −20 to −30°F [−4 to −22°C]) since 1929 and is growing in soil with a relatively high pH. It has weathered, on at least one occasion, −40°F (−40°C) without damage, whereas a nearby 'Elf' turned brown. The flower is light pink in bud and opens near white. The original plant after 70 years is broader than tall, 6 ft high and 8 ft wide (2 × 2.5 m), and has fairly dense foliage. Betty Ann Addison and her late husband Charles, of Rice Creek Gardens, Minneapolis, have micropropagated this plant and plan to introduce it.

'Emerald Sheen' (Richard A. Jaynes, 1988). This plant first flowered in 1977 and was selected and named the following year by R. Wayne Mezitt of Weston Nurseries. The seed parent is believed to be the cultivar 'Twenty'. Plants were first sold under the name 'Emerald Sheen' in 1985. The outstanding feature of this selection is the dark green, glossy foliage, which is thick, rounded, and convex and borne on a dense, broad, compact plant. It has moderate leafspot resistance. It flowers somewhat sparsely; medium pink buds open nearly white and mature to medium pink. The flowers are very large in densely packed, "frilly" clusters but are sometimes hidden by the foliage. 2.5 ft high × 3.0 ft wide (0.8 × 0.9 m)

'Freckles' (Richard A. Jaynes, *International Plant Propagators' Society, Proceedings*, 1982). Plate 40. 'Freckles' was commercially introduced by Knight Hollow Nursery in 1983. It has 10 purplish cinnamon spots (f. *fuscata*), about 0.1 in (2 mm) across on the inside of the corolla at the level of and just above the 10 anther pouches. After 24 years the original plant is attractive and only 3.5 ft (1.1 m) tall and 5 ft (1.5 m) wide. However, young plants in the field or in containers grow rapidly and may become "floppy"; hence it has lost favor among several commercial growers. Petioles and stems of new growth are sometimes lightly pigmented purplish red on the sun side. The foliage has intermediate leafspot resistance. It buds well when young and can be rooted from cuttings. 'Freckles' comes from a second-generation controlled cross (1028) I made in 1969 of 'Star Cluster' and a red-bud selection (187). 3.0 ft high × 4.5 ft wide (0.9 × 1.4 m)

'Fresca' (Greer Gardens, Eugene, Oregon, 1981 catalog; color photo in Briggs Nursery, Olympia, Washington, 1982 catalog). This cultivar was selected by J. Caperci in 1969 and propagated by John Eichelser. The open flowers have a distinct chocolate-purple band around the inside of the corolla (f. *fuscata*), also described as burgundy in color. The foliage, glossy and purplish green, is moderately resistant to leafspot. The long petioles and stems of new growth are purplish red in color. 'Fresca' is a tall, open grower, reported by at least one nurseryman to be more brittle than most selections. It is no longer in commercial production. 4.0 ft high × 3.5 ft wide (1.2 × 1.1 m)

f. *fuscata* (Rehder) Rehder (Alfred Rehder, *Rhodora*, 1910). Plate 16. This botanical form has flowers characterized by a heavily pigmented, usually continuous band on the inside of the corolla, at the level of the anther pockets, that is brownish, purplish, or cinnamon. Its common name is banded laurel. The presence of banding in the flower is under the control of a single dominant gene (*B*). Of the recognized botanical forms, *fuscata* is the one most commonly found in native stands and was first described in 1830. It also occurs sporadically among seedlings grown in nurseries. Cultivars exhibiting this trait include 'Bristol', 'Bullseye', 'Carousel', 'Freckles', 'Fresca', 'Galaxy', 'Goodrich', 'Hearts Desire', 'Kaleidoscope', 'Keepsake', 'Minuet', 'Olympic Wedding', 'Pinwheel', 'Raspberry Swirl', 'Star Cluster', 'Waxy Max', and 'Yankee Doodle'.

'Galaxy' (Broken Arrow Nursery, Hamden, Connecticut, 1994–95 price list). Plate 41. Selected from a cross I made in 1984, this is the first named selection to combine the near-petaled, 'Shooting Star'-like flower with the burgundy inner flower color of the *fuscata* forms. The corolla opens wide, displaying five deeply pigmented, petal-like lobes edged in white. Traversing to the base of the corolla, the solid pigmentation becomes speckled and then white. The plant is a vigorous, upright grower with shiny, flat leaf blades (like 'Shooting Star') and moderate leafspot resistance. My intent is to breed and select other similarly flowered plants that are more dense and compact in stature. 'Galaxy' resulted from three generations of controlled crosses. The great-grandparents were 'Stillwood' (white), CAES 137 (red-bud), 'Shooting Star', and the broad-banded selection 'Bristol'. The banded male parent used in 1980 was a seedling produced by Chuck Molnar, Vernon, Connecticut, by crossing 'Shooting Star' with a banded plant (a hybrid of CAES 137 and 'Bristol'). There is a breeder fee of U.S. $0.15 for each plant propagated and sold (Jaynes). 4.5 ft high × 3.5 ft wide (1.4 × 1.1 m)

'Golden Flush' (Richard A. Jaynes, described here). Plate 42. This was selected several years ago by Sakuo Kaneko of Saitama-ken, Japan, from a batch of standard *Kalmia latifolia* seedlings. The emerging leaves are uniform yellow borne on bright red stems. Once the leaves are fully expanded, they gradually green up, first turning a lime green. The flowers are light pink and normal for the species. Propagation has been by grafting and has been limited to date. A plant with similar yellow foliage characteristics growing on Long Island, New York, has recently been brought to my attention by Werner Brack. Mature size of this cultivar is presently unknown. 'Golden Flush' may be patented.

'Goodrich' (Richard A. Jaynes, *The Laurel Book: Rediscovery of the North American Laurels*, 1975, color photo). Plate 43. The original plant was selected by John W. Goodrich and me from a native stand at Chaplin, Connecticut, in 1972. The cinnamon-brown band (f. *fuscata*) virtually fills the inside of the corolla, except for a white border along the edge; the plant name refers to the flower color as well as to Mr. Goodrich. Vigor and growth of plants in cultivation has been disappointing when grown in Connecticut, Georgia, and Washington (Hummel et al. 1990). This poor performance surprised us because the original plant was competing successfully in a natural woodland. The foliage is often a bit mottled, and leafspot resistance is moderate. 'Goodrich' is no longer grown commercially. 3.0 ft high × 3.0 ft wide (0.9 × 0.9 m)

'Good Show' (Wright's Nursery, Canby, Oregon, 1987 catalog). Plate 44. 'Good Show' was a seedling of 'Sharon Rose' selected by Arthur Wright in about 1980. The name best describes the plant when in bloom. Flowers are a deep pink in bud, changing to rich pink when open. Leaves are large, lustrous, dark green, and leafspot resistant. Rooting of cuttings is only fair, but 'Good Show' is a vigorous grower. It does well in full sun or shade and is a promising commercial variety. 5.0 ft high × 5.0 ft wide (1.5 × 1.5 m)

'Heart of Fire' (Richard A. Jaynes, 1988). Plate 45. This cultivar was a seedling of 'Ostbo Red' grown and selected by John Eichelser, Melrose Nursery, Olympia, Washington, and named by his daughter, Lori Eichelser Gangsei, in 1986. It was previously propagated and sold by Briggs and Melrose nurseries as J-1 and John's Red. Flowers are red in bud, similar to those of 'Ostbo Red', and open wide. In addition to the flowers, the plant was selected for its better foliage and habit. It is an upright, vigorous grower and may thus be better for naturalizing than for foundation plantings. Petioles and current-season stems are purplish red. It is leafspot resistant. 4.5 ft high × 3.5 ft wide (1.4 × 1.1 m)

'Hearts Desire' (Richard A. Jaynes, 1988). Plates 46 and 47. Selected by me and introduced by Briggs Nursery in 1987, 'Hearts Desire' has flowers that are red in bud and open with a cinnamon-red pigment that almost fills the inside of the corolla (f. *fuscata*). Both the center and lip (approximately one-sixteenth inch [1.5 mm]) of the corolla are white. The flower truss is large and many flowered; it buds well, but perhaps not as well as 'Kaleidoscope'. The new growth is an attractive bronzy red, and older foliage is glossy and dark green. It is leafspot resistant. 'Hearts Desire' is not as vigorous a grower as the similarly flowered 'Kaleidoscope', but its habit is broad and densely branched. This plant was selected from a controlled cross (1283) of a deep pink (319) and a banded/red-bud selection (CAES 137 x 'Bristol'/733ap). There is a breeder fee of U.S. $0.15 for each plant propagated and sold (Jaynes). 4.0 ft high × 4.5 ft wide (1.2 × 1.4 m)

'Hoffman's Pink' (Mike Johnson, Summer Hill Nursery, Madison, Connecticut, *Additions to the Plants We Grow*, 1992). Plate 48. This is a selection that Ludwig Hoffman of Bloomfield, Connecticut, made in about 1972, most likely from Weston Nurseries' plants, and first propagated in 1977. Initially identified as Hoffman's C, it was later named and introduced by Mike Johnson. Although not a selection from the wild, its flower color is within the range of native plants; the flowers are medium pink in bud and open to a pale pink. The foliage is dense, medium green, and the plant has an upright, vigorous habit. Cuttings are comparatively easy to root. 5.0 ft high × 4.0 ft wide (1.5 × 1.2 m)

'Kaleidoscope' (Richard A. Jaynes, 1988). Plates 49 and 50. Selected by me from a cross (1299) of 'Sarah' and a sibling of 'Bullseye', this selection was introduced by Knight Hollow Nursery in 1987. The flower is red in bud and opens to display a rich cinnamon-red band (f. *fuscata*) that almost fills the inside of the corolla, much like 'Hearts Desire'. The flowers are somewhat more brilliant on 'Kaleidoscope', although in smaller trusses than those of 'Hearts Desire'. The name reflects the multicolor and intricate pigment pattern of the open flowers. There is a distinctive white lip (approximately one-eighth inch [3 mm]) on the corolla edge, and the throat of the flower is white. The foliage is dark green and lustrous. Plant habit is somewhat upright and fairly dense. Petioles and stems of new growth are purplish red, except where heavily shaded. It buds up well when young and is a promising commercial variety. There is a breeder fee of U.S. $0.15 for each plant propagated and sold (Jaynes). 5.0 ft high × 4.5 ft wide (1.5 × 1.4 m)

Kalico Kal. This is an invalid cultivar name applied by Edmond Amateis to banded (f. *fuscata*) plants in a native stand on land belonging to Sebastian Koenig of Holmes, New York. The band's pigment is largely confined to the upper third of the corolla, at and above the anther pockets. See Calico, also an invalid name.

'Keepsake' (Richard A. Jaynes, described here). Plate 51. The culmination of five generations of controlled crosses begun in 1966, 'Keepsake' is a selection from a cross I made in 1983. The parent plants include 'Bristol' and several unnamed rich pink and red-bud selections (188, 189, 319, and CAES 137). The bud color is raspberry-red; the open flower is a near-solid purplish burgundy except for a white edge (f. *fuscata*)—much like 'Kaleidoscope'. The petioles are long and new growth is reddish bronze. The broad leaves are very glossy and a deep, bluish green in color. Foliage is leafspot resistant. Plants are well branched and dense. Flower bud production has occurred on young plants. Broken Arrow Nursery has distributed plants under the number 13-83 plt 1. Stoneboro Nurseries, Stoneboro, Pennsylvania, is producing plants in their micropropagation laboratory. (It is legitimate to question whether another cultivar of this flower color is needed, but the foliage is outstanding and people's response to the plant has been very positive.) There is a breeder fee of U.S. $0.15 for each plant sold (Jaynes). 4.5 ft high × 4.5 ft wide (1.4 × 1.4 m)

'Keystone' (Richard A. Jaynes, described here). This is a selection of the native mountain laurel made by William Barbour of Stoneboro Nurseries. Flowers are light pink in bud and near white when open, and leaves are somewhat glossy and dark green. Branching is greater and growth habit denser than that of the typical native. 'Keystone' was the best of three native selections micropropagated at Stoneboro Nurseries and has been sold in the past as selection #3. The name is from the designation of Pennsylvania as the Keystone State. 4.5 ft high × 4.5 ft wide (1.4 × 1.4 m)

'Little Linda' (Broken Arrow Nursery, Hamden, Connecticut, 1992–93 price list). Plate 52. Introduced by me and named for my daughter Linda, this is the first named mountain laurel to combine miniature habit (f. *myrtifolia*) with red-budded flowers. As the flowers open, they turn pink.

Flowers are only slightly reduced in size from that of the species, whereas foliage size and rate of growth are reduced by approximately one-half, as is typical with other miniature selections. With initial pruning to stimulate branching, the plant habit is as wide as tall. Compared to 'Elf', 'Little Linda' is slower growing, better branched, and more dense. Foliage is dark green, glossy, and leafspot resistant. Leaf blades recurve and twist and are more ovate (broader) than those of other named miniatures. 'Little Linda' is fully hardy in zone 6 and should be fine in zone 5. It resulted from five generations of controlled crosses begun in 1963, with the final cross made in 1982. Parent plants included in this series were two wild types (natives) from New Jersey that were heterozygous for the recessive *myrtifolia* gene, plus two red-budded and one deep pink selection and a banded selection, 'Star Cluster'. There is a breeder fee of U.S. $0.15 for each plant propagated and sold (Jaynes). 2.5 ft high × 2.5 ft wide (0.8 × 0.8 m)

M-14. See 'Olympic Fire'

'Madeline' (Richard A. Jaynes, described here). Plate 53. This is the only cultivar with a double flower (similar to hose-in-hose on azaleas). Many of the anthers have been converted to petals. The buds are a deep rose-pink, opening near white with scattered burgundy speckles. Foliage is a dark, glossy green. The original plant grows in New Zealand in the garden of Mrs. E. M. Finch and was planted by her mother-in-law Madeline in the 1930s. The plant is about 7 ft (2.2 m) tall and fairly dense. I was alerted to its existence by Ian Donovan of Pembroke, Massachusetts, who learned of it from Os Blumhardt of Whangarei, New Zealand—a renowned breeder of camellias and rhododendrons with whom I have corresponded. Lyndale Nurseries Auck in Whenuapai, New Zealand, has micropropagated 'Madeline' and kindly sent cultures to us at Broken Arrow Nursery, but plants will not be available until it is confirmed that they remain true for the double flowers after micropropagation. Is it not amazing that the only fully double-flowered mountain laurel ever found is discovered in a garden on the other side of the world in the opposite hemisphere from its native range! Mature size of this cultivar is presently unknown.

'Minuet' (Richard A. Jaynes, 1988). Plate 54. 'Minuet' was bred and selected by me and introduced by Briggs Nursery in 1987. It is a miniature (f. *myrtifolia*) like 'Elf' but, in addition, is banded (f. *fuscata*). The buds are light pink, and the flowers are large relative to the reduced plant habit.

The broad band is a solid, bright cinnamon color. The leaves of 'Minuet' are glossier, darker green, and narrower than those of other named miniatures; they recurve from petiole to tip, and the edges curve down. Stems of new growth are thick, petioles are short, and the foliage is resistant to leafspot. Compared to 'Elf', this selection branches better, and growth and habit are somewhat diminished. 'Minuet' produces flower buds when young and is commercially promising. It was selected from a cross (1254) made in 1978 of miniature × banded ('Star Cluster')/redbud. There is a breeder fee of U.S. $0.15 for each plant propagated and sold (Jaynes). 2.5 ft high × 2.5 ft wide (0.8 × 0.8 m)

f. *myrtifolia* (Bosse) K. Koch (*Dendrologie*, 1872). This botanical form, rarely found in the wild, is characterized by slower growth and smaller leaves (myrtle-like) that are more closely spaced along stems. Habit and foliage are about one-half to one-third normal size, and the flowers are reduced proportionally somewhat less. The form *myrtifolia* is traditionally called miniature, but semidwarf or small leaved might be better descriptions. Plants of this form are quite distinct from the species; yet, like seedlings of the species, individual plants may also vary in habit and rate of growth. The expression of the *myrtifolia* traits are under the control of a single recessive gene (*m*). Its common name is miniature laurel, but it also has been referred to as minor and nana. 'Elf', 'Little Linda', 'Minuet', 'Tiddlywinks', and 'Tinkerbell' are some mountain laurel cultivars exhibiting the *myrtifolia* trait.

'Nancy' (Richard A. Jaynes, *Connecticut Agricultural Experiment Station Mimeo List*, 1984). Selected by me in 1975, 'Nancy' was commercially introduced by Bolton Technologies, Bolton, Connecticut, in 1985. It is a clear, vibrant, pinkish red in bud, opening to a clear, bright pink. There is a crisp, narrow, maroon band within and near the corolla base. Foliage and habit are normal for the species. Petioles and stems of the current season's growth are purplish red except in heavily shaded sites. Late flushes of growth are yellow-green. This selection suffers from a lack of vigor, is moderately susceptible to leafspot, and appears to be susceptible to root rot, and is, therefore, out of favor with growers. 'Nancy' is from a 1974 controlled cross (1203) of a deep pink-flowered plant (319) with pollen of 'Pink Charm'. It is a sister plant (sibling) of 'Raspberry Glow' and 'Sarah', and I named it for my coworker of many years, Nancy Kluck. It is no longer propagated commercially. 3.5 ft high × 3.5 ft wide (1.1 × 1.1 m)

'Nathan Hale' (Mike Johnson, Summer Hill Nursery, Madison, Connecticut, *The Plants We Grow*, 1986). Plate 55. Selected in 1975 and commercially introduced by Ludwig Hoffman in 1980 as his selection #4, 'Nathan Hale' has flowers red in bud and pink when open. The growth habit is symmetrical and somewhat compact. It is relatively slow and dense growing, requiring little pruning when young. Foliage is dense, shiny, dark green, and leafspot resistant; petioles and stems of new growth are purplish red. It grows well in containers and is a promising commercial cultivar. Cuttings are moderately difficult to root. Selected by the Nathan Hale Society of the Sons of the American Revolution to honor Connecticut's Revolutionary War hero, Nathan Hale. 3.0 ft high × 3.0 ft wide (0.9 × 0.9 m)

'Nipmuck' (Richard A. Jaynes, *The Plant Propagator*, 1979). Plate 56. I selected this plant in 1971 at the Connecticut Agricultural Experiment Station. The buds are vivid red in color, and cuttings root with relative ease. It is similar to 'Quinnipiac', but the foliage color is a lighter yellow-green, it branches better, and it has more vigorous growth. The leaf blades are somewhat twisted. The upper foliage often turns an unattractive purplish color in autumn, especially if the plants are underfertilized, but normal color can return in the spring. Leafspot resistance is only moderate. Petioles and stems of the current season are moderately pigmented on the sun side. It buds well when young. 'Nipmuck' has become one of the standard red-budded cultivars for some nurseries, but it eventually will be replaced by other red-buds with better foliage attributes. It is from a cross (122) I made in 1963 of a plant with deep pink flowers (189) and one with red buds (CAES 137). 4.5 ft high × 4.0 ft wide (1.4 × 1.2 m)

f. *obtusata* (Rehder) Rehder (Alfred Rehder, *Rhodora*, 1910). This rare botanical form is characterized by oval to oblong-obovate leaves that are rounded at both ends. Petioles are short, and internodes are reduced in length. The expression of these traits is under the control of a single recessive gene (*ob*). The common name hedge laurel has been applied to these plants.

'Olympic Fire' (Briggs Nursery, Olympia, Washington, 1982 catalog, color photo). Plate 57. This cultivar was selected (in 1966), propagated, and introduced (in 1978) by John Eichelser of Melrose Nursery. It is a seedling of 'Ostbo Red'. The flowers are a rich pink to red in bud and near white when open, fading to pink. The wavy, glossy, often dense foliage is highly resistant to leafspot. Cuttings are easier to root than those of 'Ostbo Red', and some growers claim that the branches are less susceptible to breakage. 'Olympic Fire' has good growth habit and foliage color, especially when grown in containers. Field-grown plants in full sun, however, may be thin—that is, carry less foliage. Petioles and stems of new growth are purplish red on the sun side. Ringspot virus is often observed on older foliage, but it results in no obvious detriment to the plant in containers. However, the virus may be the cause of this cultivar's poor performance for us when it is field grown. 'Olympic Fire' has been a favored variety of container growers, but production plants do not produce flower buds readily. Originally tested and sold as M14. 4.5 ft high × 4.0 ft wide (1.4 × 1.2 m)

'Olympic Wedding' (Richard A. Jaynes, 1988). Plate 58. This cultivar was selected in 1984 from a cross of 'Ostbo Red' and 'Fresca' by John Eichelser of Melrose Nursery and introduced in 1987 by his daughter, Lori Eichelser Gangsei. The abundant buds are rosy pink in winter and open wide in spring to reveal a broken, maroon band (f. *fuscata*). New growth is bronzy red (purple-red in winter), and fall and winter foliage color is a dark green, purplish plum color. Older leaves are dark green, broad, thick, and strongly cupped across the leaf blade. The growth habit is somewhat open. There is a breeder fee of U.S. $0.35 per plant propagated and sold (Eichelser). 4.0 ft high × 4.0 ft wide (1.2 × 1.2 m)

'Ostbo Red' (John Eichelser, *International Plant Propagators' Society, Proceedings*, 1972; briefly described in Richard A. Jaynes, *International Plant Propagators' Society, Proceedings*, 1971). Plate 59. 'Ostbo Red' was selected in the 1940s by E. Ostbo from material obtained from Charles O. Dexter. It was named by John Eichelser of Melrose Nursery. The first red-budded selection to be named, it was also sold as Ostbo's Red #5, Ostbo #5, Dexter 5, West Coast 5, and Red-Bud *Kalmia*. The color and brilliance of other red buds should be judged against this selection; its abundant buds are iridescent red and most intense when grown in the sun. Petioles and stems of new growth are somewhat purplish red on the sun side. Leaves are slightly smaller, cupped, wavy, and more twisted than those of the species and are more resistant to leafspot. In some instances, container-grown plants derived from micropropagation have been susceptible to breakage at the soil line. 'Ostbo Red' is difficult to root and is a moderate grower. Older plants in the landscape are dense and often better looking than younger plants. It is a parent of 'Heart of

Fire', 'Olympic Fire', 'Olympic Wedding', 'Pink Star', and 'Wedding Band'. 3.5 ft high × 3.5 ft wide (1.1 × 1.1 m)

Ovata. This is an invalid cultivar name applied to plants with broad, ovate-shaped leaves. See f. *obtusata*.

'Paul Bosley' (Briggs Nursery, Olympia, Washington, 1990 and 1992 catalogs). Plate 60. This was grown and selected in 1980 by the late Paul Bosley of Bosley Nursery, Cleveland, Ohio. It was micropropagated by Briggs Nursery and first distributed in 1990 as Bosley #1. Flowers are rich reddish pink in bud and medium to strong pink when open. They are borne in tight clusters on a plant of good foliage density and upright growth habit. Leaves are broad, dark green, and leafspot resistant. It buds well as a young plant. 4.0 ft high × 3.5 ft wide (1.2 × 1.1 m)

Peckham's Pink Strain (Greer Gardens, Eugene, Oregon, 1981 catalog). This is a strain of seedlings grown by George and Shirley Peckham of Pleasant Hill, Oregon, with light, bright, pastel pink flowers.

'Peppermint' (Broken Arrow Nursery, Hamden, Connecticut, 1991–92 price list). Plate 61. Selected from a cross I made in 1984, the most outstanding feature of this cultivar is the maroon-red pigmentation pattern of the open flower. A ten-spoked star radiates from the base of the corolla, at times connecting with streaks of pigment that run through the anther sacs, all on a near-white background. The cultivar name comes from the likeness in appearance of the flower to a peppermint candy. A sibling, look-alike plant received the Ames Award in the 1991 Boston Flower Show for the best plant in show. Flower buds are a blush pink. New growth is tinged reddish bronze; the last flush of the season may be yellow. Older foliage is dark green and has relatively flat leaf blades. 'Peppermint' branches well. Its parents included a plant with a distinctive star-ring at the base of the open flower; the other, collected in 1978 by Clarence Towe near the Chattooga River, South Carolina, had notable reddish burgundy streaks through the anther pockets. There is a breeder fee of U.S. $0.15 for each plant propagated and sold (Jaynes). 4.0 ft high × 3.5 ft wide (1.2 × 1.1 m)

'Pequot' (Clark's Greenhouse and Nursery, Salem, Connecticut, 1988 price list). Plate 62. This is a plant selected and named by Gerald Verkade from plant material he received from me while I was at the Connecticut Agricultural Experiment Station. 'Pequot' may be a sister plant to 'Nipmuck' and 'Quinnipiac' and, like them, was named for a Native

American tribe. Flowers are deep red in bud, opening to a light pink, and new growth is purplish red. The dark green leaves are somewhat small, twisted, cupped, and shiny; the leaf blade is acutely tapered to the base. Growth is initially somewhat upright, well branched, and dense foliaged. 3.5 ft high × 3.5 ft wide (1.1 × 1.1 m)

'Pink Charm' (Richard A. Jaynes, *International Plant Propagators' Society, Proceedings*, 1980; *Journal of Heredity*, 1981, color cover photo). Plate 63. This cultivar was selected by me in 1974 and commercially introduced by Briggs Nursery in 1982. It originated from a 1970 controlled cross (1078) at the Connecticut Agricultural Experiment Station of two pink selections (138 and 316) obtained from Weston Nurseries. Flower buds are deep pink to red, open flowers are a rich pink; it buds well when young and is prolific. The matte, cupped leaves are a medium dark green and are leafspot resistant. Stems of the current season's growth are almost entirely purplish red, and petioles are pigmented above. The habit and growth of 'Pink Charm' is somewhat open, but denser than that of 'Pink Surprise'. Cuttings are relatively easy to root. 'Pink Charm' was the pollen parent of 'Nancy', 'Raspberry Glow', and 'Sarah', and is in the parentage of 'Tiddlywinks' and 'Tinkerbell'. 3.5 ft high × 3.5 ft wide (1.1 × 1.1 m)

'Pink Frost' (Greer Gardens, Eugene, Oregon, 1981 catalog; Briggs Nursery, Olympia, Washington, 1982 catalog, color photo). Plate 64. 'Pink Frost' was selected in 1965 by John Eichelser at Melrose Nursery and commercially introduced in 1977. The large, pink buds open to white flowers that turn blush pink; young plants do not bud readily. The leafspot-resistant foliage is excellent, with wide, lustrous leaves on a well-proportioned plant. On nursery-grown plants, at least, the last flush of growth is often yellow. Scorch on leaves has been a problem in the northeastern United States on field-grown plants, but not a problem if shade grown. Cuttings of 'Pink Frost' root better than most other selections. 3.5 ft high × 3.5 ft wide (1.1 × 1.1 m)

'Pink Globe' (Clark's Greenhouse and Nursery, Salem, Connecticut, 1991 price list). Plate 60. This plant was selected by Gerald Verkade in 1976 from a cross (952) I made in 1968 between two plants with deep pink flowers (138 and 293), both of which originated at Weston Nurseries. First called "hydrangea" because of its tight, ball-like trusses of flowers, the selection was introduced as 'Pink Globe'. (Hydrangea was inappropriate, of course, as it is another plant.) Flowers are a rich, deep pink and are borne in tight clusters; it buds at a young age. Leaves are thick, broad, dark green, and leafspot resistant; plant habit is broad and dense. 3.0 ft high × 3.5 ft wide (0.9 × 1.1 m)

'Pink Star' (Greer Gardens, Eugene, Oregon, 1982 catalog). Plate 65. This is a seedling of 'Ostbo Red' selected and introduced by John Eichelser. The corolla is deeply cut to form large, star-shaped flowers that are a clear, dark pink. The leaf blades are narrow, wavy, and acutely tapered at each end. Under good growing conditions, shoots of this selection tend to extend continuously during the growing season, in contrast to the discrete flushes of most other cultivars. Heavy pruning and/or reduced fertilization is required to obtain good branching. In typical nursery culture, growth is floppy, leaving 'Pink Star' out of favor with many growers. 3.5 ft high × 3.5 ft wide (1.1 × 1.1 m)

'Pink Surprise' (Richard A. Jaynes, 1975). Plate 66. Selected by me in 1965 from a field at Weston Nurseries and commercially introduced in 1979, this is the first mountain laurel cultivar I named. Flower buds are strong pink, opening to medium pink. Foliage is dark green, and leafspot resistance has been reported from fair to good. Stems of new growth are purplish red, and petioles are pigmented above. The growth habit tends to be open and leggy; therefore, it is not grown much commercially any longer. Cuttings are relatively easy to root—that was the "surprise". 3.5 ft high × 3.5 ft wide (1.1 × 1.1 m)

'Pinwheel' (Richard A. Jaynes, 1988). Plates 67 and 68. Selected by me in 1982 and introduced by Briggs Nursery in 1987, this is a banded (f. *fuscata*) selection grown from open-pollinated seed of unknown parentage. The inside of the corolla is nearly filled with cinnamon-maroon pigment, but its center and scalloped edge are white. The color, form, and arrangement of a truss of open flowers are reminiscent of sweet william (*Dianthus barbatus*) and so "busy" that they can be compared to whirling pinwheels. Foliage is leafspot resistant, lustrous, dark green, wavy, and cupped. Growth habit is upright. Stems of new growth may have a purplish red blush on the side exposed to the sun, but otherwise they are entirely green, as are the petioles. Container plants bud well. 3.5 ft high × 3.0 ft wide (1.1 × 0.9 m)

f. *polypetala* (Nickolsen) Beissner, Schelle, & Zabel (*Handbuch den Laubgeholz-Benennung*, 1903). Plate 17. This botanical form is rarely found in nature. Typically, the corolla is cut into five straplike petals, and this form has been given the common name feather petal. I have grown numerous seedlings from controlled crosses in an attempt to obtain an apple blossom–like flower on a *Kalmia*, but the feather petal offspring typically lack vigor. The 'Shooting Star' flower trait is similar but more promising to work with. Ebinger (1974) also includes other corolla types—reduced corolla ('Bettina') and no corolla (apetala)—as expressions of this botanical form. Each of these corolla types is under the control of different recessive genes: feather petal (*p*), 'Shooting Star' (*s*), 'Bettina' (*be*), and apetala (*ap*). Because of the distinct single gene control of each of these traits, they could be separated into separate botanical forms.

'Pristine' (Briggs Nursery, Olympia, Washington, 1988–89 liner list; Woodlanders, Aiken, South Carolina, 1989–90 catalog). Plate 69. This plant was discovered in a natural laurel population by Ernestine Law in Aiken, South Carolina, and was introduced by Woodlanders. It was selected and named for its abundant, pure, crystalline white flowers that lack any trace of pink. The foliage is a medium green and the leaf blades are relatively flat; petioles and one-year-old branches are yellow-green. Late flushes of growth may turn yellow. Foliage and habit are somewhat diminutive compared to other selections. It branches well and is fairly dense. Although not apparent to the naked eye, the leaves are thicker than those of many other selections. 'Pristine' may be more heat tolerant than most other cultivars, since it was selected in zone 8; it also performs well in zone 6. It can be somewhat slow and difficult to grow for the first year or two, then it does fine. Cuttings can be rooted. 3.0 ft high × 3.0 ft wide (0.9 × 0.9 m)

'Quinnipiac' (Richard A. Jaynes, *The Plant Propagator*, 1979). I selected this plant in 1971 at the Connecticut Agricultural Experiment Station. The flower buds are a vivid red and open much lighter. It is similar to its sibling 'Nipmuck', but the foliage is darker green and growth is less vigorous. Petioles are usually pigmented purplish red above; leaf blades are wavy and twisted. Foliage is prone to purple leafspot in the fall, especially if plants are container grown. 'Quinnipiac' is from a cross (122) I made in 1963. Cuttings root with relative ease. A Connecticut nurseryman had strongly urged me to name new mountain laurel releases for local Native American tribes, hence the origin of the names Nipmuck and Quinnipiac. I soon realized that most of these tribe names were difficult for many people to spell, pronounce, or remember—good examples of bad names that do not sell. 3.5 ft high × 3.5 ft wide (1.1 × 1.1 m)

'Raspberry Glow' (Richard A. Jaynes, *Connecticut Agricultural Experiment Station Mimeo List*, 1984). Plate 70. Commercially propagated in 1985 by Bolton Technologies, Art Knuttel and I selected this from offspring of a 1974 controlled cross (1203) that I made of a deep pink-flowered plant (319) with pollen of 'Pink Charm'. When the first flowers started to open we were sure it was going to be solid red. The flowers are deep burgundy-red in bud, but they open with strong pink on the inside of the corolla and fade to a medium pink. As the name suggests, it is one of the most eye-catching cultivars in flower. The flower color is also well expressed on shade-grown plants. Foliage is dark green and leafspot resistant, and stems of new growth are purplish red. Some growers have found that it does not support itself well in containers; field-grown plants are fine. The growth habit is upright. 'Raspberry Glow' is a sibling of 'Nancy' and 'Sarah'. 4.0 ft high × 3.5 ft wide (1.2 × 1.1 m)

'Raspberry Swirl' (Clark's Greenhouse and Nursery, Salem, Connecticut, 1989 price list). Selected by Gerald Verkade, this cultivar resulted from crossing a red-bud with a banded mountain laurel, which he did by caging a bumblebee with the two plants. Flower buds of 'Raspberry Swirl' are pink; the open corolla has a broad maroon band (f. *fuscata*), with a white center and edge and a few flecks of white near the anther pockets. Foliage is medium green, with narrow, cupped, wavy leaf blades, and is leafspot resistant. Stems of new growth are golden yellow. Growth habit is somewhat upright to rounded. 3.5 ft high × 3.5 ft wide (1.1 × 1.1 m)

Red-bud. An invalid cultivar name, this is a common commercial name for cultivars and seedlings with intensely red-colored buds, such as 'Nathan Hale', 'Nipmuck', 'Olympic Fire', 'Ostbo Red', 'Quinnipiac', and 'Sharon Rose'.

'Richard Jaynes' (Briggs Nursery, Olympia, Washington, 1984 catalog). Plate 71. This plant first flowered before 1965 and was selected by Edmund Mezitt at Weston Nurseries. He named it in honor of me in 1977. Weston Nurseries originally propagated the selection by grafting and sold the plant on a limited scale for many years. The flower buds are red to dark raspberry in color. The inside of the newly opened corolla has a silvery white cast over pink. The darker color of the buds seems to bleed through to the inside of the corolla, giving a uniform dark pink-to-red color in a truss of fully open flowers. Mezitt considered this plant a major breakthrough in his crossing-selection program because it was a "bleeder" and was the first plant to show true progress toward becoming a red mountain laurel. It is a heavy, annual bloomer. Foliage is dark green and glossy, with an undulated or twisted blade; leafspot resistance has been reported from fair to good. Stems of new growth and petioles are purplish red in color. It does not grow to a salable size as rapidly and uniformly as some other selections. 3.5 ft high × 3.5 ft wide (1.1 × 1.1 m).

Rosea. This invalid cultivar name was applied to plants with deeply pigmented flowers. See also Rubra.

Rubra. This is another invalid cultivar name applied to plants with deeply pigmented flowers. Botanical forms should define a discreet class of plants. The deep, rich pink-flowered plants found in nature actually form a continuum with plants having lightly pigmented flowers. See also Rosea.

'Sandy Mountain' (Richard A. Jaynes, described here). Selected, propagated, and sold by Tom Dodd Nurseries, Semmes, Alabama, this selection was derived from a cross of sandhill laurel (*Kalmia hirsuta*) with mountain laurel (*Kalmia latifolia*) that was in turn backcrossed to mountain laurel (open-pollination), and then open-pollinated one more generation. The overall appearance of 'Sandy Mountain' is similar to that of a mountain laurel, but it is the only cultivar with some sandhill laurel in the parentage. Flowers are medium to light pink and large in size.

'Sarah' (Richard A. Jaynes, *International Plant Propagators' Society, Proceedings*, 1982). Plates 72 and 73. This form was selected by me at the Connecticut Agricultural Experiment Station, named for my wife, and introduced by Knight Hollow Nursery in 1983. The eye-catching flowers are red in bud and pink-red when open; this is perhaps the reddest selection to date. It was an easy plant to select, as the bright flowers captured my attention immediately in a field of pink and red-budded laurel. The foliage is dark green; however, it is susceptible to leafspot in shady, moist situations. Petioles and young stems are purplish red and growth habit is dense and rounded. Plants can do well in containers, but this cultivar is susceptible to high salts. Overfertilization thus causes browning of leaf tips and margins, damage often associated with winter injury. This has been a problem plant for some, but not all, container growers. The plant was selected from a controlled cross (1203) of a deep pink-flowered plant (319) with pollen of 'Pink Charm'. It is a sibling of 'Nancy' and 'Raspberry Glow' and the seed parent of 'Kaleidoscope'. 3.5 ft high × 3.5 ft wide (1.1 × 1.1 m)

'Sharon Rose' (Richard A. Jaynes, 1988). Plate 74. Selected from seedlings of richly pigmented laurel of uncertain source, this form was propagated by Arthur Wright of Wright's Nursery and named for his wife. Plants have been sold under this name since about 1979. Flowers buds are bright red, fading to pink when open. The inside of the corolla is initially near white, becoming more pink. Plant habit is dense and compact and cuttings are comparatively easy to root. Leafspot has been a problem at some locations. 3.0 ft high × 3.0 ft wide (0.9 × 0.9 m)

Sheffield Park (Gerd Krüssmann, *Handbuch der Laubgeholze*, Berlin, 1962; W. J. Bean, *Trees and Shrubs*, vol. 2, G. Taylor, editor, London, 1973). This selection is reported as a cultivar by Gerd Krüssmann and as a strain by W. J. Bean. It is apparently a strain of pink-flowered plants grown by A. G. Soames at Sheffield Park, England, which in turn came from material grown at the Knap Hill Nursery.

'Shooting Star' (Richard A. Jaynes, 1975, color photo). Plate 75. Selected in 1972 by Marjorie and Hollis Rogers from a native stand in Danbury, North Carolina, this cultivar was commercially introduced in 1982 by Briggs Nursery. The corolla is cut to give five distinct lobes that reflex after the flower opens, a unique flower form found only once in the wild. It flowers about one week later than the typical species. The leaves are shiny, broad, and relatively flat; new growth is yellow-green. 'Shooting Star' is leafspot resistant, but leaves discolor or mottle. It is a tall, lanky grower and reported by some to be brittle. This plant is some-what less hardy than the species. The near-petal trait is under the control of a single recessive gene (*s*). Plants of this flower type can be considered as belonging to the botanical form *polypetala*. See also 'Comet', an offspring of 'Shooting Star' with a similar flower. 4.0 ft high × 3.5 ft wide (1.2 × 1.1 m)

'Silver Dollar' (Richard A. Jaynes, 1975, color photo). Plate 76. Selected in 1952 at Weston Nurseries, 'Silver Dollar' was introduced in their 1977 catalog. White-to-pink blush flowers with attractive pigment markings are up to 1.5 in (4 cm) across. This is the only selection with notably oversized flowers, and the flowers are, in fact, the size of old U.S. silver dollars. It is partially sterile and may be a mixaploid (abnormal chromosome number). The leaves are dark green, large, leathery, and relatively flat in cross section, and leafspot resistance is reported from poor to excellent. It has developed little leafspot growing in woodland shade at Broken Arrow Nursery for 20 years. Container growers have had mixed results with 'Silver Dollar'. It may be more sensitive to poor drainage and more susceptible to root diseases than other selections. One commercial grower recommends that it be grown in shade. Field-grown plants are generally well branched and dense; they also develop thick, massive root systems. 3.5 ft high × 3.5 ft wide (1.1 × 1.1 m)

'Snowdrift' (Richard A. Jaynes, 1988). Plate 77. This is a compact, densely foliaged, white-flowered plant selected by Bruce Briggs and me at Broken Arrow Nursery. The name reflects its appearance in flower. 'Snowdrift' is thickly branched and has dark green leaves, and it grows at least as broad as tall. It is leafspot resistant in Connecticut, but it may be less so in the southeastern United States. Micropropagated plants are slow growing the first two or three years, but then grow vigorously. The seed parent was in a planting of white-flowered plants isolated by several hundred feet from other mountain laurel. There is a breeder fee of U.S. $0.15 for each plant propagated and sold (Jaynes). 3.5 ft high × 4.0 ft wide (1.1 × 1.2 m)

'Splendens' (Exhibited by J. Veitch and Sons, *Journal of the Royal Horticultural Society*, 1890). Plate 78. R. DeBelder described 'Splendens' plants growing at the Arboretum at Kalmthout, Belgium, as such: "flowers deeper shade than the type but 'Clementine Churchill' is definitely the best for flower colouring" (*Journal of the Royal Horticultural Society* 94: 91). 'Splendens' was the first mountain laurel selection to be named. The medium pink flowers well-highlighted with reddish pigment spots are an example of a good pink selection, which most likely originated from the wild. Foliage and growth habit are normal for the species. 4.0 ft high × 4.0 ft wide (1.2 × 1.2 m)

'Star Cluster' (Holden Arboretum, Mentor, Ohio, 1983). Plate 79. This selection originated in 1940 at the Charles Dexter Estate and was selected and released by Holden Arboretum. The flowers are similar to those of 'Fresca', but the banding is not as interrupted. The speckled, maroon band on the inside of the corolla (f. *fuscata*) contrasts with the otherwise white corolla and white buds. Leaves are cupped and medium green, and the plant is broadly spreading. 'Star Cluster' may be more tolerant of clay soils than most other cultivars. It has been propagated from cuttings as well as micropropagated. Louis Lipp sent a banded plant to me in the early 1960s, which I used in crosses (see 'Freckles', 'Minuet', and 'Yankee Doodle'); later the plant was named 'Star Cluster'. Partly because of initial mislabeling of plants in tissue culture, 'Star Cluster' has been slow to make its way into commercial production. 3.5 ft high × 3.5 ft wide (1.1 × 1.1 m)

Star-ring. This is not a cultivar name but a descriptive term for plants whose flowers have an intensely pigmented ring within and near the base of the corolla and five spokes that radiate up the creases between the five corolla lobes. The trait appears to be under the control of a single dominant gene (*Sr*). See 'Peppermint'.

'Stillwood' (Richard A. Jaynes, 1975, color photo). Plate 80. In 1962 I selected this plant with Henry I. Baldwin from a native stand in the Russell Abbott Forest, Wilton, New Hampshire. It was commercially introduced by Knight Hollow Nursery in 1983. Flower buds are white (when grown in full sun), and they open white. A very faint pink ring may show near the base of the corolla, and on close inspection, pigment specks within the corolla and near the anther pockets may be visible. Stems of new growth are yellow to yellow-green, presenting a pleasing contrast to the light-to-medium green foliage. Leaf blades are relatively flat. Growth habit and form are somewhat open and typical for the species. 'Stillwood' was likely a parent of 'Angel', and it appears to be no longer in commercial propagation. 3.5 ft high × 3.5 ft wide (1.1 × 1.1 m)

'Sunset' (Richard A. Jaynes, 1988). Plate 81. Selected and named in 1979 by R. Wayne Mezitt of Weston Nurseries, 'Sunset' has been propagated and sold at the nursery since 1985. Its flowers are bright red in bud and strong pink when open. The leaves vary in shape and size, and sometimes are narrow and twisted with recurved edges. The petioles are purplish red. The plant habit is open and spreading. 3.0 ft high × 3.5 ft wide (0.9 × 1.1 m)

'Tiddlywinks' (Evergreen Cloning, Waterford, Connecticut, 1988 price list). Plate 82. Selected by me in 1985 from a 1978 controlled cross (1260), this plant is a miniature or semidwarf (f. *myrtifolia*) mountain laurel with good branching and pink flowers. Flower buds are typically a medium to strong pink and open to a soft pink. Color intensity varies with both the season and plant exposure. Growth rate is similar to that of 'Elf', but branching is better and the plant habit is broader. Leaves are dark green and about one-half the normal size, but the flowers, as with other f. *myrtifolia* selections, are reduced less, about 20 to 25 percent. It buds well as a young plant. One of the grandparents of 'Tiddlywinks' is 'Pink Charm', the latter being the source of the genes for pink flower color. There is a breeder fee of U.S. $0.15 for each plant propagated and sold (Jaynes). 2.5 ft high × 3.0 ft wide (0.8 × 0.9 m)

'Tightwad' (Richard A. Jaynes, 1988). This plant was selected by the late Henry Wright of Highlands, North Carolina, and named by Clarence Towe of Walhalla, South Carolina. It apparently was found in the wild in western North Carolina. Its noteworthy feature is the flowers, which develop to the large bud stage and remain in good condition for a month beyond the normal bloom period, but never open. If grown in the sun, the flower buds are a good pink. It is pollen- and seed-sterile, the pistils are often short and fasciated, and foliage is leafspot susceptible. Cummins Garden, Marlboro, New Jersey, has propagated the plant. Other plants of this type have been found in the wild; see 'Tightwad Too', as well as the discussion in Chapter 16. 4.0 ft high × 3.5 ft wide (1.2 × 1.1 m)

'Tightwad Too' (Richard A. Jaynes, described here). Plates 83 and 84. Dan Cappel, a biology teacher at Wilton High School, Connecticut, alerted me to this plant in 1973. He discovered it in the Nature Conservancy's Devils Den Preserve, Weston, Connecticut, on July 4 (other laurel had finished blooming in mid-June). The buds expand one to two weeks after most laurel and remain closed and in good condition for about four weeks before turning brown. The flower buds are an eye-catching, rosy pink and winter twig color is burgundy-red. In contrast to the original 'Tightwad' selection, this plant is highly resistant to leafspot. It also has attractive dark foliage of good density on an upright, well-proportioned plant. Andy Brand of Broken Arrow Nursery has recently begun propagation in tissue culture; it is difficult to root from cuttings. The original plant was multiplied by grafting. 3.5 ft high × 3.5 ft wide (1.1 × 1.1 m)

'Tinkerbell' (Grow Tec, Glastonbury, Connecticut, 1989 catalog). Plate 85. I selected this plant in 1985 from a series of three crosses made in 1968, 1974, and 1978 (cross 1262). This semidwarf (f. *myrtifolia*) selection is similar to 'Tiddlywinks', although the flowers are heavier textured, bud color is a deeper pink, and flowers open to a medium pink. Both selections have a narrow, maroon-pigmented ring within and near the base of the corolla. Foliage is dark green and highly resistant to leafspot. The leaf blade of 'Tinkerbell' is more cup- or V-shaped in cross section than that of the flatter-leaved 'Tiddlywinks'. The growth rate is greater than that for most other f. *myrtifolia* selections, and 'Tinkerbell' grows broader than it does tall. Pink flowering genes were derived from 'Pink Charm' and a numbered selection (319). There is a breeder fee of U.S. $0.15 for each plant propagated and sold (Jaynes). 2.5 ft high × 3.5 ft wide (0.8 × 1.1 m)

'Twenty' (Richard A. Jaynes, 1988). This selection was grown from seed germinated in the 1950s by Edmund Mezitt at Weston Nurseries and selected by him in the 1960s. It was propagated and sold at the nursery as #20 beginning in 1965. The flowers are dark pink in bud and open to a medium pink. Foliage is glossy and dark green, and the leaves are long, with a distinct fold along the center rib. The plant is low and compact, growing broader than tall. Open-pollinated seedlings of this plant also tend to be more compact than the species. 3.0 ft high × 4.0 ft wide (0.9 × 1.2 m)

'Waxy Max' (Cummins Garden, Marlboro, New Jersey, 1996 catalog). This is a selection and introduction of Elizabeth Cummins. She has propagated and sold a few plants in recent years. 'Waxy Max' has glossy, broad, thick, deep green leaves on a plant of dense habit and relatively slow growth. Stems of new growth are purplish red. In tight clusters, flowers are rich pink to red in bud and narrowly banded when open (f. *fuscata*), reminiscent of the flowers of 'Yankee Doodle'. 3.5 ft high × 3.5 ft wide (1.1 × 1.1 m)

'Wedding Band' (Richard A. Jaynes, 1988). This cultivar was selected in 1984 by John Eichelser at Melrose Nursery and named by his daughter, Lori Eichelser Gangsei. A sibling of 'Olympic Wedding', it came from a cross of 'Ostbo Red' and 'Fresca'. Eventually, 'Wedding Band' was withdrawn from production because of its similarity to other cultivars.

'White Mountain' (Weston Nurseries, Hopkinton, Massachusetts, 1993 catalog). This plant was selected and named by Wayne Mezitt. Buds are white or sometimes tinged pink and open to white. Foliage is an attractive dark green, glossy, and leafspot resistant. There has been limited tissue culture propagation of 'White Mountain'. 4.0 ft high × 4.0 ft wide (1.2 × 1.2 m)

'Willowcrest' (Richard A. Jaynes, 1975, photo). Plate 86. Named by me and propagated from a large plant at the Henry Foundation for Botanical Research in Gladwyn, Pennsylvania, this selection was originally collected by Henry Wright in the mountains of North Carolina. 'Willowcrest' is a selection of form *angustata*, with linear and recurved leaves that give the plant a graceful appearance. It is leafspot resistant. The flower buds are medium pink, opening to a blush pink. Pollen is sometimes aborted and the pistils fasciated (flattened); possibly because of some of these irregularities, flowers occasionally do not fully open. The willow-leaved form is very rare in the wild and is under the control of a single recessive gene (*w*). See 'Willowood'. 3.0 ft high × 3.5 ft wide (0.9 × 1.1 m)

'Willowood' (Richard A. Jaynes, described here). Plate 87. This plant was discovered in the wild by Robert L. Mackintosh of Woodlanders, Aiken, South Carolina. It is a willow-leaved selection (f. *angustata*). The leaves are very narrow, slightly recurved, and smaller than the leaves of 'Willowcrest'. Leaf length varies greatly from 2.5 in (6.5 cm) to less than 1 in (2.5 cm) near the terminals. Occasional leaves have narrow, white-variegated stripes. The growth rate is slow to moderate, developing good branching and a dense habit. The foliage is dark, glossy, and leafspot resistant, and the texture is fine, giving the plant an overall delicate appearance. Flowers are bell-shaped and typically do not open fully. The corolla is pale pink and highlighted on the inside, with bold burgundy pigment specks at and near the anther pockets. Pollen is produced, but not seed. Cuttings can be rooted with some difficulty. Propagation has been limited to date by Woodlanders, Cummins Garden, and Broken Arrow Nursery. 2.5 ft high × 3.0 ft wide (0.8 × 0.9 m)

'Window' (Richard A. Jaynes, 1988). Formerly called Den Window, this plant was selected in the 1960s by Edmund Mezitt. It is a fourth-generation pink selection. Weston Nurseries has propagated and sold the plant since 1972. The open flowers are large and light pink, becoming progressively deeper pink as they mature. 'Window' is robust, being both wide and upright and somewhat open. The leaves are broad and slightly folded along the midrib. Foliage is bluish green or gray-green under low fertility, and new growth is glossy. The name came from the plant's location by the house. 4.0 ft high × 3.5 ft wide (1.2 × 1.1 m)

'Yankee Doodle' (Richard A. Jaynes, *Connecticut Agricultural Experiment Station Mimeo List*, 1984). Plate 88. I selected this cultivar in 1975, and it was commercially propagated and introduced by Bolton Technologies in

1985. The flowers are vivid pink to red in bud and have a narrow maroon band on the open corolla (f. *fuscata*), which contrasts well with the white background color of the open corolla. The inner pigmented ring of the corolla is crisp and burgundy-red in color. Foliage is dense on a semicompact plant. Petioles and new stems are purplish red on the sun side. Foliage is leafspot resistant. In winter the bright yellow petioles contrast well with the dark green foliage and orange-red flower buds. 'Yankee Doodle' originated from a second-generation controlled cross (1028) I made in 1969; the first-generation cross was made in 1963 (a cross of a banded and a red-budded plant, 'Star Cluster' and 187, respectively). 3.5 ft high × 3.5 ft wide (1.1 × 1.1 m)

Kalmia angustifolia Linnaeus var. *angustifolia*, Northern Sheep Laurel

f. *candida* Fernald (*Rhodora*, 1913). Plates 21 and 23. This white-flowered form has no anthocyanin. The presence of anthocyanin is controlled by a single dominant gene (*A*).

'Hammonasset' (Richard A. Jaynes, *International Plant Propagators' Society, Proceedings*, 1972). Plates 20 and 21. I selected this plant in 1961 from a native stand in Madison, Connecticut, where it grew along the Hammonasset River. It was commercially introduced in 1972. Flowers are a rich, bluish rose. Mature height is about 2 to 2.5 ft (0.8 to 0.9 m) in 10 years, somewhat less than is common for the species.

'Kennebago' (Mike Johnson, Summer Hill Nursery, Madison, Connecticut, *Additions to the Plants We Grow*, 1992). Plate 89. This selection has shiny leaves and deep rose flowers that are almost as dark as those of 'Hammonasset', but the growth is more vigorous. Mike Johnson collected this plant from Kennebago Lake, Maine.

'Poke Logan' (Mike Johnson, Summer Hill Nursery, Madison, Connecticut, *Additions to the Plants We Grow*, 1992). Leaves of this selection are glossy, growth is vigorous, and the flowers are light pink. Poke Logan is the name Native Americans in Maine gave to marshy, swampy areas. Mike Johnson found the plant in a wet area by the Little Kennebago River in an area called the Logans, hence the name.

Pumila. This is an invalid cultivar name. See 'Royal Dwarf'.

'Royal Dwarf' (Richard A. Jaynes, described and named here). Plates 90 and 91. This selection was formerly listed as "Pumila." Pumila is a descriptive term meaning dwarf that could be applied to various selections having dwarf or low habit. It is like the descriptive names ovata, nana, and rubra which, although valid if applied to a selection before 1955, are confusing because it is difficult to know if they refer to one clone or to a group of plants that may vary considerably. I received a nice low-growing plant under the name pumila years ago from the Royal Botanic Garden, Edinburgh, Scotland. The growth habit is compact and could be described as semidwarf, a characteristic associated with northern sources of the species—1.5 to 2.0 ft (0.5 to 0.6 m) in 10 years. Foliage is attractive and the flowers are a bright rose-pink with a hint of lavender. Typically, in southern New England, the plant reblooms in late summer and early fall, opening a few flowers over a period of several weeks—a very appealing trait that has little, if any, negative effect on the flower display the following spring.

Kalmia angustifolia var. *caroliniana* (Small) Fernald, Southern Sheep Laurel

A white-flowered form is known in cultivation that is similar to f. *candida* described above.

Kalmia cuneata Michaux, White Wicky

Kalmia ericoides Wright ex Grisebbach var. *ericoides*, Cuban Laurel

Kalmia ericoides var. *aggregata* (Small) Ebinger, Cuban Laurel

Kalmia hirsuta Walter, Sandhill Laurel

Kalmia microphylla (Hooker) Heller var. *microphylla*, Western Alpine Laurel

Kalmia microphylla var. *occidentalis* (Small) Ebinger, Western Bog Laurel

f. *alba* Ebinger (*Rhodora*, 1974). A white-flowered form collected near Wrangell, Alaska, and Lulu Island, British Columbia.

Kalmia polifolia Wangenheim, Bog Laurel, Eastern Bog Laurel

f. *leucantha* Schofield & Smith (*Canadian Field Naturalist*, 1953). This white-flowered form is known from one collection in Hodgewater Line, Newfoundland.

Hybrids Between Species

'Rocky Top', *Kalmia polifolia* × *K. microphylla* var. *microphylla* (Richard A. Jaynes, 1975). Plate 92. This selection is from a first-generation cross (356) made in 1974 with plants from Mount Washington, New Hampshire, and Mount Adams, Washington. It is more tolerant of northeastern growing conditions than the western alpine laurel. 'Rocky Top' has an intermediate habit, with a mature height of 1 to 1.5 ft (0.3 to 0.5 m). It is pollen- and seed-sterile and is a triploid. Vegetative cuttings are easy to root, although it has not been commercially propagated. Originally I had great expectations for this and similar hybrids as rock garden plants, but as previously noted (Jaynes 1988), they are susceptible to mites and not long-lived in eastern gardens. Recent information suggests that I may have prematurely declared the patient dead! A plant at the Arnold Arboretum of Harvard University, Jamaica Plain, Massachusetts, looked fine after more than 20 years, and Polly Hill of Martha's Vineyard, Massachusetts, says her 'Rocky Top', received in 1978, "is a survivor." Cool, maritime climates and more northern gardens would seem to be the most promising sites for this hybrid.

'Sandy Mountain'. See under *Kalmia latifolia* cultivars discussed earlier in this chapter.

Insights on Naming and Releasing Cultivars

In the early 1970s you could hardly give away new *Kalmia* selections for propagation, and virtually no new cultivars were being named. Although numerous unique and attractive selections were available, they were difficult to propagate. But tissue culture of ericaceous plants was only then beginning in earnest and was destined to make propagation easier. There was also a growing demand for mountain laurel in the marketplace. The subsequent result has not been too surprising; we have had a mini-explosion of new cultivars, going from less than 20 to nearly 80 in only 25 years.

Do we need all these cultivars? Not really.

Will more be named in the future? Most certainly.

Was it a mistake to name so many? No, each was justified in its time. The chance of uncovering some truly great selections is increased by thoroughly testing many superior plants, and naming often facilitates distribution and testing.

When is it justified to name a new selection? It should be clearly superior to other previously named cultivars in one or more traits, and there should be a potential market for the plant. When and how to judge "superior" is the problem.

What criteria do I use to name a new selection? Typically, a new selection will come from a field of several hundred other mountain laurel seedlings, all grown from controlled crosses. In addition to the seedlings in the field, it will also be compared to already named cultivars. The superior and unique attributes should jump out at you. If it takes a hand lens to see the difference, forget it. The new selection is observed for at least three years to confirm the initial judgment, irrespective of whether the superiority has to do with flowers, foliage, plant habit, or something else. The opinion of others is solicited and definitely considered.

At the time of release, my new selections have generally not been tested in climates other than that of the nursery; they may not have been container grown, nor have they been rigorously screened for common disease and insect problems. Such screening is desirable but may not be practical. It would certainly delay release by several years.

A profusion of new selections is not all bad. Sure it creates confusion, but it also creates interest. It becomes a contest to select and grow the best. If the system works properly, the best cultivars will be the survivors until they are replaced by another generation of even better ones.

The advantages of critical screening of new selections at many sites, where they are compared to existing cultivars for several considerations, is that only proven selections are then released. The following are some of the reasons not to spend too many years on screening a new selection before it is released under a name:

1. Plants sent out under number or code for testing receive scant attention at most nurseries or institutions.
2. Through the technique of micropropagation, demand can be satisfied without a long delay. After five to ten years of additional testing, it may be difficult to rekindle that same demand.

3. The marketplace is the ultimate and final testing ground. Here the winners and losers will be sorted out quickly, resulting in better cultivars sooner.

4. Plants held too tightly and too long by an individual or institution may die with that individual or disappear with the termination of a program.

Of course, none of this relieves us from the responsibility of being very honest in our claims for the virtues of new selections. Determining those virtues is a bit akin to evaluating a new girlfriend or boyfriend—they may look good, but it takes a lot of time and experience to determine real worth. So it is with plants. We need to be very selective in naming and introducing new plants, but not so cautious that we are afraid of a few failures.

In summary then, to release a new cultivar we have to be convinced that it is better than anything else available, and that means more than one year's observation. When released, let us tout the merits, but not make unwarranted claims. For those of us purchasing and growing new releases, it behooves us not to commit too heavily until we are quite certain that the plants will perform up to claims and expectations.

Cultivars Bred, Named, Introduced by the Author

The following is a list of those mountain laurel cultivars that were bred, named, and/or introduced by me. An asterisk next to the plant name indicates that a breeder fee is requested for propagation. See the individual entries in this chapter for more information on these cultivars.

'Bridesmaid'	'Keepsake'*
'Bristol'	'Little Linda'*
'Bullseye'	'Minuet'*
'Carol'	'Nancy'
'Carousel'	'Nipmuck'
'Comet'*	'Peppermint'*
'Elf'	'Pink Charm'
'Freckles'	'Pink Surprise'
'Galaxy'*	'Pinwheel'
'Goodrich'	'Quinnipiac'
'Hearts Desire'*	'Raspberry Glow'
'Kaleidoscope'*	'Sarah'

'Shooting Star'

'Snowdrift'*

'Stillwood'

'Tiddlywinks'*

'Tightwad Too'

'Tinkerbell'*

'Willowcrest'

'Yankee Doodle'

CHAPTER 4

Propagation by Cuttings, Grafting, and Layering

Today, the propagator of woody plants... has to master a diverse range of techniques from manual craft skills to the management of labour and materials. The art and science of plant propagation has been refined and developed over many generations and continues to forge ahead. It is important that such development is periodically reviewed, recorded and documented so that those involved can embrace the existing information, appraise their needs from within it and proceed along their chosen path with a foundation of sound knowledge and good technique. (Brian Humphrey, in Macdonald 1986)

Cuttings

Most broad-leaved evergreens are propagated by rooting stem cuttings, but for some, including mountain andromeda (*Pieris floribunda*) and flame azalea (*Rhododendron calendulaceum*), it can be quite difficult. Such is the situation with *Kalmia* species. Cuttings of some root readily, but mountain laurel (*Kalmia latifolia*) is generally difficult to root. The use of auxins, mist, fog, plastic tents, and/or special rooting media has helped, but as we shall see, these techniques are not always helpful enough for widespread commercial success.

Cuttings are most often rooted in a greenhouse, although a small cold frame with heating cables will do; or an indoor case, where plants depend entirely on artificial light, can be used. Since cuttings obviously have no roots with which to absorb water, they must be exposed to high humidity. Most commonly, humidity is supplied as mist or fog over the cuttings or by enclosing the propagation bench with a clear plastic film to form a humidity chamber.

Mist Propagation

The method of mist propagation relies on moisture being supplied to cuttings by intermittent applications of mist. Successful operation depends on a good supply of nonalkaline water. Atomizing nozzles that put out a low volume of water are spaced 1 to 2 ft (30 to 60 cm) above the cutting bench to insure good coverage of the cuttings (Figure 4-1). An electronic valve (solenoid) to turn the water on and off can be regulated by any one of several devices.

Electric time clocks, electronic leaves, and evaporative pans are typically used to regulate the cycling of the mist. These items, as well as the misting nozzles and electronic valves, are generally available from nursery supply houses. There are disadvantages, however: time clocks are not sensitive to light and weather conditions; electronic leaves salt up; evaporative pans tend to stick or are too readily affected by air currents. One of the most satisfactory mist controls uses a photocell so that the amount of mist supplied is dependent on available light. When a cloud passes over the cuttings, the control immediately compensates by extending the period between mist cycles. The one disadvantage of photocell control is the initial expense; but

Figure 4-1. Cuttings of *Kalmia latifolia* and *Kalmia angustifolia* being rooted under mist at Summer Hill Nursery, Madison, Connecticut. Misting nozzles are located in the water pipe over the cutting bed and are controlled by a time clock.

if it prevents even one failure, it more than pays for itself. When a mist system must be left unattended for a few days, the photocell control is the most reliable. Unfortunately, they are not easily obtained.

Whatever control device is used, the correct amount of mist must be determined by observation and testing. The aim is to keep the foliage moist without allowing the medium to become soggy. On a sunny summer day the typical requirement might be 6 seconds of mist every 3 minutes, whereas on a winter day, 5 seconds of mist every 15 minutes or longer would be adequate. These times vary with different facilities.

Mist applications are especially valuable with soft or semihard cuttings in the summer when outside temperatures are high. Mist has the inherent disadvantage of leaching nutrients from the plant and the medium, which adversely affects slow-rooting material. After two to three months in mist, unrooted cuttings tend to become "hard" as the leaf surfaces are covered with a thin layer of salts; yet in a plastic tent, mountain laurel cuttings may remain in good condition for as long as two years, with some rooting occurring throughout the entire period. Even so, some growers successfully propagate *Kalmia* from cuttings in autumn using mist. Generally their facilities are low profile and tight, meaning that a relatively small amount of mist is needed to keep humidity high.

Fog or Ventilated High-Humidity Propagation

Fog or ventilated high-humidity propagation is very similar to mist propagation except that droplet size is smaller. Therefore moisture stays suspended in the air longer and less water is needed to maintain high humidity. Daniel Milbocker, of Virginia Truck and Ornamentals Research Station, Virginia Beach, Virginia, has been instrumental in developing this method since 1974. It is proving to work well with many plants, and several firms now produce fogging devices. My experience with fog propagation suggests that it may be the best means of rooting *Kalmia* during the summer. For a small area containing a few or several flats, it is possible to use one or more of the vaporizing or humidity devices that are commercially available for home use.

Plastic Tent

One of the easiest and most reliable means of providing high humidity for cuttings is to cover the bench with a light frame of boards or wire mesh, which is in turn covered with a sheet of 4-mil clear polyethylene. The edges of the plastic should be tucked inside of the bench to allow the condensation inside the plastic to drip back into the medium. This is essentially a closed system with only drain holes under the bench to allow for the exchange of air and the elimination of excessive moisture. Such a "sweat box" requires little care. Once cuttings are stuck, watered in, and the tent is closed, no further care is needed for about four weeks. At that time the medium should be checked to see if additional water is needed. If the mix, bench, and cuttings were clean at the start, then fungal pathogens should not be a problem.

It is important to monitor the temperature, especially on sunny days. If the temperature goes above 90°F (32°C), then additional shading is necessary. Much more shading is needed in summer than in the winter.

Our plastic tents are in a greenhouse attached to the south (sun-facing) side of a barn. If I had it to do over again I would have the cutting propagation on the north side of the building. High light intensity is not needed to root *Kalmia* cuttings, and on the shady side of the building temperature swings would be much less, resulting in less stress on the cuttings.

Media

As with other aspects of propagation, there is no consensus on the best medium in which to root cuttings. One commonly used for *Rhododendron* is also good for *Kalmia*: 2 parts fibrous-sphagnum peat moss, 1 part coarse perlite.

We use this medium at Broken Arrow Nursery, but with the addition of 10 percent by volume aged pine bark. Anna Knuttle, formerly of Knuttle Nursery, East Windsor, Connecticut, recommended this to us based on her experience with rooting mountain laurel cuttings. We are also now substituting less-expensive ground styrofoam for perlite. The peat moss/styrofoam mix with bark provides an acid, light-weight, porous medium of high water-holding capacity. Normally the medium should be spread 6 to 8 in (15 to 20 cm) deep in the bench. Do not use the mix for successive batches of *Kalmia* cuttings; this often leads to problems with pathogens and reduced rooting. One other medium mix used for laurel cuttings is 1 part fibrous-sphagnum peat moss, 1 part coarse perlite, 2 parts washed, coarse sand.

Temperature

Temperatures between 70 and 80°F (21 to 27°C) are ideal for root formation and growth. In summer the main problem is holding the temperature down to this level, while in winter the problem is maintaining the temperature up in this range. Do not assume the temperature of the rooting medium is the same as the air temperature. In an open bench the mix may well be several degrees cooler.

Bottom heat, or heating the medium from below, is the preferred method for fall and winter propagation for many growers. An effective technique for small areas is the use of electric heating cables or mats under the mix. A similar but less-expensive method is passing hot water through small-diameter, flexible tubes placed under the medium, much like electric cables (Biotherm System, Biotherm Engineering, Petaluma, California). Another way directs greenhouse heat (hot air, hot water, steam) under the propagation benches, trapping it there with side curtains of plastic or felt paper. Whatever the method used, the heat radiates up through the rooting medium. In all cases the temperature should be regulated with a sensor in the mix at the level of the base of the cuttings. As long as the medium is at 70 to 75°F (21 to 24°C), it really does not matter if the air temperature is considerably lower. In fact, if foliage is kept cool until roots are formed, the cuttings will flush into growth more readily when the air temperature is later raised.

Lights

The daylight period should be extended to 16 hours during the short days of fall and early winter, because long days benefit rooting and subsequent growth. In practice, the day length can be extended by turning on the lights at dusk for a few hours. The same effect is achieved more economically by having the lights come on for less time in the middle of the night. Physiologists working with other plants have found that the length of the *dark* period is the critical factor. Hence, light in the middle of the night breaks the period of continuous darkness more efficiently. One 75-watt incandescent reflector floodlight every 12 square feet (1 square meter) of bench space should be adequate if placed 30 in (75 cm) above the plants. Critical experiments on the effects of day length on small *Kalmia* plants as well as cuttings are needed to determine the real value of supplemental lighting during the short days of winter.

Preparation of Cuttings

Summer cuttings should be taken while they are turgid. Do not collect any past mid-morning on sunny days. In fall or winter the timing of collection is less important, although collection when temperatures are much below freezing for extended periods should be avoided. Cuttings not immediately stuck in the bench can be stored in the refrigerator at 40°F (4°C) for a few days in the summer and for a few weeks in the fall or winter.

One of the mysteries of plant propagation is that some obviously mistreated cuttings root, whereas coddled ones may not. Many propagators, including myself, can tell of collected cuttings forgotten in the trunk of the car, under the work bench, or outside for a few days or weeks that rooted surprisingly well when finally placed in the bench. On occasion I have been amazed and delighted to root cuttings of mountain laurel that were badly mauled or delayed in transit. Some of the best success I have had in rooting *Kalmia angustifolia*, sheep laurel, was with cuttings that were mailed from England and shipped in a tobacco tin in the summer. The cuttings were not wrapped tightly and spent several days in transit, but root they did. So while there are certain "scientific" practices and principles that need to be followed to root cuttings, there are also many unknown factors in the art of cutting propagation.

Wounding is common practice for rhododendron cuttings and may be of benefit with mountain laurel, although with the other laurel species it seems not worth the extra effort. To wound a cutting, remove a sliver of bark and a bit of wood from either side of the cutting. Each cut should be about 0.75 in (19 mm) long and extend to or stop 0.25 in (6 mm) above the base. A recent innovative way to wound cuttings is to split the base with a knife or razor blade. New undifferentiated cells known as callus will form rapidly in the wound, from which roots are initiated.

Some propagators routinely rinse their cuttings in a water bath containing a fungicide, insecticide, and/or antidesiccant. I lean toward no treatment or spraying; hobbyists might as well skip these pesticide treatments and just rinse the cuttings in cool water. A clean bench and a clean mix are essential, however. Several days before the benches or flats are to be filled, all traces of old mix should be removed. If disease has been a problem in the facilities being used, it would be wise to disinfect the benches or flats. Rinse them with water and then douse with a nonresidual disinfectant, such as sodium hypochlorite (bleach), and allow to dry.

Kalmia microphylla, Western Laurel, and *Kalmia polifolia*, Eastern Bog Laurel

Unlike those of other laurel species, the soft or semihard cuttings of *Kalmia microphylla* and *Kalmia polifolia* are easy to root. No special cut, wound, or leaf removal is necessary. Cuttings need be only 1 to 2 in (2.5 to

5 cm) long. They can be handled in a tent or under mist, and with no auxin treatment roots will appear within three weeks. Under proper lighting and warm conditions (70 to 75°F [21 to 24°C]), the cuttings will continue to grow. The young plants may require pinching to encourage good habit—these pinched shoots make excellent cuttings.

Kalmia latifolia, Mountain Laurel

The propagation of mountain laurel cuttings has many variations. Indeed, there seem to be as many variations as propagators, and what works for one propagator does not necessarily work for another. Hence, much as I would like to, I am unable to recommend the "best" method. As an example, January, March, June, July, and August-to-December each has been reported as the best time to take cuttings for *Kalmia latifolia*.

The following guidelines reflect my own experiences along with the observations of others. A plastic tent works better for me than mist, in large part due to the length of time required for rooting. I prefer fog for soft or semihard cuttings taken in summer when temperatures are high, as the cooling effect of the water droplets is extremely beneficial. The same cooling effect in the fall and winter months tends to reduce the medium temperature to below 70°F (21°C) and so delays rooting. For amateurs or part-time growers, humidity chambers have the advantage of not having to be watched as closely as mist and fog systems. The cuttings can be left for a few days or even weeks without worrying about faulty controls or clogged nozzles. Experiments of Williams and Bilderback (1981), at North Carolina State University, Raleigh, showed no differences between intermittent mist and a polyethylene tent in the propagation of mountain laurel stem cuttings taken in autumn.

When I was at the Connecticut Agricultural Experiment Station I had best success with cuttings taken in late September to mid-October and stuck in a plastic tent. More recently, at Broken Arrow Nursery, the fall cuttings have not rooted well and have often decayed. Cuttings taken in late December and early January, however, have rooted much better. The difference seems to be not in the facilities but in the condition of the stock plants. At the Agricultural Station, all the cuttings came from field-grown stock plants that hardened off early in the fall. At the nursery, our cuttings are taken from two-year-old bedded liners, container plants, or field-grown plants, but in all cases the plants have received more fertilizer and harden off later in the fall. Other growers also have found that cuttings taken in January are among the easiest to root.

The location on a plant from which cuttings are taken also affects rooting. Less vigorous cuttings from within the plant crown often root better than the outer and upper thick, vigorous cuttings. At least one commercial grower shades his stock plants to improve success in rooting cuttings, and most wound the cuttings on one or both sides as previously described.

I have not been able to demonstrate a positive or consistent response to the auxins, fungicides, and other materials that reportedly aid rooting in other ericaceous plants. Dipping the basal 0.5 in (1 cm) of the cutting in an ethyl alcohol solution of 5000 parts per million (ppm) each of the auxins NAA (2-naphthaleneacetic acid) and IBA (indole-3-butyric acid) is beneficial in some clones. A commercial preparation of this material, called Dip'N Grow (10,000 ppm IBA and 5000 ppm IAA [indole-3-acetic acid]), is used at a dilution of 1:5 to 1:15, depending on the cultivar and the hardness of the cuttings. (Names of suppliers of Dip'N Grow can be obtained from Astori-Pacific of Clackamas, Oregon, telephone 503-655-7470.) One of the difficulties in evaluating auxins is that different clones respond differently to the same auxin treatment, and the same clone may respond differently in different years or under different propagation regimes. Most growers use auxins, and research supports the positive effect of NAA, IBA, and 2,4,5-TP (2,4,5-trichlorophenoxypropionic acid) with some clones. Growers would do themselves and others a service if along with the auxin-treated cuttings, they would leave some untreated cuttings of the same cultivar for comparative purposes.

John McGuire at the University of Rhode Island had excellent success (96 percent) in rooting 'Pink Surprise' from semihardwood cuttings in the summer under outdoor intermittent mist. The cuttings were dipped in a talc dust of Hormex 45 (4.5 percent IBA) and placed in flats of peat moss and vermiculite. They were heavily rooted in eight week's time.

The technique of rooting softwood cuttings from forced plants in winter has been used by some growers. Alfred Fordham, former propagator at the Arnold Arboretum of Harvard University in Jamaica Plain, Massachusetts, has reported success with this method, and a note in an old gardening magazine indicates that a nursery in New York was rooting cuttings from young wood of plants grown indoors as long ago as 1893 (Trumpy 1893). This method, which has also worked extremely well with Exbury azaleas, is particularly suitable for container-grown stock plants.

The stock plants are allowed to go into their usual fall dormancy until mid-January, at which time they are heated and forced into growth. The new shoots are then rooted under mist or plastic, with the following advantages: 1) cuttings root more readily; 2) unlike with fall cuttings, the cold-treatment requirement is fulfilled; and 3) once rooted, they have a full, normal growing season ahead. Unfortunately and for reasons that are not entirely clear, my attempts to root cuttings of mountain laurel with this procedure were unsuccessful, and I am not aware of others currently using it.

Stock Plant Age

One important and often overlooked factor in rooting mountain laurel and other difficult species is the age of the stock. It has been known for years that cuttings from young plants generally root more readily than those from older plants. The classic example is the difference in the rooting ability of juvenile and mature English ivy, *Hedera helix*. The juvenile vine form roots readily, but the mature, shrublike form is difficult to root.

Several years of experimentation have demonstrated that the same is true in rooting cuttings of *Kalmia latifolia*. Indeed, the success rate for rooted cuttings of one-year-old seedlings receiving no auxin treatment was 90 percent, whereas the rate of rooting dropped off rapidly with older plants, diminishing to 20 percent when cuttings were taken from flowering plants. Cuttings from two- and three-year-old seedlings also root more readily than those from older, flowering plants, and they also flush into growth more rapidly. Cuttings from flowering plants have the disconcerting tendency of producing flower buds in the propagation bench. These flower buds occupy the sites where vegetative growth should occur, and they are best removed.

Cuttings from rooted cuttings and cuttings from young grafts also root more readily than those from the original stock plant (Jaynes 1971e). For example, cuttings of the red-budded selection CAES 137 taken from cuttings rooted the previous year rooted much better (94 percent) than cuttings from flowering plants of the same clone (30 percent).

Cuttings from young plants started in tissue culture is another source of material that root more readily than cuttings from the parent plants. The process of tissue culture appears to increase juvenility in the plantlets, thus making it easier to root cuttings, more so than in comparable plants started from normal stem cuttings.

Clones vary in their ability to form roots on cuttings. 'Pink Surprise', for example, consistently rooted 80 percent or better from fall cuttings, whereas 'Silver Dollar' and 'Bristol' often failed to root or rooted poorly (Figure 4-2). Once rooted plants are obtained, cuttings should be taken from these and not the original plant in order to maintain as much juvenility as possible. If necessary, cuttings can also be taken from one- to two-year-old seedlings, if the seedlings are of known pedigree and flower color.

Cuttings, especially those from older plants, taken in the fall may show a reluctance to flush into growth after rooting. If possible, provide such rooted cuttings with a cold period—35 to 50°F (2 to 10°C) for six weeks—with no artificial light to extend day length. For cuttings taken in October, try this cold dormancy treatment during February and March. Then in April, when the rooted cuttings are sufficiently warmed, they should burst into growth. In situations where it is not possible to cool the greenhouse because of other plants, I have moved flats of rooted cuttings to a cool area, where they were exposed to temperatures just above freezing and received eight hours of light daily. After six to eight weeks of this "winterization," the plants were brought back into the warm greenhouse to resume growth. Another alternative is to take cuttings in the first two weeks of January after the stock plants have received some cold. About the time at which the cuttings root, they begin to flush new growth.

It does take patience and perseverance, but by carefully selecting and manipulating the stock and then properly treating the cuttings, mountain laurel cuttings can be rooted. Other things being equal, the most important

Figure 4-2. Comparison of root development in two *Kalmia latifolia* selections: *left*, 'Pink Surprise' is an easy-to-root cultivar; *right*, 'Bristol' is difficult to root and is representative of most mountain laurel selections. Both sets of cuttings were taken in October and placed in a humidity case for 12 weeks.

decision is in selecting the cultivars to propagate—some are much easier to root than others. Among the best for rooting are 'Bullseye', 'Carousel', 'Nipmuck', 'Olympic Fire', 'Pink Charm', 'Pink Surprise', 'Quinnipiac', and 'Sharon Rose'. As for the other factors—timing, wounding, auxin, fog or tent, media, and so on—no one recipe is guaranteed as better than another.

Kalmia angustifolia, Sheep Laurel

Sheep laurel cuttings are somewhat easier to root than those of mountain laurel. Softwood cuttings taken during the summer can be rooted, but firmer cuttings taken from late summer through January are easier to handle and to root. Treat the hardwood cuttings with the same auxin dip as mountain laurel cuttings (Dip'N Grow, 1:7 dilution).

Whenever possible, choose cuttings that lack flower buds. They are easier to root and they flush into growth more readily. Cuttings should be 2 to 3 in (5 to 7.5 cm) long and have two leaf whorls. Strip off the lowest leaves, and wound lightly on each side. Newly rooted cuttings will begin growth without first receiving a cool rest period.

Kalmia cuneata, White Wicky, and *Kalmia hirsuta*, Sandhill Laurel

Kalmia cuneata and *K. hirsuta* are rarely grown commercially, so our experience with these species is limited. Greenwood cuttings and semihardwood cuttings taken in late summer or early fall will tend to root. Auxin treatment is beneficial. Cuttings of white wicky taken too late in the fall will lose their leaves. Extension of the day length in late summer and fall will extend the rooting and growing period. As with mountain laurel, use juvenile wood whenever possible.

Grafting

Outstanding mountain laurel specimens that are inordinately difficult to root are good candidates for grafting. *Kalmia latifolia* can be grafted with little difficulty, and suckering of the stock is not a serious problem on established grafts. Late winter or early spring is the normal grafting time. Vigorous seedlings 4 to 8 in (10 to 20 cm) tall make good stocks. Stock plants should be placed in pots or flats in the fall and then exposed to cold temperatures until January or February, at which time they can be warmed up and forced into growth. They should not be grafted until clear signs of root activity are observed by tipping the plant out of the container and looking for new white rootlets on the surface of the root ball. This should occur two to three weeks after they are provided with heat.

Dormant scions should be either whip-, cleft-, or side-veneer-grafted onto the stock as low as possible (Figures 4-3, 4-4). Wrap the graft firmly, but not tightly, with a rubber band or a rubber budding strip. The grafted plants must be kept under humid conditions until new cells knit the stock and scion together. A plastic tent makes for the easiest and best environment. Individual humid chambers can be created simply by enclosing each potted and grafted plant in a plastic bag. After four to six weeks, the tent can be gradually ventilated for a week or two for the plants to adjust to the less-humid conditions of the greenhouse. Mountain laurels knit slowly; if you are in doubt as to whether the graft union has knitted, leave the tent for the longer period of time. Most of my failures have come from not allowing the union to callus long enough. When there is no longer any danger of frost, plant the grafts outdoors. An advantage of late-winter and early-spring grafting is that the grafts put out one flush of growth before the normal growing season even begins.

June grafting can be successful and is most valuable for propagating new selections identified in flower or in cases where it may be inconvenient or impossible to obtain scions the next winter. For June grafting, use scions of the current season's growth, firm but not woody. Stock should be chosen from small plants that grew vigorously the previous year.

Graft scions onto the previous year's growth on the smoothest part of the stem with few leaves. Tie the unions with budding strips or cut rubber bands, and handle the grafts the same as in early-spring grafting. Approximately seven weeks after grafting, the plants can be set outside in shaded beds. Since June-grafted clones often do not put out a flush of growth until the following spring, the only advantage over grafting the same plants next spring is that of necessity or convenience.

One rooting method used with difficult-to-root rhododendrons and certain other plants is to graft the difficult-to-root scion onto a stem section of an easy-to-root selection. Then treat the graft like a cutting, placing the union below the medium surface in the propagation bed. The easy-to-root "stock" will form roots while the graft knits, and months later the scion itself roots. Some combinations have a delayed incompatibility that will cause the graft union to eventually fail, but not until after the scion roots.

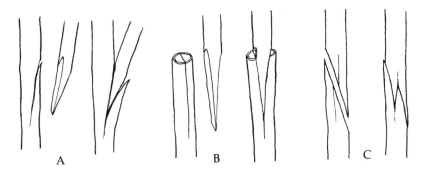

Figure 4-3. Three kinds of grafts used with *Kalmia latifolia*: (A) side veneer, (B) cleft, and (C) whip. A sharp knife and steady hand are essential to making smooth cuts and a good match of the cut surfaces.

Figure 4-4. A cleft-grafted *Kalmia latifolia* wrapped with a cut rubber band. In this example, it would have been better if the graft were lower to limit sprouting below the union and to produce a plant from the grafted scion with branching close to the ground.

I tested this approach by grafting mountain laurel selections onto eastern bog laurel and sheep laurel. Several of the grafts on sections of underground stems of sheep laurel were successful, but on the whole the method is unreliable and impractical.

Layering

Laurels spread and propagate in the wild by natural layering. Bent-over branches covered with leaf litter and humus eventually root along the portion that is covered and in contact with the soil. All species will layer, but *Kalmia latifolia* is the slowest to respond. Heavy snows, broken branches from trees, weak stems, and other circumstances will cause the branches of mountain laurel to bend down so that layering occurs. If the process occurs repeatedly for many years, small thickets arise that have their origin in a single plant. I have observed clumps of banded mountain laurel—readily identifiable by their unique flowers—that measured nearly 20 ft (6 m) edge to edge. It is easy to imagine a single plant spreading over a much larger area.

To layer a selection of your own, remove 1 in (2.5 cm) or so of soil beneath a low-lying stem and then bend it to the ground (Figure 4-5). Rooting can be facilitated by girdling: with one or more loops of wire, firmly bind the stem where it comes in contact with the soil; bend the stem to break it partially; or make several shallow, encircling knife cuts. Then peg the stem down and cover it with leaf mold or peat moss and soil. Finally, water and mulch. Do not allow the layer to dry out. If started in the spring, roots may form by fall, but a second growing season is often necessary for good rooting. Once roots have formed, sever the layer from the mother plant and move it to a protected location. If the roots are not strong, prune back the top when transplanting it to reduce the stress on the new plant.

Layering is a slow and laborious method, yet it is one that fascinates many gardeners. To propagate just a few plants, the technique is as practical as any; however, it has little or no appeal at the nursery where more efficient methods are needed.

Figure 4-5. Layering. Lateral branches are placed and pegged in depressions dug alongside the plant. Each layered branch is wounded, covered with a mix of peat moss and soil, and kept moist. After rooting—about 6 to 18 months for mountain laurel—the layers are cut from the mother plant and transplanted. The number of layers per stock plant is determined by the number of branches that can be pulled to the ground.

CHAPTER 5

Micropropagation of Mountain Laurel

Andrew J. Brand, Horticulturist, Broken Arrow Nursery

Grateful acknowledgment is given to Keith Jensen, who authored this chapter in the 1988 edition of *Kalmia: The Laurel Book II*.

> The rate of multiplication [of *Kalmia*] appears adequate for commercial purposes. Producing an average of 30 shoots per culture in 8 weeks yields at least 7000 shoots per 1 sq ft [900 sq cm] of culture shelf space per year. With a 73 percent rooting success, this represents approximately 5000 useable propagules [per square foot per year]. (Lloyd and McCown 1980)

> [Imagine devoting 1 acre (0.4 hectare) to such a method: 200,000,000 plantlets could be produced in one year!]

As discussed in Chapter 4, we have found that propagating mountain laurel (*Kalmia latifolia*) from cuttings can be frustratingly unreliable. Tissue culture has made the large-scale propagation of *Kalmia* not only possible but highly successful, and commercial growers have quickly picked up on its benefits. Cultivars that many people previously found difficult to obtain are now readily available because growers can produce sufficient quantities of the best laurel cultivars shortly after they are introduced. Briggs Nursery of Olympia, Washington, is the largest producer of mountain laurel in the world; they list about 30 cultivars and produce approximately 225,000 liners a year. It is also possible now for amateurs to set up small laboratories and experience the pleasure of producing their own plants. But remember micropropagation is not for everyone. I would recommend this method only to those individuals interested in producing hundreds of plants. Grafting and other propagation options are more practical for production of only a few plants.

The purpose of this chapter is to educate the novice and hopefully to encourage others to try mountain laurel micropropagation. It is not my intention to present a full, scientific review of the subject. Rather I will describe the techniques with which I have had success, as well as some methods used by other propagators. As you will see there are many different procedures that may be followed to achieve the same results. Each propagator develops his or her own style and procedures and will continue to refine them as he or she gains more experience.

Although easy-to-follow methods have been established for *Kalmia* micropropagation, a period of training is needed to acquire the skills necessary to be successful. It is helpful for beginners to have had basic chemistry and botany courses, an understanding of metric measurements, and some experience with sterile techniques. Familiarity with common chemical names and abbreviations as well as certain scientific terminology will make the learning process much easier. Several excellent books describing methods for growing plant tissue under sterile conditions *in vitro* are available; one of the best for beginners is *Plants from Test Tubes: An Introduction to Micropropagation* by Lydiane Kyte and John Kleyn (Portland, Oregon, 1996).

Simply stated, micropropagation is a form of asexual (vegetative) propagation that allows for multiple plants (literally thousands) to be produced from a single bud or cutting. Plant cultures are grown under sterile conditions on a gelled medium containing essential macro- and microelements required for growth, as well as growth regulators to stimulate shoot and/or root formation.

Twenty-five years ago micropropagation of broad-leaved evergreens was not widely practiced nor was it very successful. The standard preparations of mineral salts and vitamins, like that developed by Toshio Murashige and Folke Skoog (referred to as MS medium and first published in 1962), which have continued to serve so well for culturing of tobacco, orchids, small fruits, vegetables, herbaceous perennials, and other plants, produced poor results when used with various genera of Ericaceae such as *Rhododendron* and *Kalmia*. Recognizing this problem, W. C. Anderson published a new formulation in 1975 that was significantly better for the woody Ericaceae. He also found that among the cytokinins (plant growth regulators) tested, shoot formation in rhododendrons was best induced using 2iP—which is also sometimes known as IPA and has the full chemical names of N^6-(2-isopentenyl)adenine or 6-(γ,γ-dimethylallylamino) purine. Additional modifications to the media formulations were made by Greg Lloyd and Brent McCown (1980). Their medium, commonly referred to as woody plant medium or WPM, worked exceptionally well for *Kalmia* micropropagation and has since become the standard formulation used for mountain laurel as well as many other plants.

Getting Started: Facilities and Equipment

Space

The area required for tissue culture depends mostly on the size of the operation anticipated. Large or small, the space must be clean and should have wall and floor surfaces that can be scrubbed periodically. Basements or small bedrooms have conveniently been converted into adequate starter laboratories. Media preparation and sterile transfer work are typically isolated from culture growing rooms. Closets make excellent growing areas; shelves and lighting can be easily installed and temperature can be readily controlled in the confined space. Such rooms have also been used as rooting facilities for microcuttings. Kitchens can easily be used for media preparation and cleaning and sterilization. Access to water will often determine the location of the laboratory and, more specifically, where the media will be made. Proper electrical capabilities also play a factor in location decisions. Additional space should be planned for storage of supplies and refrigeration.

Commercial growers who do not want to invest thousands of dollars in new laboratory facilities may want to consider using a remodeled mobile home or trailer. Again, the size of the trailer needed will depend on anticipated production. Prides Corner Farms, Lebanon, Connecticut, has successfully used this approach and currently produces approximately 40,000 tissue cultured *Kalmia* per year from a trailer of about 700 sq ft (65 sq m).

Sterile Air Hood

Every time culture vessels are opened, uninvited microbes in the air can enter the media and quickly form colonies, overtaking hapless plants. Because of the rich nutrient content of tissue culture media, a multitude of bacteria and fungi will thrive there. To reduce the chances of contamination, all sterile (aseptic) operations should be performed in a sterile hood or box cabinet. Several laboratory equipment suppliers offer laminar-flow hoods in which all the air flowing into the work area of the hood first passes through special filters that remove all microbes. Commercial hoods are somewhat expensive (U.S. $2000 to 3000); a cheaper alternative is to build your own. The necessary components can be easily acquired and design plans have been published by Martin Meyer (1986). Although most plant tissue culture laboratories use hoods, a more primitive alternative is a box cabinet. Typically, these are made of rigid clear plastic or glass on top and three sides, enclosing a space large enough to allow easy manipulation of cultures, but remaining relatively aseptic. Kyte and Kleyn's book (1996) provides sketches of such cabinets.

Growth Rooms

The growth room is the area in which the cultures and plantlets grow under controlled conditions (Figure 5-1). Two kinds of rooms should be planned: one for growing the cultures in sterile media and the other for rooting the microcuttings in a nonsterile peat mixture.

Culture rooms should be designed so that they can be easily cleaned to reduce microbial contamination. It is also vital that the temperature can be maintained in the range of 70 to 80°F (21 to 27°C) and that the area can be illuminated with fluorescent tubes. Ordinary cool-white bulbs have worked fine for me, but other propagators prefer the wider spectrum obtained from Gro-Lux tubes. Many laboratories use timer switches to achieve a 16- to 18-hour photoperiod, and others employ continuous 24-hour lighting. During the phases of micropropagation, most mountain laurel cultivars perform best under light intensity not exceeding 10,000 lux or 100 footcandles. These levels can be obtained either by diffusing light through opaque plastic or by adjusting the distance between the light source and the cultures. Lighting fixture ballasts produce excess heat that can damage cultures placed directly over them; some propagators have gone to the trouble of wiring the ballasts outside the growth room. Shelves should be constructed from materials that allow for good air circulation, such as

Figure 5-1. Racks of baby-food jars in the expansive growth room at Briggs Nursery, Olympia, Washington. Photo by Briggs Nursery.

expanded metal screens, plastic-coated closet shelving, or 0.5-in (12-mm) grid "egg-crate" panels used for fluorescent light fixtures.

The rooting phase requires both high humidity and controlled lighting. Closed plastic containers can provide adequate humidity. Shelves must be able to support the weight of several containers filled with moist rooting media and should be constructed of materials that allow free air flow. Generally the light intensity can be greater than is supplied to growing cultures, but rooting plantlets need no more than 200 to 300 foot-candles. Excessive light may cause leaves to turn red. I have also rooted microcuttings directly in the greenhouse using fog—during the winter months supplemental lighting is required.

Sterilizers

Plant tissue culture's #1 enemy is the airborne microbes that are everywhere present and must be eliminated before cultures can be grown. Decontamination or sterilization of containers and culture media is best achieved using autoclaves or pressure cookers. All microbes and spores are killed by heating at 250°F (120°C) under pressure.

Forceps, scissors, and scalpels used on sterile plant tissue can be disinfected by immersion in 70 percent ethyl alcohol. The alcohol can be removed by flaming over an alcohol lamp or propane burner. After seeing one close call with an alcohol lamp (a lamp was knocked over and its contents caught fire), I have since used an electrical heater known commercially as Bacti-Cinerator. As an extra precaution, one should also sterilize forceps, scalpels, and petri dishes in a pressure cooker prior to using them in the flow hood.

Containers

Although glass test tubes were once the standard vessel for tissue culture, they have since been replaced in most laboratories by reusable jars (baby-food or home-canning) and autoclavable plastic containers. Test tubes can still be good for experimental work or for initiating cultures, but for multiplication they really are not large enough. Regardless of the container selected, a tight-fitting closure that allows air exchange but inhibits microbial passage is essential. Magenta Corporation manufactures lids for baby-food jars called B-caps, as well as different sizes of polycarbonate boxes. I prefer the $3 \times 3 \times 3$ in ($7.5 \times 7.5 \times 7.5$ cm) box for laurel; it is short enough for easy transferring, yet still provides ample room for shoot development. These boxes are also convenient for nurseries involved in large-scale production. Polycarbonate, egg-shaped containers have been used by some laboratories. I have found that media in these eggs dry out quickly, requiring more frequent transferring than with other vessels. Also, they are small and too poorly shaped for efficient use of space. Single-use, disposable plastic containers are also available from several sources for those who do not care to wash dishes. This option may become expensive, depending on your intended scale of production. Additional types of containers are continuously becoming available. Select one or two that optimize your production yet keep your expenses down. Parafilm M, a pliable plastic film available from most chemical supply companies, is usually used to seal the vessels, decreasing the chances of contamination while still allowing air exchange.

Propagation Media
Formulation and Preparation

The woody plant medium described by Lloyd and McCown is now standard for *Kalmia* micropropagation. Tissue culture media supply houses, such as Sigma Chemical Company, offer WPM mixtures in either powder or liquid preparations. Most propagators choose to make their own, however, using the formulation presented in Table 5-1. This original formulation has been modified by some propagators by substituting potassium nitrate (KNO_3) (at 1150 milligrams per liter) for the potassium sulfate (K_2SO_4)— this formulation is commonly referred to as modified WPM.

Stocks A and B in Table 5-1 are made in 500-milliliter (ml) volumes; stocks C through H in 200-ml volumes. They can all be stored under refrigeration at 40°F (4°C) for six to eight weeks. Before preparing a medium,

Table 5-1. Components of Woody Plant Medium (Lloyd and McCown 1980).

Stock	Chemical	g in stock	mg/liter in medium
A (20 ml per liter of medium)			
	NH_4NO_3 (ammonium nitrate)	10.0	400
	$Ca(NO_3)_2 \cdot 4H_2O$ (calcium nitrate)	13.9	556
B (20 ml per liter of medium)			
	K_2SO_4 (potassium sulfate)	24.75	990
C (5 ml per liter of medium)			
	$CaCl_2 \cdot 2H_2O$ (calcium chloride)	3.84	96
D (5 ml per liter of medium)			
	KH_2PO_4 (potassium phosphate)	6.80	170
	H_3BO_3 (boric acid)	0.248	6.2
	$Na_2MoO_4 \cdot 2H_2O$ (molybdic acid)	0.01	0.25
E (5 ml per liter of medium)			
	$MgSO_4 \cdot 7H_2O$ (magnesium sulfate)	14.8	370
	$MnSO_4 \cdot H_2O$ (manganese sulfate)	0.892	22.3
	$ZnSO_4 \cdot 7H_2O$ (zinc sulfate)	0.334	8.6
	$CuSO_4 \cdot 5H_2O$ (cupric sulfate)	0.01	0.25
F (6 ml per liter of medium)			
	$FeSO_4 \cdot 7H_2O$ (ferrous sulfate)	1.114	27.8
	Na_2EDTA	1.49	44.76
G (5 ml per liter of medium)			
	Thiamine HCl	0.04	1.0
	Nicotinic acid	0.02	0.5
	Pyridoxine HCl	0.02	0.5
	Glycine	0.08	2.0
H (5 ml per liter of medium)			
	myo-Inositol	4.0	100

inspect the stocks for microbial contamination (cloudiness) and discard contaminated ones. Pay particular attention to the organic stocks, G and H.

To make stock F, prepare 100 ml of each component, add several drops of a 0.1-normal (*N*) solution of hydrochloric acid (HCl) to each chemical to acidify, then heat both to dissolve, but do not boil. While stirring the Na_2EDTA (ethylenediaminetetraacetic acid, disodium salt), slowly add the ferrous sulfate ($FeSO_4$). A clear, pale golden color should develop. This complex provides for slow release of iron to the plant cultures. Do not add Na_2EDTA to $FeSO_4$—it will not work.

An alternative to this stock preparation, which I learned about from Dr. Mark Brand of the University of Connecticut—and find more convenient to work with—is presented in Table 5-2. In this case only two stocks are prepared, one for macronutrients and the other for microelements and organics. I also substitute KNO_3 (at 480 mg/liter final) for K_2SO_4 in stock A. This amount is less than is used by others, but it is identical to the level used by Anderson. The iron complex should be prepared separately and then added to the remaining stock solution. Both stocks are made in 1000-ml volumes and can be dispensed into smaller vessels (I use 200-ml aliquots) and frozen until needed. Stock B will need to be briefly heated and stirred once thawed to dissolve any precipitates. Once dissolved, precipitates will not form again.

After deciding on the amount of medium you want to prepare, add distilled water to the appropriate volume of stocks and stir. Cane sugar (sucrose) is added at 20 to 30 grams (g) per liter. After the addition of the growth regulators and antibiotics (if desired), distilled water is added to produce the final volume. Next the pH must be adjusted to 5.2 to 5.4 using 1 *N* potassium hydroxide (KOH) or sodium hydroxide (NaOH). If the medium is to be solid, the desired amount of gelling agent is then added and stirred while heating to a mild boil until a clear liquid is observed. An alternative is to cover the container with plastic wrap and place it in a microwave oven. The amount of time in the microwave will depend on the volume of solution and the power of the unit. Typically, 1 liter of medium will require 12 to 14 minutes to boil in most microwaves, but keep a close eye on it so that it does not boil over. Place two or three small holes in the plastic wrap to allow the steam to escape while cooking. Once clear, the medium can be dispensed into selected vessels and sterilized.

Table 5-2. Alternate Stock Preparation for Woody Plant Medium.

Compound	final concentration (mg/liter)	for 1 liter of 20× stock (g)
Stock A (macronutrients)		
NH_4NO_3	400	8.0
$MgSO_4 \cdot 7H_2O$	370	7.4
KH_2PO_4	170	3.4
K_2SO_4	990	19.8
Stock B (micronutrients)		
$Ca(NO_3)_2 \cdot 4H_2O$	556	11.1
$MnSO_4 \cdot H_2O$	22.3	0.445
$CaCl_2 \cdot 2H_2O$	96	1.92
$ZnSO_4 \cdot 7H_2O$	8.6	0.17
H_3BO_3	6.2	0.125
$CuSO_4 \cdot 5H_2O$	0.25	0.005
$Na_2MoO_4 \cdot 2H_2O$	0.25	0.005
$FeSO_4 \cdot 7H_2O$	27.8	0.555
Na_2EDTA	37.3	0.745
Thiamine HCl	1.0	0.02
myo-Inositol	100	2.0

Growth Regulators

The most important variable additives to media are the growth regulatory substances called cytokinins and auxins. Early in the history of mountain laurel micropropagation it was unclear which was the best cytokinin to use, but currently most propagators depend on a synthetic form called 2iP. Usually stock solutions are prepared by adding small amounts of dilute acid (0.1 N HCl) to weighed amounts of the powder, gently heating while stirring to dissolve, then bringing the solution up to the desired volume by adding distilled water. The above procedure can be used for most cytokinins. I find 100-ml stocks (at 1 mg/ml concentration) to be convenient, as I can usually use them all before they become contaminated. All stocks, including the macro- and microelements, must be refrigerated or frozen until needed after they are prepared. As noted earlier, cloudiness in the solutions indicates microbial contamination and such stocks should always be discarded.

A naturally occurring cytokinin, zeatin, has been used on occasion to stimulate shoot growth, but it is usually not chosen because it is very expensive and is not very heat-stable, requiring ultrafiltration through special filters (0.22 micron pore size) for sterilization. The loss of potency due to heat sterilization can be accounted for by adding 10 percent more zeatin (an expensive option).

Some propagators find the addition of an auxin to be beneficial. The usual choice is indole-3-butyric acid, commonly referred to as IBA. As with all auxins, IBA can be dissolved in dilute base, such as KOH, following heating and stirring. After bringing the volume up to its final level with distilled water, vessels can be frozen until needed.

Although not used very often, gibberellins are used by some propagators to improve culture growth. The gibberellin used for tissue culture is known as gibberellic acid, or GA_3. As with auxins, GA_3 can be dissolved in a base and then treated exactly like other growth regulator stocks.

Nowhere is it carved in stone what quantities of cytokinins and auxins should be added to culture media for propagating *Kalmia*. Usually individual propagators will have their own concentrations with which they are comfortable. I have had success growing all *Kalmia* cultivars on 1.5 mg/liter 2iP with no auxin added. Prides Corner Farms grows many cultivars on a medium containing 1.6 mg/liter 2iP, but they report that certain ones respond favorably to a slight increase in concentration. I use a higher concentration of 2iP (up to 3.0 mg/liter) when initiating new cultures. Extremely high levels of cytokinin will result in many spindly, poorly developed shoots, so concentrations should usually be reduced once cultures are growing.

Some larger laboratories have the capability of setting up small experiments using different combinations of cytokinins and auxins to determine the optimum concentrations for a particular cultivar. Smaller facilities usually will try their current medium and, if it does not work, will then look to other alternatives. One logical alternative would be to increase the 2iP concentration or add additional growth regulators such as zeatin or IBA. As the saying goes, "If at first you don't succeed, try try again."

Other Additives

Most cultures are grown on gelled medium. Agar (a mixture of polysaccharides derived from species of red algae) is the most common gelling agent. Many propagators have a favorite brand of agar and prefer a certain concentration in their media. Phytagar, a high-purity-grade agar sold by GIBCO, is used by several laboratories. Other propagators like myself are more than satisfied with lower grades. I buy the cheapest agar available that works, but there is a multitude of brands and grades to select from. Sigma Chemical Company alone offers eight different types of agar. Agar substitutes, such as the gellan gums Gelrite (produced by Kelco) and Phytagel (produced by Sigma Chemical), are also commonly used either alone or in combination with agar. These agar substitutes produce a more translucent medium, which allows for easier detection of bacterial contamination than would be possible with agar alone.

Sometimes small amounts of antibiotics and/or fungicides are added to control microbial contamination introduced by the plant tissue. These materials typically need to be filter sterilized to retain their potency. Unfortunately, these materials rarely eliminate the microbes completely, but rather keep their levels low. It may be both time- and cost-effective to initiate new, clean cultures.

Sterilization and Storage of Medium

Both liquid and gelled media must be sterilized before being used. Again, sterilization is achieved using an autoclave or pressure cooker and heating the medium to 250°F (120°C) under 15 lbs (7 kg) of pressure for 15 to 30 minutes. As the volume of the medium increases, the length of time of autoclaving also must increase. I frequently leave the cooker on for 5 to 10 minutes longer to ensure complete sterilization. Typically, a medium is first dispensed into selected vessels and then sterilized, but some propagators prefer to autoclave the medium and containers separately and to pour the liquid into the vessels in the sterile environment of the flow hood. Media stored in a refrigerator will remain good for up to six to eight weeks; however, containers should be stored in plastic bags to prevent drying and to reduce possible contamination. I do not refrigerate my media, but rather place it in zip-lock bags and store on separate shelves in the growth room away from growing cultures. No noticeable loss of potency has been observed. Freezer storage should be used for fluid media only; the gelling properties of agar are altered by freezing.

Micropropagation Procedures

The process of micropropagation involves many steps and procedures, from selection of a piece of plant to tissue culture—the explant, which is cleaned, placed on sterile media to induce growth and multiplication, and then transferred to a soil mix that will foster rooting—to acclimation and transplanting to the field or greenhouse where the tissue cultured plantlet can grow on to a full-grown plant. The following section describes the procedures and protocol followed by different propagators, beginning with the stage of culture initiation and proceeding to the establishment of rooted plantlets.

Collection and Storage

Many considerations must be made when selecting the plant part to use as a source of explants (the tissue used *in vitro*), including the health of the stock plant and its physiological state (actively growing versus dormant). Cuttings taken any time during the year can be a source of explants, but I and others have had more success using succulent, actively growing tissue rather than dormant shoots. The former tend to be cleaner and more responsive in sterile culture, possibly due to endogenous hormone levels.

Terminal apices, axillary shoots, and flower buds all have been used to initiate cultures, but the buds are generally more difficult to disinfect. There is also some concern about possible variation in plants produced from flower buds. I prefer to initiate cultures from shoots taken from actively growing plants that have been forced into growth in a greenhouse. The tissue is much cleaner and easier to disinfect. Immediately after cutting, explants should be placed in a container to prevent drying. A plastic bag containing moistened (not wet) paper towel works well. Cuttings can generally be held in a refrigerator crisper drawer for several days.

Disinfection

Before tissue cultures can be initiated, it is essential to remove microbial contaminants from the explants. The methods for treating plant tissue vary with every laboratory, but a typical sequence of steps is presented here.

1. Trim off leaves and most of the petioles, and cut stems in 1- to 3-node segments.
2. Shake or stir pieces in a mild detergent solution (add a few drops of any dishwashing liquid to 100 ml of water) for about 5 minutes.
3. Rinse with demineralized (sterile) water.
4. Place in 70 percent ethyl alcohol for 5 to 10 seconds and rinse again with sterile water.

5. Shake or stir for 10 to 20 minutes in a 10 to 15 percent liquid bleach solution (most common bleaches contain 5.25 percent sodium hypochlorite, an excellent oxidizer-disinfectant). Add a drop of Tween 20 (a wetting agent) or dishwashing liquid to the solution.
6. Rinse three times in sterile demineralized water.
7. Hold in sterile demineralized water until dissection.

Steps 5 through 7 should be conducted under the sterile hood. When using dormant tissue, most propagators will extend step 2 to 45 minutes and increase the bleach concentration used in step 5 to 50 percent and the time in solution to one-half hour. Regardless of the steps one chooses to follow, it is advisable to use several explants (8 to 10) when initiating cultures, to increase your chances of success.

Dissection and Culture Initiation

There is a great deal of diversity in dissecting techniques followed by different micropropagators. Some people, including myself, do very little cutting after disinfection, removing only the bleached ends, and place the segments onto gelled medium without further manipulations (Figure 5-2). Other propagators choose to dissect the buds and work only with the meristematic tissue of each bud (Figure 5-3). In either situation, the sterilized tissues are usually dissected in sterile petri dishes or on some other sterilized surface and then placed on either liquid or solid medium. If all goes well, some buds should begin to produce shoots in four to six weeks. At this time, segments that have been on liquid medium can either remain on liquid or be transferred to a gelled medium. An alternative technique, first described and successfully practiced by Dr. Hindera Palta at the New York Botanical Garden, is to cut out the bud carefully with a sharp-pointed scalpel and, after momentarily drying the bud, float it on the surface of a liquid medium. This technique is tedious and time consuming and should be left to those with a great deal of patience and skill. Keith Jensen has also had success initiating cultures from flower buds. He cuts the flower buds in 10- to 15-mm segments and places them on a gelled medium or floats them in a liquid medium on rafts of nonwoven fabrics, such as Pellon or Lelux, sold by fabric stores for garment interfacing. Sigma Chemical Company sells membrane rafts that fit into Magenta boxes to be used with liquid medium. It is important to re-emphasize here the necessity of culturing several explants from each cultivar for each medium used. This will allow for losses due to contamination as well as damage incurred during the disinfection process.

Figure 5-2. A stem segment that included a bud at the base of the still-attached petiole. Shoots are beginning to form from the bud. Photo by Keith Jensen.

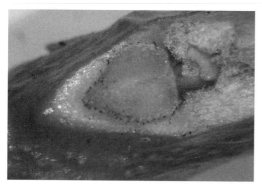

Figure 5-3. A dormant bud on a mountain laurel stem that has been uncovered by removing the leaf petiole. The bud, about 0.04 in (1 mm) in diameter, is all that is needed to initiate cultures of a new selection.

Transfers to Multiplication Media

Once the initial shoots are well formed it is time to begin the multiplication process (Figures 5-4, 5-5). These shoots can be handled in several ways to encourage multiplication. A common practice is to cut off entire shoots, remove most of the leaves and petioles, and lay the shoots on new multiplication medium. New shoots will form from buds in the petiole axils. Alternatively, small shoot clumps (3 to 5 mm in diameter) can be removed and the base pressed into the medium. Masses of shoots will form from the clumps. Some propagators frown upon this latter technique because many of the new shoots develop from callus tissue—which is thought to occasionally produce plants not true-to-type (this is discussed later in the chapter). Yet another method of transfer, which I prefer, is to cut shoots in three- to four-leaf sections and stick them upright in the medium; shoot tips are frequently placed in separate vessels because they grow at a faster rate and do not possess the same multiplication potential. Only healthy, normal-looking shoots should be transferred. I usually discard any disfigured shoots and basal clumps of tiny, glassy looking shoots.

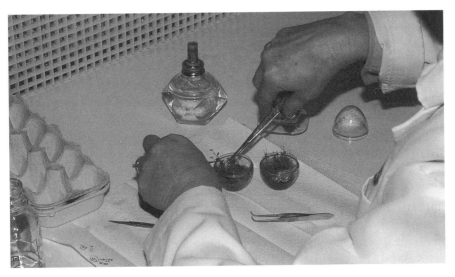

Figure 5-4. Making transfers in a laminar-flow hood. Photo by Keith Jensen.

Figure 5-5. Close-up of a well-established mountain laurel culture in a baby-food jar, with many shoots large enough to harvest for sticking and rooting. Remaining clumps could be subdivided into other containers for growing on. Photo by Greg Lloyd and Brent McCown.

Browning or dead tissue should also be removed, as toxins produced from dying tissue can poison neighboring healthy tissue. Any contaminated cultures should be discarded. Occasionally, shoot tips can be salvaged from valuable but contaminated cultures without spreading the contaminants, although success is not common. Transfers should be made at intervals of three to four weeks to keep shoots growing vigorously. If left longer, cultures will begin to decline (turn brown) as their nutrient supply is depleted.

Cultures can be stored in the refrigerator (do not allow them to freeze) for 6 to 12 months without transferring. Containers should be wrapped in Parafilm or placed in sealable plastic bags. After their stay in the refrigerator, shoots will be spindly and creamy white (etiolated), but they will fatten up and turn green once back in light.

Baby-food jars have been the preferred container used, but I find 3 × 3 × 3 in (7.5 × 7.5 × 7.5 cm) autoclavable plastic boxes (Magenta Corporation) to be very convenient as well. Not only do they hold more plant material, but the shoots are able to grow larger. The large shoots provide both cuttings for rooting as well as pieces for additional multiplication.

Rooting Microcuttings

In general, microcuttings are not rooted in sterile culture. Cuttings rooted in culture must have the medium carefully cleaned off the fragile roots, a time-consuming process. Also, when rooting in culture there is always the greater risk of contamination. I have not found major differences among cultivars in their ability to root in peat mixtures without any pretreatment in culture, and I find it more practical than rooting in culture. Typically, I can expect at least 80 percent rooting four to six weeks following harvest, a value I am satisfied with. Some cultivars, however, do not root readily in a peat mixture and may show improved rooting in culture. The medium formulation that is used for multiplication needs to be adjusted to encourage root formation. Some effective adjustments include reducing the macronutrient concentration to half strength along with the sugar concentration, removing 2iP and any other cytokinins, adding IBA or other auxins, and including activated charcoal to absorb cytokinins produced by the plantlets. Not all cultivars will respond similarly to these changes, so some experimentation may be needed.

Once an adequate number of shoots has been produced, they can then be harvested and prepared for sticking. *Harvesting* refers to cutting from established cultures shoots considered ready for rooting. *Sticking* is the process of putting these cuttings in a peat mixture for rooting.

The ideal length of the shoots to be harvested varies among propagators. Some people only harvest shoots that are 1 to 2 in (about 3 to 5 cm) long; others have had no problems rooting smaller sizes (1 to 2 cm). I feel that if the shoot looks healthy and can be conveniently handled, then stick it. I have found no difference in rooting ability depending on shoot size. Whether you select long or short shoots, all must be kept moist until they are stuck. A beaker of water works fine if the shoots will only be held for a few hours. Sometimes a fungicide can be added to the water to inhibit fungus growth. If refrigerated, cuttings placed in a covered container with wet paper towel can be held for at least 24 hours prior to sticking.

Composition of rooting media varies greatly. Materials that are used either alone or in assorted combinations include peat moss, milled sphagnum, composted and screened pine bark, vermiculite, perlite, and styrofoam. I use a mixture of screened peat moss and styrofoam (or perlite) at a ratio of one to one. Wetting agents such as mild dishwashing liquid (1 to 2 drops per liter) or a commercial material like Aquagro (2 ml per liter) can be added to the medium but are usually not needed. It is crucial that the medium not be too wet so as to discourage rooting and encourage rotting. Ideally the medium should be moist enough so that when squeezed in a fist it stays together but water does not drip out.

There is no standard for containers to use for rooting (Figure 5-6). A clear plastic box 5.5 × 7 in (14 × 18 cm) with a tightly fitting lid is favored by many growers. Usually 1 to 1.5 in (2.5 to 4 cm) of medium can be used in this container and up to 200 cuttings placed in each. Wooden or plastic seedling flats have also been used. The flats are placed on greenhouse benches lined with wet perlite and covered with plastic sheeting to prevent evaporation. If a mist system is available, the plastic is not necessary. Prides Corner Farms has developed another technique for rooting microcuttings. Plastic plug trays (200 cells per tray) are filled with a peat moss and perlite mix (2:1) and the cuttings are stuck directly in each cell (Figure 5-7). The trays are then placed in a separate area of the greenhouse. This area is equipped with a fog-producing Humidifan and timer to provide adequate moisture. Once the plants are rooted, the trays are moved to the main section of the greenhouse for hardening off. An advantage of this method over the others mentioned is that there is very little root disturbance during transplanting, as each plug is removed individually.

Figure 5-6. A variety of small containers used to root microcuttings under a 4-ft (1.2-m) fluorescent light fixture. There are over 1000 microcuttings in this photo.

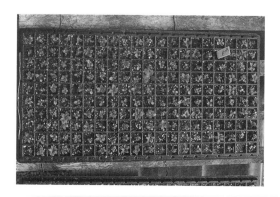

Figure 5-7. A plug tray used to root up to 200 microcuttings. Photo by Andrew Brand.

Typically, forceps are used to hold and guide each cutting into the rooting medium. The bottom two or three leaves are often removed prior to sticking. The practice of dipping the microcuttings in a solution containing IBA or other auxin usually is not necessary for mountain laurel. However, a dilute solution of a commercial auxin can be used for cultivars that are very difficult to root. Place the solution in a shallow container and dip only the cut end of the cutting before placing it in the rooting medium.

Good root production typically occurs after three to six weeks, although some cultivars may take longer. Once rooted, the cuttings must be acclimated to lower humidity conditions. Lids on closed plastic containers should be gradually opened a little each day and removed completely after 7 to 10 days. If the flats in a tent cannot be removed all at the same time, individual flats can be removed for increasingly longer periods of time each day over a one-week period, at which time they should be able to be left out. Keep an eye on the cuttings during the first two days for signs of low-humidity stress (wilting). Overcast days are good for hardening off plants. When all flats are to be hardened off together, either gradually remove the plastic cover or reduce the mist until it can be shut off entirely. At Prides Corner Farms, trays are removed from high humidity and are covered with a mesh cloth that is kept moist and gradually removed.

Once hardened off, the small plants can be transplanted to small 2- to 4-in (5- to 10-cm) pots or similar containers and moved to the greenhouse for further growing. At Broken Arrow Nursery, acclimated microcuttings are placed in wooden flats 10 × 21.5 × 2.5 in (25 × 54 × 6.5 cm). Each flat holds 80 plants, which remain there until they reach 2.5 to 4 in (6.5 to 10 cm), at which time they are planted in liner beds outdoors (Figure 5-8).

Figure 5-8. Mountain laurel cultivars growing in wooden flats at Broken Arrow Nursery.

Variation in Micropropagated Plants

Like other methods of vegetative propagation, micropropagation is used to produce clones of desired plants. Sometimes with tissue culture, however, aberrant plants can be produced. At Broken Arrow Nursery we have noticed a few instances of plants not coming true-to-type. For example, micropropagated plants of 'Pinwheel' have produced flowers with an array of color patterns (Plate 93), and this variation in flower color has appeared in several plants of the same clone as well as within a single plant. Similar flower color alterations have also been observed on other banded laurel cultivars, such as 'Goodrich' (narrow to thick bands) and 'Kaleidoscope' (no band). Interestingly, the original 'Keepsake' also produced flowers with different patterns, indicating a possible genetic basis for these differences that the tissue culture process may enhance somehow (Plate 94). It would appear that the banding-pattern characteristics of *fuscata* forms may be less stable than most other flower and foliage traits.

Besides changes in flowers, unusual plant habits have also been observed in micropropagated plants. Plate 95 shows two growth habits present in a group of 'Tinkerbell' plants. Several plants showed a very dwarf and dense habit as compared to the compact growth typical for 'Tinkerbell'. This diminutive habit has persisted for five years and appears very stable. Micropropagated offspring of 'Bridesmaid' have also been found with dwarf habits, reduced internodes, and small rounded leaves. Besides their pink flowers, these plants show little resemblance to the original 'Bridesmaid'. Other propagators have reported very dense habits and reduced internodes on micropropagated plants of 'Yankee Doodle' and 'Elf'. Again, these characteristics seem to be stable. Twisted, crinkled leaves have been observed on entire branches of 'Kaleidoscope' (Figure 5-9), but unlike the above-mentioned abnormalities, the plants appear to grow out of this leaf condition.

Figure 5-9. Abnormal and normal foliage on branches from the same plant of 'Kaleidoscope' produced in sterile culture.

Tissue proliferation (TP) is a recent problem observed on some micropropagated elepidote (large-leaf) rhododendrons. Afflicted plants typically produce abnormal calluslike growths at or near the crown of the plant, which may be accompanied by a proliferation of small shoots or buds. Some instances of small, highly meristematic regions have been observed at the base of micropropagated mountain laurel plants. Whether this is analogous to the TP found in some rhododendrons remains to be determined.

Although tissue culture can on occasion yield a few plants that are not true-to-type, by no means should this be a reason to dismiss micropropagation as an effective method of producing *Kalmia*. Any aberrant plants can often be discovered early on and then discarded or evaluated for market potential if the characteristic is considered worthy.

The recent surge in popularity of mountain laurel among the gardening public can be attributed not only to the wonderful new cultivars but also to the success of micropropagation. In the future this technique is sure to continue expanding the possibilities for breeders, growers, and gardeners by making rare cultivars more readily available.

Plate 1. *Kalmia polifolia*, eastern bog laurel, in Secretts Garden, England. Photo by Alan Pullen.

Plate 2. *Kalmia latifolia* 'Carousel' doing well in Secretts Garden, England. Photo by Alan Pullen.

Plate 3. *Kalmia latifolia* 'Sarah' growing in England with a holly *(Ilex)* to the left and a maple (*Acer japonicum* 'Aureum') to the right. Photo by Alan Pullen.

Plate 4. The mountain laurel *Kalmia latifolia* 'Clementine Churchill' in a garden in England. Photo by Pamela Harper.

Plate 5. A nice pink-flowered selection of *Kalmia latifolia* growing in Japan. Photo by Hideo Suzuki.

Plate 6. *Kalmia latifolia* growing in a nursery outside of Tokyo, Japan, with azaleas in the foreground. Photo by Hideo Suzuki.

Plate 7. *Kalmia latifolia* 'Sharon Rose' growing in Seoul, South Korea. This is one of many mountain laurel selections doing well in Ferris Miller's garden. Photo by Ferris Miller.

Plate 8. A well-grown *Kalmia latifolia* at the Royal Botanic Garden, Melbourne, Australia, with *Rhododendron* in the background. Photo by Stirling Macoboy.

Plate 9. *Kalmia microphylla* var. *microphylla*, western alpine laurel, from the Cascade Mountains of Oregon. Total plant height, including flowers, of this high-altitude form is about 2 in (5 cm).

Plate 10. *Kalmia latifolia*, mountain laurel, is the state flower of Connecticut and Pennsylvania and is one of our most beautiful native plants.

Plate 11. Natural variation in flower color from near white to pink on native mountain laurel plants growing side by side.

Plate 12. Native *Kalmia latifolia* can grow in some truly difficult sites, as seen here among rocks and native ferns along a roadway.

Plate 13. Although *Kalmia latifolia* will not grow in water-logged soils, it can often be found close to water.

Plate 14. An older plant of mountain laurel with a graceful and artistic form on the edge of a woods and pond.

Plate 15. Old stems of *Kalmia latifolia* have a special charm and beauty, as seen here highlighted by a snow cover on the ground.

Plate 16. A fairly typical expression of the banded mountain laurel, form *fuscata*.

Plate 17. *Kalmia latifolia* f. *polypetala*, feather petal mountain laurel. Each flower typically has five petals; the petal edges are often rolled more and are therefore less attractive than the one pictured here.

Plate 18. *Kalmia latifolia* apetalous selection, which lacks a corolla (or petals).

Plate 19. A particularly attractive sheep laurel, *Kalmia angustifolia*, photographed in Newfoundland. Photo by Dick Redfield.

Plate 20. Sheep laurel in a garden setting. The one pictured here is the selection named 'Hammonasset'.

Plate 21. *Kalmia angustifolia* branches from three flowering plants, illustrating the range of flower color within the species: *left*, the white-flowered form *candida*; *center*, the cultivar 'Hammonasset'; *right*, an unnamed seedling.

Plate 22. A red-flowered selection of *Kalmia angustifolia* often listed and sold as the cultivar 'Rubra'.

Plate 23. The white-flowered northern sheep laurel, form *candida*, grown from seed collected at Madison, Connecticut.

Plate 24. *Kalmia cuneata*, white wicky, an endangered species.

Plate 25. Fall color of *Kalmia cuneata*, the only deciduous *Kalmia* species.

Plate 26. Close-up of the hairs on the stem and leaves of *Kalmia hirsuta*, sandhill laurel, and the reason for the Latin name of the species "hirsuta".

Plate 27. *Kalmia hirsuta* with leaves about 0.5 in (12 mm) long. The pigment spots in the flower are more prominent in this plant than in most.

Plate 28. View of a relatively new planting of *Kalmia latifolia* cultivars at the Highstead Arboretum, Redding, Connecticut. A place to see and compare many named selections.

Plate 29. 'Alpine Pink' is a soft pink form and is notable for the two-tone appearance of the open flowers. The buds just before opening are a deeper pink. Photo by Briggs Nursery.

Plate 30. Although described as having coral-colored flowers by the introducer, 'Bay State' has an overall floral appearance similar to other red-budded selections.

Plate 31. 'Bridesmaid' is rich pink in bud and in open flower, but with a lighter center.

Plate 32. 'Bristol' is a banded selection (form *fuscata*) where the pigment nearly fills the corolla. It was used by the author as a parent to produce other cultivars such as 'Bullseye' and 'Kaleidoscope'.

Plate 33. 'Bullseye', like 'Sarah', 'Kaleidoscope', and some other deeply pigmented selections, displays new growth with red stems and bronzy foliage.

Plate 34. 'Bullseye' flowers are banded. The plant grows into a large and sometimes open plant.

Plate 35. 'Carol' is red to deep pink in bud, opening near white and then darkening to a medium pink.

Plate 36. 'Carousel' has an intricate banding pattern. The color and width of the band will vary some with year and exposure.

Plate 37. 'Clementine Churchill' is a rich pink selection with nice markings in the corolla. It was named in Great Britain and is highly thought of there.

Plate 38. 'Comet', an offspring of 'Shooting Star', was selected for improved foliage and growth habit, along with its deeply lobed white flower.

Plate 39. 'Elf' was the first of the miniature laurels (form *myrtifolia*) to be named. The flowers are essentially white when open.

Plate 40. 'Freckles' is actually a banded laurel where the band of pigment is interrupted.

Plate 41. 'Galaxy' is the first selection to combine the lobed 'Shooting Star'-like flower with the banded trait.

Plate 42. 'Golden Flush' is a new selection from Japan. The new foliage is yellow in color and contrasts nicely with the red stems. Photo by Hideo Suzuki.

Plate 43. 'Goodrich', a banded selection from the state forest in Chaplin, Connecticut.

Plate 44. 'Good Show' is a relatively new and handsome selection with pink flowers.

Plate 45. 'Heart of Fire' flowers are firey red in bud and borne on an upright-growing plant.

Plate 46. 'Hearts Desire' has raspberry-red buds opening to display flowers with a burgundy interior with a white center and white edge.

Plate 47. 'Hearts Desire' close-up. Note that these flowers, from the same plant as in the previous photo but in a different year, have a broader band.

Plate 48. 'Hoffman's Pink' has intermediate to soft pink flowers, equatable to the rich pink end of the spectrum of flower colors found among native plants.

Plate 49. 'Kaleidoscope' flowers combine the raspberry-red flower bud color with the broad burgundy band in the open flower. The miniature 'Tiddlywinks' is to the left. Photo by Chuck Molnar.

Plate 50. The white edge on the 'Kaleidoscope' corolla contrasts well with the rich band and bud color.

Plate 51. 'Keepsake' is a newly named selection with flowers much like those of 'Hearts Desire' and 'Kaleidoscope'. The foliage is especially glossy and dark green.

Plate 52. 'Little Linda' is a recent selection combining the traits of red-budded flowers with a miniature growth habit.

Plate 53. 'Madeline' is a double-flowered selection found in a New Zealand garden and only recently brought to the United States. Photo by M. J. Chappell.

Plate 54. 'Minuet' is a banded miniature with dark, glossy, narrow leaves. Photo by Mike Hayman.

Plate 55. 'Nathan Hale' is a red-budded selection that requires little pruning when young.

Plate 56. 'Nipmuck' is red in bud, has light green foliage, and cuttings are relatively easy to root.

Plate 57. 'Olympic Fire' is a red-budded selection that has been popular with container growers of mountain laurel.

Plate 58. 'Olympic Wedding' is lavender-pink in bud and maroon banded when open.

Plate 59. 'Ostbo Red' was the first named red-budded selection and is still one of the best for bright, orangey red (non-blue) flower bud color.

Plate 60. 'Paul Bosley', *right*, displays strong pink to red-budded flowers on an attractive upright-growing plant. 'Pink Globe', *left*, with rich pink flowers on a globe-shaped truss, grows as broad as tall and has wide, thick leaves.

Plate 61. 'Peppermint' has an enhanced inner ring with streaks of pigment running up the corolla creases. Photo by Mike Hayman.

Plate 62. 'Pequot' has dark red flower buds and smallish and often twisted leaves.

Plate 63. 'Pink Charm' flower buds are strong pink to red in bud and open a rich pink.

Plate 64. 'Pink Frost', with flowers that are a soft pink when open, performs best when grown in light shade.

Plate 65. 'Pink Star' is a deep pink in bud and open flower and was selected for its strongly lobed, star-shaped corolla. Photo by Briggs Nursery.

Plate 66. 'Pink Surprise' has a pleasing pink flower with crisp, dark pigment accents within the corolla.

Plate 67. 'Pinwheel' has vibrant, banded flowers borne on an upright growing plant.

Plate 68. Close-up of 'Pinwheel' flowers showing the interesting pigment pattern.

Plate 69. 'Pristine' has pure white flowers borne on a somewhat diminutive plant, and was selected from the southern part of the natural range.

Plate 70. 'Raspberry Glow' has deeply pigmented flower buds that open to strong pink. Photo by Mike Hayman.

Plate 71. 'Richard Jaynes' has red-budded flowers that open light but soon turn a strong pink.

Plate 72. 'Sarah' has striking red flowers in bud that are borne on a rounded, dense-growing plant.

Plate 73. As the flowers of 'Sarah' open and age, the red coloring is lost and the flowers become pink.

Plate 74. 'Sharon Rose' is a rounded, densely branched, red-budded selection.

Plate 76. 'Silver Dollar' has near-white, oversized flowers that are enhanced with distinctive pigment markings.

Plate 75. 'Shooting Star' has a unique flower form that has been found only once in the wild.

Plate 77. 'Snowdrift', with clean white flowers and dark green foliage on a rounded plant, is slow growing at first but destined to grow large.

Plate 78. 'Splendens' was the first mountain laurel cultivar to be named, in 1890. It represents the pink end of the color range found among native plants.

Plate 79. 'Star Cluster' is a banded selection exhibiting greater tolerance to heavy soils than one usually associates with *Kalmia*.

Plate 80. 'Stillwood' is a nearly pure white selection from New Hampshire.

Plate 81. 'Sunset' is one of the most deeply pigmented selections.

Plate 82. 'Tiddlywinks' is a pink-flowered miniature. It is a bit more compact and slower growing than 'Tinkerbell'.

Plate 83. 'Tightwad Too' has pink flowers that never open but hold in the bud stage, as seen here in mid-July, one month after the normal peak bloom period in Connecticut.

Plate 84. 'Tightwad Too' offers prominent flower buds in winter that are reddish bronze in color and darker than those of most other selections.

Plate 85. 'Tinkerbell' is a pink-flowered, vigorous-growing miniature that might best be referred to as semidwarf.

Plate 86. 'Willowcrest' is a distinctive willow-leaved form. The light pink flowers do not always open fully, especially if the plant is stressed.

Plate 87. 'Willowood' is similar to 'Willowcrest', but its foliage and growth habit are diminutive.

Plate 88. 'Yankee Doodle' has flowers that are red in bud and open to reveal a narrow burgundy band.

Plate 89. *Kalmia angustifolia* 'Kennebago', selected in Maine, has deep rose flowers.

Plate 90. *Kalmia angustifolia* 'Royal Dwarf' is a brightly colored sheep laurel of low stature that has previously been called pumila, meaning dwarf.

Plate 91. *Kalmia angustifolia* 'Royal Dwarf' characteristically has scattered flowers in late summer and early fall.

Plate 92. 'Rocky Top' is a selected hybrid of the eastern bog laurel *(Kalmia polifolia)* and the western alpine laurel *(Kalmia microphylla* var. *microphylla)*.

Plate 93. Variation in flower color pattern in micropropagated 'Pinwheel' plants.

Plate 94. Variation in flower color pattern in a plant *not* produced through tissue culture—this is 'Keepsake'.

Plate 95. Two growth habits found in micropropagated 'Tinkerbell' plants: *right*, typical habit; *left*, unusually dense, compact growth.

Plate 96. Field-grown *Kalmia latifolia* mulched with wood chips: *left*, native, collected laurel; and *foreground*, a few small 'Sarah' plants.

Plate 97. Different color forms of naturalized *Kalmia latifolia* planted on the edge of a lawn, with grey birch, *Betula populifolia*, to the right.

Plate 98. An old, single-stemmed, native *Kalmia latifolia*. Here the stem and seed capsules add charm through the dormant season.

Plate 99. Woodland scene of *Kalmia latifolia* selections.

Plate 100. A mixed planting of named mountain laurel cultivars. Photo by Mike Hayman.

Plate 101. Pink, white, and other selections of *Kalmia latifolia* bordering a stonewall on a property line.

Plate 102. A backyard scene. The mountain laurel cultivars 'Pink Globe' and the white-flowered 'Angel', with the fullmoon maple *(Acer japonicum)* and Japanese maple *(Acer palmatum)* 'Crimson Queen' in the background.

Plate 103. Native *Kalmia latifolia* used to screen a roadway at a public golf course.

Plate 104. A collection of mountain laurel selections in a private garden in Connecticut. Photo by Dick Redfield.

Plate 105. Selected mountain laurel seedlings used to screen a greenhouse and shed.

Plate 106. Twig blight dieback and drought stress are intertwined. Drought stress may look like winter injury, with browning of leaf tips and edges, or, as shown here, it may appear as discoloration and death of entire branchlets. The latter is often the result of infection by the twig blight organism on the stressed plant.

Plate 107. Yellow leaves may be normal on *Kalmia latifolia*, as seen here during a brief period in autumn just before the old foliage falls off. This photo was taken in Connecticut on 1 October, about the time our deciduous trees and shrubs begin to show their fall colors.

Plate 108. *Kalmia latifolia* forced for a late-winter or early-spring flower show. High temperatures are usually required for six to eight weeks after a period of cold dormancy.

Plate 109. The fine-grained wood of *Kalmia latifolia* is beautiful. Here are a pair of candlestick holders, a bowl, and a spoon, each produced by different craftsmen. The bowl was turned from a burl and shows a bird's-eye pattern. Note the sprite carved on the spoon handle to ensure good luck.

Plate 110. An example of a *Kalmia angustifolia* heath near Botwood, Newfoundland, where apparent allelopathic effects of the laurel prevent seedling regeneration of black spruce (*Picea mariana*). The black spruce seedling was planted 14 years earlier but is only 1 ft (30 cm) tall. The previous spruce stand was clearcut and natural regeneration is absent. Photo by Brian Titus, Canadian Forest Service.

Plate 111. Another example of a sheep laurel heath in central Newfoundland impeding the natural regeneration of black spruce (*Picea mariana*). These spruce seedlings were planted 11 years earlier and are about 1 ft (30 cm) tall. Note the size of the stumps of the previous stand, indicating good growth and productivity, in stark contrast to the stunted planted seedlings! Photo by Brian Titus, Canadian Forest Service.

Plate 112. Selfing sometimes reveals recessive genes for such traits as compact growth, as is seen with these seedlings from the self-pollination of a native *Kalmia latifolia*.

Plate 113. Typical wild native *Kalmia latifolia*, growing at Weston Nurseries, Hopkinton, Massachusetts—compare to the next two plates.

Plate 114. A field of mountain laurel seedlings grown from seed parents selected for deep flower color at Weston Nurseries. There are some red-budded and rich pink-flowered plants in the field.

Plate 115. Mountain laurel seedlings from controlled crosses made by the author at the Connecticut Agricultural Experiment Station. The rich color of the plants in this photo demonstrates the advantage of controlling not only the seed parent but also the pollen parent to obtain offspring with richly colored flowers.

Plate 116. The segregation in seedlings from a cross can be remarkable. Here is a sampling of the variation in flower color found among seedlings from a single cross of two plants having diverse backgrounds. There was also great variation in growth habit, segregating for normal and miniature.

Plate 117. The F_1 hybrid of sandhill laurel and sheep laurel (*Kalmia hirsuta* × *Kalmia angustifolia*) with characteristics intermediate between those of the parent species.

Plate 118. A first-generation hybrid of mountain laurel and sandhill laurel (*Kalmia latifolia* × *Kalmia hirsuta*). Of the many seedlings grown from this cross, this is the only one ever to produce good seed.

Plate 119. Young first-generation seedlings of the cross between sheep laurel (*Kalmia angustifolia*) and mountain laurel (*Kalmia latifolia*). The new growth lacks chlorophyll, emerging a pale yellow-green, but the leaves turn green as they mature.

Plate 120. Flowering hybrid of sheep laurel and mountain laurel.

Plate 121. The F$_1$ hybrid of eastern bog laurel and western alpine laurel (*Kalmia polifolia* × *Kalmia microphylla* var. *microphylla*).

Plate 122. A putative hybrid of *Kalmia latifolia* and *Rhododendron williamsianum* produced by Halfdan Lem and named 'No Suchianum' by Lawrence Pierce. Photo by Gwen Bell (*Journal, American Rhododendron Society*, 1994).

Plate 123. 'Stillwood' crossed with another white-flowered selection (*center*). Flowers of the offspring are all white, as shown in the 12 surrounding clusters.

Plate 124. 'Stillwood' crossed with the red-bud CAES 137. All the offspring were white flowered (nine are shown here).

Plate 125. A rich pink, very dwarf selection that is 25 years old. It was selected from a controlled cross of two deep pink plants but is too slow growing to propagate commercially.

Plate 126. Flowers from 13 representative seedlings of a controlled cross of two red-budded mountain laurel plants, in which all the offspring were red budded. The parent flowers are in the center. This is an example of a trait that can be bred true from seed.

Plate 127. There is always room for improvement of existing cultivars. This is a deeply pigmented red-bud selection with dense, dark, glossy foliage.

Plate 128. A solid red *Kalmia latifolia* still eludes us, but selections like this one bring us closer.

Plate 129. A nicely pigmented selection from the wild made by Clarence Towe and used in the parentage of 'Peppermint'.

Plate 130. A hybrid similar to 'Peppermint' but having an enhanced inner ring. This selection is not named.

Plate 131. A selection similar to 'Galaxy', combining the deeply cut lobes of 'Shooting Star' and a banded corolla.

Plate 132. Another mountain laurel selection combining the traits of a deeply cut corolla and banding, except in this case the pigmentation of the band is more pink than burgundy.

Plate 133. The reduced corolla of the 'Bettina' type flowers *(left)* and the near-petaled form of the 'Shooting Star' type *(right)* combine to form a plant with ministar flowers, as is shown in the plant in the middle, the result of a second-generation cross.

Plate 134. Even the apetala form of *Kalmia latifolia* is attractive when in full "flower." I like to think that this is the blue- or yellow-flowered mountain laurel, if only it had petals!

Plate 135. The first seedling to flower that combines 'Shooting Star' type flowers on a plant of miniature (f. *myrtifolia*) growth habit.

Plate 136. A seedling from a controlled cross that combines two single-gene recessive traits: *Kalmia latifolia* forms *myrtifolia* and *angustata* (miniature and willow-leaved, respectively). Note the miniaturization in comparison with a branch of normal mountain laurel to the left.

Plate 137. A seedling with the compact growth and broad leaves of *Kalmia latifolia* f. *obtusata* that was selected from the second-generation cross of a normal mountain laurel with the *obtusata* form.

Plate 138. Sarah Jaynes, the author's wife, standing next to a very compact *Kalmia latifolia* plant that is approximately 30 years old.

Plate 139. An unusual variegation pattern in the foliage. The sectors are streaked or splashed along the leaf. Photo by Clarence Towe.

Plate 140. Not all crosses produce great plants. 'Nathan Hale' crossed with 'Sunset' produced an unusually high percentage of seedlings with chlorotic or crinkled leaves, as well as slow-growing plants.

CHAPTER 6

Seeds and Their Germination

Although a native of our woods, the cheapest and easiest mode of procuring [mountain laurel] plants is to import them from England, where they are raised from seed in large quantities. Nice, bushy plants, about a foot high, cost only twenty-five dollars per hundred landed here, and, as they grow rapidly, soon form large plants. (Rand 1876)

Laurel seed is small and requires careful handling for good germination. The seed of each species has a characteristic size and shape (Figure 6-1) and specific germination requirements. The sandhill laurel, *Kalmia hirsuta*, has the smallest seeds—as many as five million to the ounce (28 g)—even smaller than those notoriously small-seeded garden flowers *Petunia*, *Nicotiana*, and *Begonia*.

Seed Harvest and Cleaning

Maturation time of seed capsules will vary a bit from year to year—even in the same area—and also will vary among plants. As the capsules mature they change from green to brown. If capsules are harvested too soon, the seed will not be ripe and it may not shed readily from the capsule, even if mature enough to germinate. If left on the plant too long, the capsule will dehisce (split) and scatter its seeds. Yet, with mountain laurel (*Kalmia latifolia*) and sheep laurel (*K. angustifolia*) it is often possible to extract a few seeds from capsules left on the plant in the spring or summer, six to nine months after they have ripened. The approximate flowering

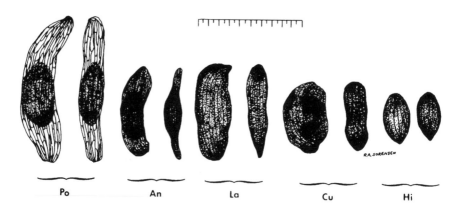

Figure 6-1. Typical seeds of five *Kalmia* species, showing two views of each seed (left to right): *Kalmia polifolia, K. angustifolia, K. latifolia, K. cuneata,* and *K. hirsuta.* The scale is 1 mm (0.04 in) in length. Drawing by Rita Sorensen-Leonard.

period, days to seed harvest, and harvest period in Connecticut (USDA zones 5 and 6) for the six *Kalmia* species are given in Figure 6-2. Each species is distinct from the others, either in time of flowering, time of seed harvest, period of flowering, or period required for seed maturation.

To extract small quantities of seed, place the harvested capsules in a coin envelope, paper bag, or other small container and allow them to air dry for a few days. The capsules will then open and seeds can be shaken loose. A small piece of window screen can be used to separate the capsules and larger pieces of debris from the seed, which will be mixed with dust and chaff. Clean the seeds of any other material that came through the screen by gently funneling them down a trough-shaped piece of white paper and letting them fall a short distance onto another piece of paper. Most of the chaff will move down the paper more slowly than the seed. With each pass, some chaff can be discarded. Repeat the process several times, and most of the debris will separate from the seed.

Due to a fear that capsules on the plant will open prematurely, resulting in seed loss, I have too often collected capsules from my controlled crosses too soon. In such cases the seed is mature, but it does not readily release from the capsule when dry. The solution is to crush the capsules on paper

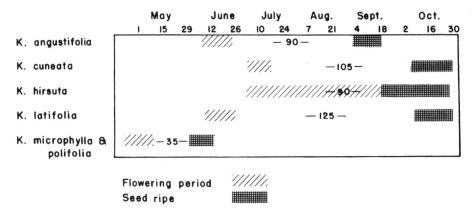

Figure 6-2. Relative periods of flowering and seed ripening, and time from flowering to seed maturation in days. The dates will vary according to location, but the general pattern will hold. Note that there is an almost fourfold difference in the time required for *Kalmia latifolia* seed to mature as compared with *K. microphylla* and *K. polifolia*; also note that *K. hirsuta* tends to be ever-blooming.

between a table top and a small wooden block. The seed will contain more debris and the cleaning will be more laborious, but the seed can indeed be recovered by this method.

Sieves are also effective for cleaning seed, especially if the seed is dirty or large quantities are involved. Most mountain laurel seed will pass through a 0.5-mm round-holed sieve. I use a #1 (0.508 mm) and #2 (0.610 mm) sieve obtained from D. Ballauf Manufacturing Company in Laurel, Maryland. Even with this sieve method, a final cleaning on white paper is recommended, because any debris left with the seed increases the chance of contamination and will support fungal growth at the time of germination.

Other cleaning methods take advantage of the specific gravity of laurel seed. Seedsmen can use commercial air separators to winnow the heavier, viable seed from the dust and chaff. Alternatively, the fresh, filled mountain laurel seed can be placed in water, where the chaff and unfilled seeds float and the viable seeds sink to the bottom. Decant the debris and remove the good seed and dry for sowing.

Seed Storage and Longevity

Laurel seed maintains its viability for several years if stored under cool, dry conditions. I store seed in glassine or coin envelopes in enclosed but unsealed trays in a household, frost-free refrigerator at 40°F (4°C). Exact longevity of seed from different species is difficult to determine because of variability among seed lots and departures from ideal storage conditions.

A summary of seed germination results for five laurel species is given in Table 6-1. Mountain laurel seed is long-lived. Of 28 lots of seed stored more than 10 years, 21 of them, or 75 percent, had a germination rate above 50 percent. It came as a surprise to me that such small seed would stay alive so long. Numerous tests suggest that mountain laurel seed kept dry and refrigerated remains in good condition for 15 years or longer. Some seed stored 20 years is still capable of producing seedlings.

Tests with the other species were less extensive, but the evidence suggests that seed of sheep laurel (*Kalmia angustifolia*), bog laurel (*K. polifolia*), and white wicky (*K. cuneata*), like that of mountain laurel, can also be stored for many years and remain viable. Seed of sandhill laurel (*K. hirsuta*) would appear to be shorter lived.

Table 6-1. Summary of Seed Germination of *Kalmia* Species Stored for Many Years.

Species	number of lots of seed	years stored	percent germination
Kalmia angustifolia	1	16	22
Kalmia cuneata	1	3	29
	1	10	46
Kalmia hirsuta	6	7–16	0
	2	14	< 1
Kalmia latifolia	28	10–20	3–90 (avg. > 50)
Kalmia polifolia	7	8–17	0
	1	8	51
	1	12	27
	1	15	59

General Requirements for Germination and Early Growth

The best temperature for germination and initial growth is between 70 and 75°F (21 to 24°C). Constant temperatures above 80°F (27°C) will reduce survival, whereas temperatures below 70°F (21°C) slow growth dramatically (Figure 6-3). A cool, wet germination and growing medium, especially during cloudy, low-light periods in winter, may result in ammonia buildup and root injury.

Various media can be used for germination, including pure sphagnum peat moss (Canadian peat) or milled sphagnum moss as well as media recommended for *Rhododendron* and *Pieris*. I prefer the following mixture for small batches of seed germinated in closed but not airtight plastic boxes (proportions by volume): 2 to 3 parts Canadian (sphagnum) peat moss (screened 0.25 in [6 mm]), 1 part perlite (screened one-eighth in [3 mm]).

For each gallon (3.8 liters) of mix, add 1.5 teaspoons (8 g) of ground limestone to raise the pH slightly. Peat moss often has a pH near 4.0, which is too low even for these acid-loving plants. A pH of about 5.0 is desired, and it really should be checked; reliable, accurate, and relatively inexpensive pocket pH meters are readily available. Good drainage and aeration are required for good seed germination as well. Avoid using soil, and if vermiculite is used keep the proportion to 15 percent or less by volume because problems have been known to occur at higher rates. Fine, milled, aged pine bark could substitute for perlite or vermiculite. By using a medium without

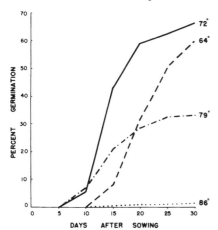

Figure 6-3. Seed germination of *Kalmia latifolia* at four temperatures: 64, 72, 79, and 86°F (19, 21, 23, and 26°C). Note the low germination rate at the two high temperatures.

soil, one minimizes the danger from soil-borne pathogens and, in addition, the peat (and sphagnum moss if used) contributes some antibiotic activity.

Clear plastic boxes, 3.5 × 7 × 1.75 in (9 × 18 × 4 cm) high and placed 9 to 12 in (23 to 30 cm) below fluorescent lights, have served me well. Certainly a variety of other metal and plastic containers can be substituted. Trays without tops can be placed in clear plastic bags. A few pencil-sized holes will allow for air exchange without excessive drying. Large quantities of seed can be germinated in standard flats.

The following is a mix I have used for the successful germination of seedlings in flats. It is virtually the same as that used in the small containers and can be restated as follows:

2 bushels (70 liters) Canadian peat moss
1 bushel (35 liters) perlite
0.5 bushel (17 liters) coarse sand (optional)
2 to 3 ounces (56 to 84 grams) ground limestone

After filling the flats, use a board to gently firm the surface. The medium should be wetted thoroughly prior to sowing by setting the flats in a shallow tray of water (a sheet of plastic placed on a level surface and bounded by 2-in (5-cm) high boards works well). Excessive initial watering from above tends to compact the media and leaves a layer of perlite on top; if the surface appears too rough, sprinkle a thin layer of screened sphagnum peat on top before sowing the seed.

These and other mixes exhibit an unusual property: when stored, they do not support good seed germination and growth. Though difficult to believe, this virtually aseptic, nonsoil mix, stored in near dryness, deteriorates as a germination medium in a few months. I have observed this deterioration of the medium time and again; and one of my colleagues, who used a quite different medium for germinating *Gloxinia*, had the same difficulty with his stored mixes. Possibly, the natural antibiotic qualities of the sphagnum peat oxidize and deteriorate when mixed with other material and stored warm and enclosed. My advice, then, is to not prepare more germination mix than will be used within two months, and try not to use peat that has been allowed to become extremely dry for the same reasons.

The seeds should be sown on the surface of the mix and *not covered*—they need light and will not germinate in the dark. A moist medium and high humidity are necessary for germination. Once the seed is germinated and well rooted, however, the surface of the medium should be allowed to dry occasionally to retard algal and moss growth.

It is not necessary to fertilize the mix until true leaves begin to emerge, at which time a solution of soluble fertilizer, such as 20-20-20, prepared at the rate of 1 teaspoon per gallon (1.25 grams per liter) should be sprinkled or misted over the mix. This concentration is approximately 200 parts per million (ppm). Reapply at two- and three-week intervals, testing the mix from time to time to prevent overfertilizing and to detect possible nutrient imbalances or changes in pH. Those familiar with the seedling growth of azaleas, rhododendrons, and *Pieris* will note that *Kalmia* seedlings are generally slower growing.

The seedlings can be left in flats for two months to even a year (Figure 6-4), provided they do not become too crowded or matted by algae and moss. As noted above, once small seedlings have become established, the surface of the medium should be allowed to dry every few days, because algae, moss, and liverworts are difficult to control once established. Should a heavy mat of these plants become established, it is best to transplant the seedlings, leaving behind as much of the "weeds" as possible.

Most seeds will germinate in 10 to 21 days. Light intensity should be at least 100 foot-candles, or 50 microeinsteins per square meter per second. A pair of closely spaced standard fluorescent tubes with a white reflector will furnish this much light when placed 9 to 12 in (23 to 30 cm) above the seeds; the bulb length will depend on the area to be covered. Because light intensity drops sharply near the ends of fluorescent tubes, light distribution is better with one 8-ft (2.5-m) fixture than with two 4-ft (1.2-m) fixtures.

When growing the seedlings indoors, I have used 16 hours of light, from 8 AM to midnight. In the greenhouse during the winter, I extend the day length with 20-watt fluorescent floodlights from 10 PM to 2 AM. These incandescent lights are used not to increase growth (by photosynthesis) but

Figure 6-4. Seedlings nine weeks after sowing in a small tray and kept under fluorescent lights (white bar is 0.4 in or 1 cm).

to keep the seedlings from becoming dormant. The reflector bulbs are spaced every 4 ft (1.2 m), 30 in (75 cm) above the plants, so that the plants receive only 8 to 10 foot-candles of artificial light in the middle of the night. To save energy, the lights can be set by timers to flash on for five seconds every minute.

Much of the logic for this day-length extension is based on work done with other greenhouse crops. The procedure outlined here has worked well indoors under lights. However, we do not fully know the best conditions for maximizing growth of seedling laurel in greenhouses during the short days of winter, when growth is often disappointing. (See Chapter 7 for a further discussion of this.)

Experiments with mountain laurel and sheep laurel seed demonstrate that germination can be hastened by starting the seeds under an atmosphere enriched with carbon dioxide (CO_2). The benefits of CO_2 on increasing plant growth is well known and is discussed in the next chapter, but its effect on stimulating germination is less well understood. Apparently the translucent seed coats of laurel allow the seed leaves to green up, and in the presence of high CO_2 levels, their development and growth is accelerated, resulting in faster germination.

Time of Sowing

Seeds from even late-maturing species can be harvested and cleaned by late fall. If seeds are planted indoors under lights by 1 December, husky seedlings can develop by late spring. After danger of frost passes, the seedlings can be moved outdoors and, in late spring or summer, planted in beds where they will continue to thrive throughout the normal growing season.

An alternative is to sow the seed outdoors in the spring after the soil warms up. The seed should still be sown in flats and shaded from full sun. Protect the plants from extreme cold the first winter by placing the flats in a cold frame or by covering them with conifer branches. If the seedlings are large enough (1.5 in [4 cm] tall or more) they can be bedded or potted individually the following spring.

Mycorrhiza—Fungi Associated with the Roots

Many species, especially in the family Ericaceae, have beneficial fungi, called symbiotic mycorrhiza, that are intimately associated with the roots.

These fungi are dependent on the plant, and in turn they may in some way assist the plant in assimilating nutrients and water or in preventing attacks from other fungi. Indeed, native and field-grown *Kalmia* plants have been described as normally having mycorrhizal associates within (endophyte) and outside (ectophyte) the roots. They are not carried in the seed or on any other parts of the plant growing above ground.

A helpful paper by William Flemer (1949) of Princeton Nurseries, New Jersey, deals with isolating these fungi and growing mountain laurel seedlings with and without them. Under sterile conditions, Flemer isolated pure cultures of various root-associated fungi and then inoculated the root area of aseptically grown seedlings with the fungi. He observed a positive growth response by the seedlings to the presence of the most commonly isolated endophyte. On the basis of Flemer's work one may conclude that there is an important mycorrhizal association beneficial to the growth of mountain laurel.

Fortunately, it seems unnecessary for most of us to inoculate seedlings. The beneficial organism(s) is likely present in peat or sphagnum moss, and the plants become naturally inoculated. It is also possible that mycorrhizal association does not occur and/or is less important to seedling growth in more complex media than in the sterile, defined environment of the laboratory. More research in both laboratory and field is needed to determine how to manage these fungi to our benefit in growing seedlings.

The Seeds and Their Germination

Kalmia angustifolia, Sheep Laurel, *Kalmia microphylla*, Western Laurel, and *Kalmia polifolia*, Eastern Bog Laurel

Kalmia angustifolia, *K. microphylla*, and *K. polifolia* are the easiest laurel species to germinate because their seed has no strong dormancy requirement, although there has been just a hint of a partial dormancy requirement for sheep laurel seed from plants in the southern part of the range. Interestingly, these three species are the ones that have elongated and winglike seeds (see Figure 6-1). Dormancy may be related to the tighter, harder-appearing seed shape, or the relationship may be entirely coincidental. The number of seeds per capsule varies from a few up to about 200 in the western laurel and eastern bog laurel, and to about 300 in sheep laurel. The number of seeds per capsule is less when pollination is poor or when there are large numbers of flowers on a plant.

Kalmia latifolia, Mountain Laurel

Fresh mountain laurel seed will germinate without any special treatment, although cold stratification for eight weeks or merely soaking the seeds overnight in 200 ppm gibberellin (a naturally occurring plant hormone) will increase germination by 50 percent. Seed stored for a year or two will germinate even better than fresh seed, because simple dry storage overcomes the partial dormancy requirement of fresh seed. As noted previously, seed stored dry in a refrigerator may remain viable for 15 to 20 years. Recently I had good germination of seed saved from controlled crosses between miniature mountain laurel plants that was harvested 20 years earlier.

Dormancy requirements probably evolved as an adaptation to prevent all the seed from germinating at once in the wild. For example, if there were an extended warm period in the fall after the seed capsules had split, the seed lacking a dormancy requirement would germinate (and would thus be vulnerable to freezing), while the rest would remain quiescent during the winter until more favorable conditions occurred in the spring.

Treatment to break dormancy of mountain laurel seed is necessary or valuable only when seed is in short supply, such as seed from controlled crosses, or when the expectation is that germination percentages of fresh seed will be abnormally low. Untreated fresh seed usually has a 20 to 50 percent germination rate in three to four weeks. By treating with gibberellin, the germination rate is higher and a bit faster, and emergence is more uniform (Figure 6-5).

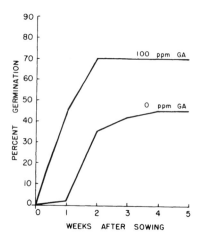

Figure 6-5. Germination of freshly harvested *Kalmia latifolia* seed is enhanced by treating the seed with 100 ppm of gibberellin (GA). The germination rate of untreated seed was 45 percent, compared to 70 percent for the GA-treated seed.

In the wild, mountain laurel seeds germinate on bare mineral soil or on low-growing moss. Since the soil cannot be allowed to dry, seedlings are commonly found on north-facing slopes of road cuts with mature plants above—the source of the seed that is dispersed by gravity and wind. Some long-distance spread occurs from the release of seed in winter when blown across the surface of hard-packed snow.

Kalmia cuneata, White Wicky

Freshly harvested seed of white wicky (*Kalmia cuneata*) has a poor rate of germination, usually less than 5 percent. However, seed treated in a moist-cold environment (stratified) for 8 to 16 weeks shows a tenfold increase in germination rate. To stratify such fine seed, mix it with a small quantity of moist sand in a polyethylene bag and place in a refrigerator at a constant temperature of 40°F (4°C). Alternatively, simply sow the seed on the moistened germination mix and refrigerate at a few degrees above freezing. The latter technique works well for small quantities of seed sown in small plastic containers that are taped shut to prevent evaporation during the cold treatment. Seed harvested in late fall or winter often has been naturally stratified sufficiently to satisfy the dormancy requirement.

A short treatment with gibberellin can be used instead of the stratification procedure; a solution of 500 to 1000 ppm is effective (Figure 6-6). Before the seeds are sowed, place them on a piece of filter paper or paper towel saturated with the gibberellin solution for 12 to 24 hours in an enclosed container to prevent evaporation. The effect of this treatment on germination is the same as if the seed had received eight weeks of moist-cold treatment. Since it is difficult to remove the seed from the wet paper immediately after treatment, let the paper and seeds air dry. Then the seeds simply will roll off the paper and can be handled normally.

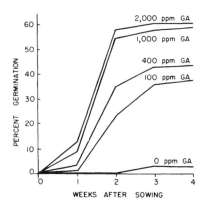

Figure 6-6. Soaking *Kalmia cuneata* seed in gibberellin (GA) substitutes for several weeks of moist-cold stratification. Here rates of 100 to 2000 ppm were effective, although the high rates cause the seedlings to elongate excessively.

Although white wicky seed capsules may hold as many as 200 seeds, the average is closer to 100. They are a bit lighter than mountain laurel seed, at 1.7 million seeds per ounce (28 g).

Kalmia hirsuta, Sandhill Laurel

Kalmia hirsuta exhibits the most unusual requirement for germination, and its seed is the most difficult to germinate. The seed of sandhill laurel is incredibly small—as many as five million to the ounce (28 g). Only a few other plants in the world have such minute seeds. Yet because they are round, they roll easily on paper and so can be readily separated from the chaff. The difficulty encountered with this seed is in fulfilling the dormancy requirement to insure germination. Seed sown on the usual mix will not germinate for three or more months, often with less than 20 percent success.

In experiments I improved this success rate by treating the seed with heat and high humidity prior to sowing. Seeds were placed in small open vials set in a closed jar containing 0.5 in (12 mm) of water. These jars were then heated in an incubator or constant-temperature water bath. The higher the temperature, the shorter the treatment time (Figure 6-7). At the unusually high temperature of 176°F (80°C), the seed needed to be treated for 10 to 20 minutes. At 140°F (60°C), however, the treatment had to continue for about 12 hours. Temperatures up to 195°F (90°C) were effective but dangerous, because boiling kills the seeds. Seed treated with a solution of gibberellin (2000 ppm) for 48 hours had a positive effect on the germination of both untreated and heat-treated seeds.

The heat-humidity treatment that stimulates *Kalmia hirsuta* seed germination would surely kill seeds of most other plants. During the early stages of these seed germination experiments, I corresponded with T. S. Shinn of Leicester, North Carolina, who had been frustrated in his many attempts to germinate sandhill laurel seed. I explained what we were doing, and he

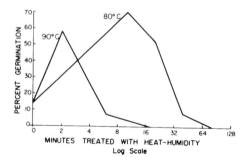

Figure 6-7. Germination of *Kalmia hirsuta* seed after treatment at near-boiling temperatures (90°C = 195°F and 80°C = 176°F) and high humidity. Even with this treatment, seed of sandhill laurel germinates slowly. The data shown are for 11 weeks after sowing.

treated the seed at about 176°F (80°C) for 20 minutes in his oven. He thus succeeded in germinating sandhill laurel for the first time, and I was delighted to learn that we were not dealing with a mere laboratory effect.

Heat-humidity treatments with sandhill laurel have been performed many times, and although often successful, unfortunately they are not always effective. Therefore other treatments need to be established that will assist us in obtaining maximum, fast, reliable germination rates with this species. One thing I have noted is that untreated seed, which has a low germination rate in plastic boxes under lights, will often germinate after several weeks on the surface of the same medium when top watered regularly in a flat in a greenhouse. Perhaps either sunlight, bacterial action, or leaching of water triggered germination.

This unusual dormancy requirement of sandhill laurel seed could have evolved in the natural environment as a response to recurrent ground fires. During a fire, soil temperature near the surface often reaches 170°F (77°C). Humidity and vapor pressure in the top layer of the soil increase as the fire passes, because water vapor is forced downward from the burning litter and condenses there, like vapor in an inverted still. A seed adapted to germinate after a fire would find itself on a seedbed of bare mineral soil. It would be relatively free of competition, since the fire would destroy seeds of most other plants on or near the soil surface. Yet after a ground fire, shade from large shrubs and especially trees would frequently be present. This shade would lessen temperature extremes and moisture stress on young seedlings and would thus aid in their survival.

Fire is accepted in the southeastern coastal plain as a natural part of the environment. Other plants in the area are adapted to fire, although often not in the same way. Longleaf pine (*Pinus palustris*), for example, loses its competitive advantage unless there are occasional ground fires that, while killing many plants, allow the survival of very young pine seedlings in the "grass stage" and mature trees with fire-resistant bark.

The unique dormancy requirement of sandhill laurel seed may have been a key factor in the spread of *Kalmia* onto the coastal plain. If this is true, the Cuban laurel, *Kalmia ericoides*, which represents a further extension of the genus, might have a similar seed dormancy requirement, but to date we have had no opportunity to confirm this hypothesis.

CHAPTER 7

Growing Laurels

Kalmia latifolia (mountain laurel)... is without argument one of the most beautiful ornamental shrubs, but I would rather put a chastity belt on a bull than try to grow one! (Sabuco 1990)

Whether growing laurel to establish later in one's own landscape or to sell, the task should be somewhat easier than the bulldogging and belting of bulls alluded to by John Sabuco in the above quote. Growing *Kalmia* may not be easy; yet Mother Nature seems not to have a problem, and with certain precautions one should not have great difficulty.

In the wild, it is not speed but survival and reproduction that are of the essence. Ernest Kurmes (1961) found that the annual growth of 20 wild laurel seedlings under forest trees averaged only about 0.4 in (10 mm). Mountain laurel would not be a viable nursery or landscape garden plant if this was a general characteristic, but fortunately, by improving the growing environment we can do much better.

One often overlooked aspect of growing a plant like *Kalmia* is the optimum growing temperatures. As indicated in Chapter 1, *Kalmia latifolia* grown in Great Britain, the Canadian west coast, and Korea are not noted for vigorous growth. A number of reasons for this have been suggested, including less sun during the growing season. Research by David Carden at Horticultural Research International, East Malling, England, showed that outside temperatures there are too low and that the size of *Kalmia* plants increased by approximately 200 percent when grown in a polytunnel (plastic-covered greenhouse). Some of the details of this research are proprietary and not available; nevertheless, the results are remarkable and need to be considered by cool-climate growers. Are there practical and economical means to raise the temperature of plants grown in cool-climate areas? The opportunities for manipulating the temperature of container-grown plants would seem much greater than for plants grown in the ground.

Carden found that water quality is also important. Hard water—that is, water high in salts and especially calcium—as is found in the southeast of England, increased the incidence of leaf damage and stunted growth as compared to pure water. So if the water is hard, thought should be given to purifying it; and hard water is not an uncommon problem.

As for the substance in which the plants are grown, a growing medium with no soil is considered optimum by most commercial growers. Intuitively this may seem wrong, but it works. Soils are highly variable, they carry pathogens, and they compact in containers. Growers have done much better with artificial mixes, most often using combinations of peat moss, aged pine bark, perlite, and coarse sand, with adjustments for pH and fertilizer needs. Whether one is growing a few plants for the yard or thousands for resale, the needs of the plants remain the same and the basic techniques remain similar. Rarely do two growers follow the same regimen, however. Media, containers, facilities, and cultural practices vary greatly from nursery to nursery. The following practices therefore are suggestions of what has worked and probably will work, but certainly do not exclude other methods. They were designed largely for mountain laurel (*Kalmia latifolia*) but are quite satisfactory for the other species of laurel.

Small Plants: Seedlings, Rooted Microcuttings, and Conventional Cuttings

Small plants less than 2 to 3 in (5 to 7.5 cm) tall are best handled in flats or small containers. As they grow larger, the plants can be planted in the ground in beds and then field planted, or they can be transplanted (stepped up) into ever-larger pots.

Many micropropagation laboratories have adopted a 2-in (5-cm) square mesh pot as the standard container in which to establish their just-rooted microcuttings. Because laurel roots are fine and tend to form a discrete "ball," I have found it practical to plant young seedlings, rooted microcuttings, and conventionally rooted cuttings in flats.

To insure the best growth, seedlings should be transplanted two to six months after germination when they have just a few true leaves. Nurseries, however, commonly leave their seedling plants in the flats for a full year after germination, which probably delays flowering an additional year. If seed is sown in late fall in a greenhouse or indoors under lights, the seedlings should be ready for transplanting in mid-winter. I generally prick them out with forceps when they have two to three true leaves and space them 1.5 to 2 in (4 to 5 cm) apart in another flat. I use a dibble board the size of the flat, with 60 to 80 nails equally spaced to mark the position for planting each seedling. The choice of mix varies from grower to grower, but I have found the following satisfactory for small transplants:

> 3 bushels (105 liters) Canadian peat moss
> 2 bushels (70 liters) perlite or styrofoam
> 1/3 lb (150 g) dolomitic limestone
> 2 tablespoons (30 g) 20-20-20 soluble fertilizer
> micronutrients, such as Sierra's Micromax, at rates recommended on
>   container

If the growing conditions are good, with bright light and daytime temperatures of about 75°F (24°C), then the plants can be sprinkled about every three weeks with a dilute solution (200 parts per million nitrogen or less of soluble, complete fertilizer such as 20-20-20 [that is, 1 teaspoon per gallon or about 1.25 grams per liter]). A pH of about 5.0 is good. The amount of limestone can be increased or decreased in future mixes to adjust the pH, if necessary. See the next chapter for additional cultural information.

Despite the avowed potential problems with using soil in growing media, I confess to often using the above mix with an addition of loam (10 percent by volume) that has been fumigated with Vapam. This small amount of soil adds exchange and buffering capacity as well as micronutrients. It is also just further evidence that individual growers adapt basic media to their perceived needs.

Fertilizing the Air with CO_2

Enrichment of the atmosphere around seedlings with carbon dioxide (CO_2) is an economical means of achieving a dramatic increase in plant size. Carbon dioxide is an essential raw material for plant growth, and its low ambient concentration is often the critical factor limiting plant growth. Ambient air contains 300 to 350 ppm CO_2, but some plants are capable of using up to 10 times that amount if water, light, and fertilizer are optimum.

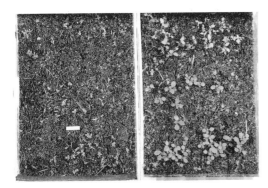

Figure 7-1. Effects of enriched carbon dioxide atmosphere on *Kalmia latifolia* seedlings after seven weeks. The plants on the left were exposed to normal air and most have only one true leaf; the plants on the right, however, were exposed to 2000 ppm CO_2 and they are much larger and many have four true leaves.

An increased rate of laurel seed germination and a large increase in seedling size were achieved by exposing the sown seeds to an atmosphere of 2000 parts per million CO_2 for seven weeks (Figure 7-1) (Heichel and Jaynes 1974).

Greenhouse operators have used enriched CO_2 atmospheres for many years, and therefore several techniques are available for increasing CO_2 concentration. Peter Hickenton has authored a handbook titled *CO_2 Enrichment in the Greenhouse* (Timber Press, Portland, Oregon, 1988). In large greenhouses CO_2 is produced by generators burning propane or natural gas; dry ice, compressed gas, or combustion are commonly used in smaller greenhouses (Mastalerz 1968). Even the decomposition of organic materials has served as a source of CO_2. Each method has its advantages and disadvantages; the source of the CO_2 makes no difference to the plants, unless of course it contains toxic impurities, not likely with any of these methods. Plants themselves give off CO_2 at night or on dark, overcast days and utilize a CO_2-enriched atmosphere only on bright or sunny days. The CO_2 source should be operated only during the day and only on days when the greenhouse vents are closed most of the time. Therefore, winter is generally the most practical time to add CO_2 to the atmosphere of growing plants.

An increased concentration of CO_2 alone will not stimulate plant growth. Other conditions, including light, nutrients, and temperature, must be equally favorable. In fact, when the CO_2 concentration is increased, plants are able to utilize more light and nutrients. We have found that 600 foot-candles of light (or 250 microeinsteins per square meter per second at 400 to 700 nanometers) are required for good growth with CO_2 enrichment. This level was attained in the laboratory using high-output fluorescent tubes and in the greenhouse by supplementing natural daylight in winter with fluorescent light to extend day length and to supplement day-light on cloudy days. Somewhat lower light intensities are adequate in air not enriched by CO_2, but growth is, of course, reduced. Low light intensity produces spindly seedlings.

The most advantageous time to expose laurel to an enriched CO_2 atmosphere is from the time of seed germination until after several true leaves are formed—that is, from December until March in the northern hemisphere. Many seedlings can be handled in a relatively small space, and the rapid increase in plant size in the first few months is valuable in reducing the time before the plants reach flowering age. Obtaining a 3-in (7.5-cm) plant from seed sown outdoors under natural conditions takes two to three years, whereas the same size can be realized in a single winter and spring under controlled greenhouse conditions. With a winter head start the young seedlings are already one-year-size or more in spring and are ready to take advantage of the full growing season outdoors.

Alcohol Burning

The least expensive and perhaps simplest means of supplying carbon dioxide is to burn methyl or ethyl alcohol. To obtain 2000 ppm CO_2 per 100 sq ft (9 sq m) of greenhouse space, 2 to 3 fluid ounces (60 to 90 ml) of ethyl alcohol or 3 to 4 fl oz (90 to 120 ml) of methyl alcohol must be burned per nine-hour day. To lessen the danger of fire, a kerosene lantern or similar device should be used to enclose the alcohol flame. A small lamp with a 0.25-in (6-mm) diameter wick and a low flame burns about 1 oz (30 ml) of alcohol in nine hours. One disadvantage of the combustion method is the production of heat and water vapor. Neither is a serious problem, unless the heat necessitates increased ventilation, which would disperse the CO_2. It is often practical to partition off, with clear plastic, the area where CO_2 enrichment is desired.

The actual concentrations of CO_2 achieved with any one of the methods will vary somewhat depending on the size and tightness of the area treated. Anything between 400 and 3000 ppm will help the plants. If the 2000-ppm level is maintained, you should have no qualms about working in the enriched atmosphere.

With careful management, the grower can enjoy substantially larger plants in much less time utilizing CO_2. Check with the floriculture special-ist at a nearby state university, with other experts, and with other growers for more information and suggestions on the use of CO_2 to stimulate plant growth. The value of using CO_2 to increase the growth of plants was demonstrated long ago, but most of us have been remiss in adopting this technology.

Light and Day Length for Growth

Rhododendrons, azaleas, and laurels typically do not grow well in greenhouses in the fall and winter (October through February). This is due largely to the short day length (long, uninterrupted periods of dark) and low light intensity. Increasing the day length with low levels of incandescent or fluorescent light (50 to 100 foot-candles) often has little positive effect. Research by Professor Mark Brand (1996) at the University of Connecticut has shown that high light intensities (500 foot-candles from high-intensity discharge [HID] lights), a 16-hour photoperiod, and 1500 ppm CO_2 in a windowless room has a dramatic effect in maintaining growth and increasing size of young laurel plants in the winter. In contrast, similar plants in a greenhouse receiving natural light plus 500 foot-candles to extend the photoperiod did not do nearly as well. It is as if the greenhouse plants receiving normal sunlight, up to 10,000 foot-candles on a sunny day, still recognize the short days of winter and go dormant. This despite the extension of day length to 16 hours with the HID lights.

Additional research is required to determine the most effective combination of temperature, day length, light intensity, and CO_2 to maximize growth, especially in greenhouses. Brand concludes that for high-value, high-density crops such as *Kalmia*, windowless, HID-illuminated rooms with CO_2 enrichment may be economically feasible to optimize growth of young plants during winter.

A Chemical Stimulant for Stagnant Seedlings

Even in the proper growing environment, growth of mountain laurel seedlings may stagnate for two or three months after germination. Such seedlings can be stimulated to elongate and grow by spraying them once or twice with a 200-ppm water solution of gibberellic acid (Gibrel, 80 percent potassium gibberellate). The cause of the poor growth, however, should be determined and corrected; likely causes include low temperature, crowding, insufficient nutrients, low light, short days, and/or compacted media.

Container Plants

The conventional way for commercial growers to produce *Kalmia* plants up to 30 in (75 cm) in size is to grow them in containers. This is a practical way to optimize the growth of plants: containers are easy to plant into and out of; digging and burlapping are eliminated; the mechanisms of the operation become almost independent of weather conditions; and more plants can be grown per unit area.

Container-grown plants have their drawbacks, of course. In climates where temperatures are likely to be well below freezing for extended periods, the containerized plants have to be protected in overwintering shelters. Many years ago Dr. John Havis, at the University of Massachusetts, found that the minimum safe root temperature for mountain laurel was 15°F (−9°C); the killing root temperature is presumably between 5 and 10°F (−15 and −12°C). Also, *Kalmia* requires media that are especially well drained and well aerated. Growing in containers allows less room for error with regard to fertilizing and watering as compared to growing in the field. Summer sun can heat media in containers to such high levels that roots are killed on the sunny side. Finally, plants grown in containers in a nonsoil mix can be more difficult to establish in soil than field-grown plants.

There is little agreement on the ideal container medium. However, research horticulturists Richard Bir and Theodore Bilderback of North Carolina State University have canvassed successful growers to learn of their methods, and with this information, they and others have tested and compared some of the most promising media and growing techniques (Bir and Bilderback 1989). Of the many nurseries they visited, Bir and Bilderback found most growing good mountain laurel, but only two growing excellent laurel. Media used by the growers varied from pure peat to pure aged pine bark. Either of these, aside from not being ideal for mountain laurel, are likely to make it especially difficult to establish the plants in the landscape.

By observing *Kalmia latifolia* in the wild as well as in gardens, Bir and Bilderback rediscovered some of the basics: mountain laurel does not thrive in wet, poorly drained places, it grows best in acid soils, and high fertility can be a detriment. I particularly like their observation about planting a healthy mountain laurel on the edge of a loamy, fertile vegetable garden: "it seems to slowly look worse and worse until it reaches the point where you may wish it would die. However, it usually lingers, reminding you of your mistake."

When such observations are translated to container media, it usually means that the plants need to have air around the roots (lots of pore space) and easily available water. Bir and Bilderback compared the porosity and water availability of the two media growing the best laurel plants with the two media that grew the worst, but still quite good-quality, mountain laurel. They found that the best plants grew in the media that were lighter and more porous and had more water available to the plants under normal growing conditions.

Some of the best media ranged from 1:1 to 1:4 pine bark:peat or 1:1 to 1:4 fir bark:peat. The ratios were not critical. Indeed, media components that Bir and Bilderback found to be successful in their nursery survey included hardwood bark, pine bark, fir bark, redwood sawdust, composted hardwood leaves, composted brewery sludge, composted municipal sludge, sand, granite tailings, loamy soil, peat (at least three grades), perlite, styrofoam, and vermiculite. At least one grower in the northeastern United States found that the bark from conifers native to the area (*Abies*, *Picea*, and *Tsuga*) was unsatisfactory. Sand and other mineral matter have value largely as weight to prevent plants from tipping over, although they can cost growth and add to shipping costs.

Proper irrigation of container plants can be even more important than the porosity of the medium. By watering only when plants need it, it is possible to compensate for media with less-than-ideal pore space. Nurseries that irrigate blocks of azaleas and mountain laurel equally often have nice azaleas but lower-quality mountain laurel; laurel needs to be grown drier. Laurel plants tolerate drought better in the wild than many other ericaceous plants and respond well to less-frequent watering in the nursery. Of course, excessive drought and wilting must be avoided. And when irrigating the plants, they need to be watered thoroughly. Successful commercial growers of *Kalmia latifolia*, therefore, all seem to agree that separating *Kalmia* from the other plants is best, especially to control irrigation.

There are many ways to water plants, including overhead sprinklers, drip irrigation, soaker hoses, and flooding. For details on methods and available equipment, contact nursery supply dealers, agricultural agents, and other growers. Publications such as *Irrigation Design* by Larry Hawes and David Kier (1993) are also useful.

Testing various media and fertilizer treatments on opposite sides of the United States, researchers Hummel, Johnson, and Lindstrom (1990) found that the conditions most favorable to the plants were the same in Washington in the Northwest as in Georgia in the Southeast. They and others have demonstrated that weekly liquid fertilization at 100 ppm nitrogen provided for significantly more growth than at 50 ppm. Doubling the rate to 200 ppm nitrogen neither adds to the growth nor produces injury. The 100-ppm rate is equivalent to the medium rate of 18-6-12 slow-release Osmocote during the middle of the growing season. The source of fertilizer is not as important as the rate and management. Mountain laurel, like other ericaceous plants, responds best to a combination of nitrate (NO_3) and ammonia (NH_4) nitrogen, compared to either form used alone (Hummel et al. 1990). The 60/40 ratio of NO_3 to NH_4 produced the best shoot and root growth. Results from unpublished research by Dr. Stuart Warren of North Carolina State University at Raleigh were similar: ammonium nitrate (NH_4NO_3) was the best nitrogen source, urea ($CO[NH_2]_2$) was a close second, and the poorest response was with nitrate alone.

Dr. Warren's research also suggests that among several phosphorus rates applied as a liquid feed three times a week, 10 ppm was best. This is a *higher* rate than that maintained by many controlled-release fertilizers. Several different potassium rates were also tested, and large plants were produced with a 5- to 15-ppm rate applied as a liquid feed three times a week, leading to the conclusion that *Kalmia* either requires little potassium or is very efficient in taking it up.

Medium pH and the availability of minor elements are also important factors. The following is a commercial mix for containers that has performed well:

1 part Canadian peat moss

2 parts pine bark

5 to 7 lbs per cubic yard (2.3 to 3.2 kg per cubic meter) dolomitic limestone

commercially available minor elements at rates suggested on container

In the Piedmont of the southeastern United States the best mountain laurel are grown in 50 percent shade supplied by lath or shade fabric. In the mountains of the South, Northeast, or Northwest no shade is required. In hot areas it may be best to shade with white instead of black shade because it is cooler underneath the white.

The speed at which plants can be grown to flowering and market size will vary depending on local climate and growing conditions. Growers with a long season, as in United States zones 7 and 8, can get more annual growth than can growers in colder areas. At least two successful growers receive branched 2- to 4-in (5- to 10-cm) liners from a tissue culture laboratory on the first of October, and the liners are put in pots or flats in plastic-covered greenhouses (hoop houses) for the fall and winter, with minimal heat to keep the plants from freezing (Figure 7-2). The plants grow new roots and establish a nice root ball during this period. By late February, when the cold-chilling requirement of the plants has been met, the temperature in the houses is raised to flush growth. When the danger of frost is over, they are then re-potted in larger containers. In the past the practice has been to place them in 1-gallon (3.8-liter) pots for one year's growth, but some growers plant immediately in 2- or even 3-gallon (7.5- or 11.5-liter) pots and the plants are sold at the end of the second growing season (Figure 7-3). Growers will have to determine if immediately planting liners in large pots produces as large a plant as when they are transplanted each year. Plants may stagnate if started in too large a pot. It generally takes a minimum of three years to produce a 24- to 36-in (60- to 90-cm) tall plant in a 5-gallon (19-liter) container (Figure 7-4). Further north at least one more year is required to produce these larger plants.

Figure 7-2. Tissue culture produced liners received in the early fall, potted and held in polyethylene-covered houses at Historylands Nursery, Montrose, Virginia. Minimal heat is supplied as necessary to prevent hard freezing through the winter.

Figure 7-3. Tom Huggins of Historylands Nursery, Montrose, Virginia, with some red-budded *Kalmia latifolia* in containers ready for sale.

Figure 7-4. Container-grown *Kalmia latifolia*. *Left foreground*, tissue cultured liner as potted in the fall; *left to right*, one, two, and three years later.

In-Ground Growing

The nursery production of small to mid-sized plants in the ground is almost becoming old fashioned—but some of us are still doing it, and there are some definite advantages. Unlike those grown in containers, the plants do not need to be babysat each day—that is, checked for water or straightened up after winds blow them over. Plants in the ground are more forgiving as to watering and fertilizer requirements. And as already indicated, plants grown in soil re-establish more readily when transplanted to the landscape; without the discontinuity between the artifical mix and native soil, the roots move from the soil ball into the native soil more readily.

Maximizing plant growth is usually not one of the advantages of field growing, nor is it as economical for large-scale production of mid-sized plants. However, the economics of producing large plants, plants over 3 ft (1 m) in size, probably reverts back to field-grown plants.

Transplant Beds

Once plants are 2 or more inches (5 or more cm) in size they can be planted in the soil, relatively close to one another in what are called beds. At Broken Arrow Nursery, our beds are usually about 5 ft (1.5 m) across, so that the middle can be readily reached from the aisles for mulching, weeding, and pruning. We prepare the soil by tilling in peat, aged pine bark, or aged wood chips (obtained from arborists; see next section, Field Culture, for amounts to incorporate), and the beds are raised 3 to 6 in (7.5 to 15 cm) from surrounding soil to enhance drainage. The plants are set approximately 4 in (10 cm) apart in rows 7 in (18 cm) apart.

To prevent compaction, do not transplant when the soil is wet. Plants need to be set in the ground at about the same depth at which they were previously growing. Immediately after planting, cover the soil with an organic mulch to lessen weed growth, retain moisture, and maintain lower soil temperatures.

Shading benefits small plants during the first summer. We use poles and wire or twine to support 50 percent shade fabric set high enough off the ground to allow walking underneath. Irrigation with sprinklers is also easier under this high shade, which is removed the first of September. Typically, the plants need no winter protection, but a thin cover of conifer branches can be used over especially small or tender plants. These boughs also lessen the danger of frost heaving. We usually leave the plants in the beds for two growing seasons and then transplant to the field in the fall or early spring.

Field Culture

Field soil is prepared in much the same way as the transplant beds. The incorporation of aged organic matter can be a great aid to the success of the laurel plants. Bir and Bilderback (1989), however, found that incorporating peat in clay soils could cause problems during wet seasons, because the soil retains too much moisture. Aged pine bark is notably better. Leaf mold and other composted vegetation are also helpful. I have had excellent success with aged wood and bark chips from mixed hardwoods, tilling in 2 to 4 in (5 to 10 cm) of material (equivalent to 268 to 536 cubic yards per acre or 205 to 410 cubic meters per hectare) to a soil depth of 6 to 8 in (15 to 20 cm); see Table 8-1 for volumes required for smaller areas.

The space between plants depends in part on the size of the plant to be sold. A 2 × 2 ft (60 × 60 cm) spacing allows nice 18- to 24-in (45- to

60-cm) plants to grow. The best plants are dug, and the remaining ones then have room to become larger over the next year or two.

Field plants respond well to organic mulches (Plate 96). Immediately after planting we cover the soil with wood chips, using more than enough to prevent sunlight from reaching the soil, thereby reducing weed seed germination. Overhead irrigation can be used, but less water and lower pressure are required with drip irrigation. With this system, water is distributed in small tubes throughout the field. Emitters are spaced near the plants and they drip water onto the ground when the water is turned on. Typical rates are one-half gallon (2 liters) per hour per emitter.

Weed Control with Herbicides

Herbicides are relatively modern inventions that, for many of us homeowners and nursery people, have taken much of the drudgery out of controlling weeds. As with a hoe or tractor, herbicides can be misused, but given proper respect and understanding, they are nothing short of miraculous in their efficient control of weeds.

A short overview will acquaint you with some of the herbicides that can be used around *Kalmia*. Since no single herbicide will control all weeds safely, your choice will depend on many factors, including size and type of plants, kinds of weeds, and time of year. Some products are designed for the home gardener; others are restricted and should be used only by professionals. New products enter the market constantly, and preferences and laws governing use change. Therefore, prior to purchasing any herbicides, check with your horticultural service or other agricultural authority for the latest information on materials and proper usage in your locality.

Classification of Herbicides Based on Activity

Pre-Emergence Herbicides

Pre-emergence herbicides are chemicals that affect weeds at a very early stage of growth and are selective in their effect on different kinds of plants. Crabgrass killers used on established lawns and applied in the spring are a pre-emergence type. They are long lasting, effective for a few months to a year or more depending on the material and rate of application.

Pre-emergence herbicides typically fall into two groups: those that primarily control grassy seeds and those that primarily control broadleaf weeds. Best results are obtained by using a combination of grass and broadleaf herbicides, provided the crop is tolerant of both. New product mixes containing two active ingredients are designed to provide broad-spectrum weed control.

Simazine (Princep) is one of the most useful pre-emergence herbicides and is sold as an 80 percent wettable powder (80W), a 90 percent dry flowable (Caliber 90), a flowable liquid (4L), or a 4 percent granular preparation (4G). It kills many weeds as they germinate and is also effective on many established weeds and grasses when applied during the dormant season. Simazine is safe when used around established plants if applied properly but may lead to injury when applied around new transplants or small seedlings. It has residual action throughout the growing season and a small persistent residue into the second year. The effect of simazine, which is best on broadleaf weeds, can be improved by applying it together with other pre-emergence herbicides such as DCPA (Dacthal), napropamide (Devrinol), trifluralin (Treflan), oryzalin (Surflan), prodiamine (Factor), or metolachlor (Pennant). The latter are especially effective on grasses and are packaged in liquid, wettable, or granular forms. Like simazine, DCPA, oryzalin, and metolachlor, are applied on the soil surface before weed germination. Trifluralin, on the other hand, is volatile and must be mixed into the soil for best results. These materials possess moderate residual activity but, when applied at the proper rates, will not leave soil residues harmful to the growth of laurel. Metolachlor is particularly effective in controlling annual grasses and nutsedge. Derby is a granular combination of 1 percent simazine and 4 percent metolachlor for nursery or landscape use.

Isoxaben (Gallery 75DF) is a new pre-emergence herbicide that is effective in controlling many broadleaf weeds and thus can substitute for simazine in the field, in containers, and in landscape plantings. It controls seeds for three or four months and has little effect when sprayed on plant foliage and, like simazine, has little effect when sprayed on weeds that have already emerged.

Oxadizon (Ronstar 2G) is a pre-emergence herbicide that has been widely used by commercial growers on newly planted or established container-grown *Kalmia*. This granular herbicide has long residual activity against broadleaf weeds as well as grasses; chickweeds (*Cerastium* and *Stellaria*), however, are resistant. The material lasts two to three months in containers and a full season in the field. In addition to outdoor use, it has proved effective on container-grown *Kalmia* in greenhouses and can be combined with napropamide (Devrinol) for broad-spectrum control.

Rout 2+1G is a granular combination of oxyfluropfen (Goal) and oryzalin (Surflan). This combination provides better pre-emergence control of annual grasses than Goal alone and provides a broader range of safety on deciduous plants and broad-leaved evergreens than Goal sprays. One application should control weeds for up to three months in containers or in the field. Granules should be applied when foliage is dry and followed by irrigation.

Snapshot 80DF is a mixture of 20 percent isoxaben and 60 percent oryzalin that has long residual control and can be used in containers, landscape ornamentals, and field-grown nursery stock.

Post-Emergence Herbicides

As the name implies, post-emergence herbicides control weeds after they have emerged. Dichlobenil (Casoron) is effective on established perennial weeds in established plantings, with pre-emergence activity usually lasting until early summer. Nursery people use it, but unfortunately, it injures the roots of newly planted laurel. Applications are usually made on the soil surface during the late fall, winter, or early spring, when soil and air temperatures are low—preferably just before a rain or snow, or just before renewing mulch.

Nonselective Herbicides

Glyphosate (Roundup, Kleenup) is a chemical hoe—but instead of the weed being cut out it is sprayed out. Roundup is quickly inactivated in soil and therefore it is safe to plant in that soil soon after treatment. Glyphosate is systemic and moves from foliage to roots to kill rhizomes and underground plant parts. It has low toxicity to mammals and so is quite safe to use. Glyphosate may also be used as a directed spray around established plants with care to avoid spraying the plant foliage. Most annual and perennial weeds and deciduous woody plants are controlled by glyphosate applied at the proper stage of growth and at the proper concentrations. Woody plants, including poison ivy (*Rhus toxicodendron*) and brambles (*Rubus*), are most susceptible to glyphosate sprays from mid-summer to early fall. Glyphosate provides no residual control of weeds from seed and must be combined or used in sequence with a pre-emergence herbicide for all-season control. A combination of Roundup at 1 fl oz (30 ml) plus Surflan 75W at one-third cup per gallon (42 ml per liter) as a directed spray on weed growth 4 to 6 in (10 to 15 cm) tall has provided excellent kill and long residual control in landscape plantings of woody shrubs. Sulfosate (Touchdown) is a new foliar-absorbed systemic herbicide much like glyphosate in its chemistry and mode of action, and thus is a possible substitute.

Glufosinate (Finale) is another new, nonselective, foliar-applied systemic herbicide that controls most annuals and herbaceous perennials, but it is less effective on woody plants. It kills weeds faster than glyphosate and is not affected by rain four hours after application. It cannot be safely sprayed on bark. Glufosinate has low toxicity to animals.

Fumigants

General sterilants, called fumigants, are sometimes used for treating soil in commercial nurseries. Types such as metham (Vapam) and methyl bromide (Basamid, Dowfume) have value in sterilizing soil for mixes or in treating beds prior to planting seedlings. They kill not only weed seeds but also perennial root stocks, fungi, and nematodes. The expense of fumigation generally precludes treating large areas. For information on the use of fumigants, consult local agricultural authorities.

I have had limited experience with fumigants, but I did get excellent results with Vapam. As noted earlier, we use some soil in our greenhouse potting mixes. So in early fall, before soil temperatures are too cool, I sprinkle a solution of Vapam and water on a 10 × 10 ft (3 × 3 m) area of top soil and cover it with a sheet of plastic for a few days. Then the plastic is removed and the Vapam is allowed to break down and dissipate a few more days before shoveling off the top 4 to 6 in (10 to 15 cm) of soil and storing it in a bin for future use. On rare occasions I have used Vapam to treat a bed that was going to be planted with seedlings when the soil was known to be loaded with weeds and weed seeds. Such treated soils remain weed free until new seeds blow in or are carried in by birds and other animals.

Pruning Plants

Pruning is an integral part of growing mountain laurel (*Kalmia latifolia*), for attractive structure of mature plants is dependent on multiple branches formed near the ground. This is accomplished in the case of most mountain laurel by pruning young plants. The most effective means of stimulating multiple breaks is to prune late in the first dormant season, just before the spring growth starts. In the case of plants started in tissue culture or seedlings grown under lights in a greenhouse for up to 18 months, however, it is advisable to prune before that first dormant phase—that is, when the plants are 1 to 2 in (2.5 to 5 cm) tall. Successive pinchings are usually required to obtain good branching on growing plants. The amount to prune off depends in part on legginess and the height of the plant. Retain a few leaves below the pruning cut. On tall, spindly plants, prune low enough so that the newly formed branches will be within a couple of inches (about 5 cm) of the soil.

Under good growing conditions in containers—and even in the field—shoot extension may be excessive during the growing season and must be pruned to prevent the growth from flopping. Unfortunately, a single shoot rather than multiple shoots typically break below such pruning cuts, but lateral bud formation is enhanced, and these are much more likely to break into growth on successive prunings. See the next chapter for a further discussion of pruning laurel.

Growth Regulators to Initiate Flowers and Control Growth—Especially for Commercial Growers

Many nursery people have succeeded well in overcoming the obstacles to growing *Kalmia latifolia* in containers. Large, handsome, bushy plants will grow in two to four years, but with one apparent fault: they often fail to produce flower buds. The rule of thumb with these plants is the better the growth rate, the poorer the flower bud set. High phosphorus, low fertilization, and withholding water are means to encourage flower bud set, but these methods are often ineffective or at least difficult to manage for practical and consistent results.

Many years ago I had success in reducing growth and stimulating flower bud set using the growth retardants Phosphon and Cycocel (CCC). The results were inconsistent, however, and at least in the case of Phosphon, the treatment severely retarded growth for at least two years after application. More growth regulators are available now, and some, like B-Nine and Cycocel, are routinely used on poinsettias (*Euphorbia*), Easter lilies (*Lilium*), chrysanthemums (*Dendranthema*), and greenhouse azaleas (*Rhododendron*). The ideal growth regulator would eliminate the final flush of growth (often the third growth in nursery production and the one that is late and chlorotic) and in its place stimulate the production of flower buds.

Of the newest growth regulators on the market, Bonzi and SuMagic are the most active. They are effective at concentrations 100 to 1000 times more dilute than their predecessors. These materials are called triazoles; paclobutrazol is the active ingredient in Bonzi and uniconazol is the active ingredient in SuMagic.

At least three groups of researchers have been testing the effectiveness of these substances on mountain laurel in recent years: Dr. Martin Gent, who has led the research at the Connecticut Agricultural Experiment Station, New Haven, Connecticut; Dr. Tom J. Banko, at Virginia Polytechnic Institute and State University, Agricultural Research and Extension Center, Virginia Beach, Virginia; and Dr. Richard E. Bir, North Carolina State University, Mountain Horticultural Crops Research and Extension Center, Fletcher, North Carolina. All three groups have been conducting similar experiments and all are working closely with growers in their respective states.

Although much remains to be done, the results are promising. There is no question that Bonzi and SuMagic can reduce growth and stimulate flowering in *Rhododendron* and *Kalmia*. Typically, the material is drenched or sprayed on the plants during the second growing season to achieve flowering the third year. Further testing will determine how consistent and reliable the results are from year to year. To date, the following conclusions have been learned:

1. Stem growth is reduced and flower bud production increased when these materials are applied at low concentrations. The effective rates have varied tremendously for the different investigators; from 4 to 400 ppm for Bonzi and from 1 to 100 ppm for SuMagic.

2. Different cultivars respond differently to the same concentration of the same material, unfortunately a commonly observed phenomenon with growth regulators. 'Bullseye' and 'Olympic Fire' are two mountain laurel cultivars that seldom produce flower buds when grown in containers for two or three years; however, these cultivars were induced to produce flower buds when treated with Bonzi and SuMagic (Figure 7-5).

3. Applications early in the growing season (April and May) are more effective in producing flowers than those applied later (June, July, and August).

4. *Kalmia* is far more sensitive to Bonzi than is *Rhododendron*, but the sensitivity of the two plants to SuMagic is similar.

5. Growth is also reduced in the year following application—that is, in addition to the effect seen the first year. This prolonged effect may be greater on *Kalmia* than on *Rhododendron*.

6. Mechanical pruning is not required when either of these two compounds is applied at the appropriate rates. Indeed, pruning inhibited flower bud formation on both treated and untreated plants.

Figure 7-5. 'Bullseye' treated with 200 ppm SuMagic, *right*, and untreated 'Bullseye', *left*. Notice the reduced growth and heavy flower bud set on the treated plant. Photo by Tom Banko.

These materials translocate somewhat differently than most other growth regulators. They move in the same direction as water—up the stems and out—not downward from the leaves. Thus, it is important that stems be thoroughly covered. Drenches may work better than sprays.

The question of whether these and similar compounds can be used instead of mechanical pruning to obtain good branching, especially on very young plants, is yet to be determined.

Growers of large numbers of mountain laurel will certainly welcome a means to reliably stimulate flower bud formation. Simultaneous elimination of the final flush of growth, which is often yellow, would be a real benefit. Research with growth regulators on other plants suggests that fine tuning the application of these materials is required for practical, consistent results. An ideal solution would be some cost-effective cultural modification that would achieve the same results as a squirt of Bonzi or SuMagic, or even the breeding and selection of cultivars with attributes that would negate the need for such cultural manipulations.

Chemical Deadheading

The nursery grower wants flower buds on salable plants, yet for plants to be held and grown to larger sizes, the presence of flowers is a disadvantage because seed capsules that develop after flowering inhibit new flushes of growth, and plant growth is slowed. Removal of these seed capsules by hand is laborious (disbudding by hand is discussed at the end of Chapter 8). Research with other plants suggests that the development of seed capsules can be prevented with sprays of growth regulators like Ethephon (2-chloroethylphosphonic acid).

Trials conducted by Dr. Richard Kiyomoto of the Connecticut Agricultural Experiment Station in New Haven are promising. Ethephon rates of 500 to 2000 ppm, sprayed to run off when 25 to 50 percent of the flower buds had opened, inhibited 75 to 95 percent of the seed capsules from developing, and in addition, new shoot growth was dramatically enhanced as compared to that on untreated plants (Figure 7-6). Tests with three different cultivars provided similar results. Of course, repetition of these tests another year, along with varying dates, concentrations, and cultivars, is necessary to further verify the results. Other growth regulators may also be found that are even more effective than Ethephon.

Kiyomoto's data from the first year's results are impressive. I can hardly overemphasize the value that chemical deadheading could have in the more

Figure 7-6. Inhibition of seed capsule development and stimulation of new growth by spraying *Kalmia latifolia* flowers with Ethephon: (A) control sprayed with water—many seed capsules developed and little new growth was initiated; (B) 500 ppm Ethephon—few seed capsules developed and many new shoots emerged; (C) 2000 ppm Ethephon —most of the spent flowers fell off and many new shoots emerged. Photos taken eight weeks after treatment.

efficient growing of large plants in the field and possibly even in containers. At Broken Arrow Nursery we presently deadhead all our field-produced plants by hand, but we would find it much more efficient to spray a single application of a growth regulator.

Measuring Soil Aeration in Containers

Materials needed for measuring soil aeration in containers include a measuring cup, masking tape, a pencil, the pot (at least 1 gallon or 4 liters) to be used, a bucket or pan, water, and the medium to be tested (Botacchi 1980).

1. Measure the volume of the pot. Tape the holes outside securely at the bottom of the pot. Fill the pot with water to within about 0.5 in (about 1 cm) of the lip or at the normal soil line. Mark this line with a pencil. Carefully pour the water from the pot into the measuring cup and count the number of cups of water held by the pot. This is the *total volume* of the pot.

2. Dry the inside of the pot, but do not remove the tape. Fill the pot with your dry potting mix and pack it as you would when potting a plant.

3. Using the measuring cup, carefully wet the medium. Add water until the medium is thoroughly saturated, keeping track of the number of cups of water it takes for saturation. When a thin film of free water appears at the soil line, the medium is water saturated.

   Since dry peats are difficult to wet, add water a little at a time. If the medium tends to float, seal the top of the pot with plastic film or foil to reduce surface evaporation, as several hours may be required to wet the medium.

   The total amount of water added is the total *porosity*—the pore space of the medium which can be occupied by water or air. A porosity of 60 to 80 percent is good for *Kalmia*.

$$\text{Percent Porosity} = \frac{\text{Cups of water required to saturate the medium}}{\text{Total volume of the pot, in cups}}$$

4. After the medium is thoroughly saturated, elevate the pot over the bucket or pan and remove the tape from the holes. Water will drain from the pot. Allow the pot to drain until no more water comes out. Measure the amount of water collected in the receptacle. This

amount of drained water is equivalent to the *air space* in the drained medium. Air space should be 20 to 25 percent for *Kalmia*.

$$\text{Percent Air Space} = \frac{\text{Cups of drained water}}{\text{Total volume of the pot, in cups}}$$

This is the percentage of the total volume of the drained medium that is occupied by air. Note that not as much water drained from the medium as was applied to saturate it. The difference between the amount applied and the amount drained is the *water holding capacity* of the medium. For *Kalmia* the water holding capacity should be about 40 percent.

Percent Water Holding Capacity = Percent Porosity minus Percent Air Space (Percent of total drained medium occupied by water)

CHAPTER 8

Garden Care of Laurels

Since mountain laurel was first discovered by colonists coming to America, perhaps no other woody native shrub has more excited and frustrated gardeners worldwide. When it is in full bloom, nothing quite compares. (Bir 1992)

Site Selection

I once said that there was probably a *Kalmia* plant that could be grown someplace in every one of the 50 United States. I do not say that anymore. Although technically it may be true if one includes all the species, this statement leads to the assumption that these plants are very cosmopolitan and can adapt to a wide range of conditions. They do grow over a broad area and on some absolutely wretched sites, but there are specific requirements that have to be met. These needs are similar for all the species, but the following is written with *Kalmia latifolia*, mountain laurel, especially in mind. That said, anyone who has enjoyed success with azaleas and other ericaceous plants should have little trouble with laurel. Their requirements are, in fact, quite similar.

An initial consideration is whether the plant will be hardy. This can be determined by knowing where the species normally grows and how other specimens have done in your area. Locally grown plants have the advantage of having been exposed and acclimated to the local environment. Species like mountain laurel, with its extensive range both in latitude and altitude, may vary greatly in their hardiness. Plants native to the southern areas and lower elevations of the range are not adapted to the shorter growing season in the north. They may not stop growing soon enough in the fall and may thus be susceptible to late-fall and early-winter freeze damage. Young plants are more susceptible to such damage, whereas older plants in the landscape typically harden off earlier in the season and thus are "hardier." In spite of these considerations, some mountain laurel selections from zone 8 appear to do well as far north as zone 6 and may even be satisfactory in protected areas of zone 5.

Most of us are limited in our choices of planting sites, so we must survey the conditions carefully before selecting a planting location. None of the laurels will thrive in an exposed location where the soil is left bare and the ground freezes deeply in winter or where there is no snow protection. But with some mulch and a little protection against winds, all do well in bright to full sunlight. The more sun they receive, the more dense their growth and the more prolific their flowering. On the other hand, partial shade from an overstory of widely spaced trees is beneficial in prolonging the life of the flowers and thus extending the bloom period, especially in the case of *Kalmia latifolia*. Shade becomes even more important for mountain laurel in the middle to southern part of its range, where the combination of summer sun and heat is particularly harsh.

Avoid planting mountain laurel in low, open areas. On clear nights, heat is radiated to the open sky from the ground, plants, and air. If there is no breeze, the cold air settles and moves down slope where it collects in depressions, valley bottoms, and along streams—or so-called frost pockets. A change of just a few feet in height may mean a difference of several degrees in minimum temperature. Because a canopy of trees, even with bare branches, will moderate the effects of heat loss, sites under trees offer good locations for mountain laurel and other ericaceous plants. Other laurels are more resistant to frost injury—as would be expected from their natural habitat, which includes low and sometimes wet areas.

You might assume the southern side of a house (the side facing the sun, for the northern hemisphere) to be a preferred location for laurels. Not so, unless there are some high trees. Plants on the south side of a building are exposed to the full winter sun and reflected heat in the day, then suddenly subjected to the cold air temperatures of night. Excessively high daytime temperatures and frozen ground can literally mean death to broad-leaved evergreens, because water is lost from the leaves and cannot be replaced from the roots. A southern exposure, however, can be tempered to the plant's benefit if the plant is moved several feet away from the building, or if overhead trees break up the sun's intensity. The angle of the sun changes greatly during the course of a year, so do not be fooled: trees that shade a bed in June may not do an effective job in December.

The northern side of a house (southern in the southern hemisphere) is one of the best locations for mountain laurel. Here the plants are shaded in winter because of the low sun angle, daytime temperatures are moderated, and the ground is subjected to less freezing and thawing. In summer they receive early-morning and late-afternoon sun but are shaded from the intense midday sun. Adequate light is available even if the plants receive no direct sunlight but are exposed to open sky. On the other hand, if the plants receive no direct sunlight and the sky is blocked by a canopy of tree foliage, flowering will be limited. Heavy shade does not only consist of a lack of direct sun but also a loss of direct sky light. If these plants see plenty of sky but no sun, they will still have adequate light for growth and flowering.

Ground slope is not of concern as long as other conditions are met. A southern slope is warmer and drier than one facing north; hence, on the south-facing slope a good mulch is essential and dappled shade is more beneficial. Likewise, in warmer climates a northern or northeastern slope would be preferred for their cooler, moister conditions.

Eastern bog laurel (*Kalmia polifolia*), mountain laurel (*K. latifolia*), and sheep laurel (*K. angustifolia*) are all found in the wild fairly near the coastline, but only the eastern bog and sheep laurels might be considered salt tolerant. Mountain laurel cannot withstand salt; in the northeastern United States, where roads are kept clear in winter with applications of sodium chloride, plants close to the road often die. Where mountain laurel does survive along such roads, it is up a bank and/or beyond the splash or drainage zone of the road bed. Clearly they will not thrive near the shore, where they would be regularly exposed to salt spray.

Soil

Plant growth depends on soil moisture, and soils vary greatly in their water-holding capacity and their ability to release water to plants. Coarse, sandy soils admit water rapidly but have limited storage capacity. Fine-textured soils, on the other hand, have a much larger capacity, but when compacted, they have slow water infiltration and increased surface runoff. In addition, water is tightly held to fine clay particles, and therefore less moisture is released to plant roots in clayey soils than in sandy soils.

Laurels prefer well-drained, acid soils and suffer in heavy, poorly drained, alkaline soils. Even bog laurel and sheep laurel, which can tolerate wet soil, do better in well-drained locations. Inhospitable soils can be modified, but considerable effort may be necessary. Richard Bir and Theodore Bilderback (1989) have clearly demonstrated the benefits of incorporating 3 to 4 in (7.5 to 10 cm) of aged pine bark or wood chips into heavy mineral soils for improving growth and survival rates of mountain laurel. Incorporation of peat moss was also found to be beneficial, except when there was excessive rain; then the soil retained a detrimental amount of water. The volume of material to be incorporated in areas of varying sizes is given in Table 8-1. Note that at the higher rate and for just one landscape plant utilizing 10 sq ft of soil surface (approximately 3 × 3 ft, or just under 1 sq m), one 3-cubic-foot (0.1-cubic-meter) bag of pine bark should be incorporated in the soil. It is suggested that the material be tilled or dug into the top 8 inches (20 cm) of soil. At these rates, a large planting requires a lot of material—advisable on heavy mineral soils but not required on well-drained soils already containing organic matter.

In clayey soils, a shallow dishlike hole, whether small or large, acts as a catch basin for water, thus causing the roots to rot. It is best to prepare an area much larger and deeper than that required for the root ball. Incorporate aged pine bark, leaf mold, wood chips, or other coarse, partially decayed organic matter (10 to 30 percent by volume) into the soil to a depth of about 8 in (20 cm) and four or five times that across to help improve drainage. Then mulch the soil surface. The bed should also be raised several inches (Figure 8-1). Another approach for heavy soils is to set the plant on the soil surface and bring well-drained soil up to and around the plant root ball.

Table 8-1. Volume of Organic Material Required as a Mulch or to Incorporate in Soil.

Area	Depth of compost to be applied	
	1 in (2.5 cm)	4 in (10 cm)
10 ft^2 (0.9 m^2)	0.8 ft^3 (0.023 m^3)	3.2 ft^3 (0.091 m^3)
30 ft^2 (2.8 m^2)	2.5 ft^3 (0.071 m^3)	10 ft^3 (0.283 m^3)
100 ft^2 (9.3 m^2)	9.0 ft^3 (0.25 m^3)	35 ft^3 (1.0 m^3)
1,000 ft^2 (92.9 m^2)	90 ft^3 (2.5 m^3)	335 ft^3 (9.5 m^3)
10,000 ft^2 (929 m^2)	900 ft^3 (25 m^3)	3,350 ft^3 (95 m^3)
43,560 ft^2 (1 acre; 4,047 m^2)	3,600 ft^3 (102 m^3)	14,500 ft^3 (410 m^3)

(ft^2 = square feet, ft^3 = cubic feet, m^2 = square meters, m^3 = cubic meters)
(To obtain cubic yards, divide ft^3 by 27.)

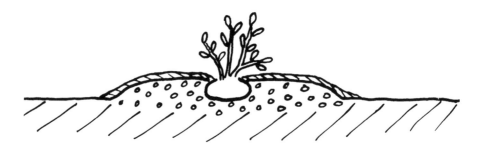

Figure 8-1. To improve heavy soils for *Kalmia*, raise the entire bed or, at least, the area for each *Kalmia* plant.

Established laurels are tolerant of drought conditions but do best when soils are kept moist—but not wet. Conditions vary, but during the growing season plants need at least 1 in (2.5 cm) of water per week; if this amount is not released by the soil or provided by rains, then irrigation is necessary. Since daily waterings may waterlog the soil, and sprinklings may be superficial, a good soaking every one to two weeks during dry periods is preferred. For new transplants the watering cycle should be shortened to every three to five days. Two simple ways to check for water stress is to check for wilting on neighboring annuals, herbaceous perennials, or weeds, or by probing the soil in and around the roots with your finger. The look and feel of dry soil is generally pretty obvious, once actually examined.

The availability and intake of nutrients by plants is determined by the acidity or alkalinity of the soil. Acidity or alkalinity is measured by the concentration of the hydrogen ion (H^+) and is referred to as pH. The pH scale is numbered from 0 to 14, with 7.0 being neutral. Acid soils have a pH lower than 7.0, while alkaline soils have a pH higher than 7.0. Few natural soils are more acid than pH 3.5 or more alkaline than pH 9.0. The soil pH of wild laurel stands generally ranges between 4.0 and 5.5.

If the soil pH is 5.6 or higher, large amounts of Canadian peat moss thoroughly mixed throughout the soil profile will help to acidify it. Acidifying materials such as aluminum sulfate, ferrous sulfate, or sulfur can also be added to lower the pH. Table 8-2 gives approximate amounts needed to acidify (lower pH) for silty loams. On coarse, sandy soils, 50 percent less material should be applied.

If aluminum sulfate is used excessively, aluminum toxicity may occur in some soils. David Leach, in his book *Rhododendrons of the World and How to Grow Them* (1961), strongly recommends ferrous sulfate, but the average

Table 8-2. Material and Amount Needed to Lower pH of Soil.

To change pH		Add pounds (kg) of material per 100 sq ft (9 sq m) of soil					
Start	Desired	Aluminum sulfate		Ferrous sulfate		Sulfur	
from 8.0	to 5.5	13.3	(6.1)	25.9	(11.8)	5.5	(2.5)
from 7.5	to 5.5	11.5	(5.2)	23.5	(10.7)	5.0	(2.3)
from 7.0	to 5.5	9.0	(4.1)	16.5	(7.5)	3.5	(1.6)
from 6.5	to 5.5	6.5	(3.0)	11.8	(5.4)	2.5	(1.1)
from 6.5	to 5.0	10.5	(4.8)	18.8	(8.6)	4.0	(1.8)

garden center or nursery supplier often does not stock this material. They may be able to order it, however, and it is available from chemical supply houses. Ferrous sulfate usually costs more than aluminum sulfate. Both sulfates are quick-acting, producing results in two to three weeks, compared with six to nine weeks or more for sulfur. Sulfur dust can be difficult to apply because it is so fine and if it gets in your eyes it forms sulfuric acid and burns. Pelletized sulfur is now available, however, and it disperses quickly in the first rain.

Soils are formed over long time periods from various kinds of rock. Parent rocks determine the soil pH, so even though additives can modify it, the soil always tends to return to its original pH over time. Soils around building foundations often have a pH too high for ericaceous plants, because calcium leaches from the concrete walls or because plaster or other limestone material was left in the soil at the time of construction. Even the careless application of lime to an adjacent lawn can have a similar effect.

Some soils are very low in available calcium. In such cases, lime or calcium sulfate (gypsum, land plaster) can be applied. The latter should not affect pH but will increase available calcium.

Fertilizing

Normal plant growth depends on at least 14 elements supplied by the soil. Of these, nitrogen (N), phosphorus (P), potassium (K), calcium (Ca), magnesium (Mg), and sulfur (S) are required in sufficient quantities to be called major or macronutrients. The remainder, including iron (Fe), boron (B), and zinc (Zn), are utilized by plants in smaller quantities and are called minor or micronutrients. Deficiencies or excesses in either major or minor nutrients can cause abnormal growth and may even be fatal to plants.

Most soils contain less-than-optimal amounts of one or more of the elements. Such deficiencies must be determined to know when fertilizer is needed. Fertilizer is likely needed if new growth is weak and foliage color is yellow-green. Plants in soils with adequate or better nutrient reserves have a lustrous green to blue-green foliage color, good growth, and good leaf retention. Those in soils lacking nutrients grow slowly, have poor color, and lose their leaves prematurely. An excess of one or more nutrients may cause leggy, floppy growth and eventually injure the roots, leaves, and shoots. Composition and vigor of weeds are good indicators of soil fertility, a fact often overlooked by gardeners. When even the weeds are not doing well, there is surely a problem. And, of course, the soil or the laurel leaves may be chemically analyzed to determine nutrient needs.

Soil testing, although not an exact science, is the easiest and most reliable means of measuring soil fertility. Soil testing services are available through most state universities or horticultural experiment stations as well as private firms. Kits are also available for do-it-yourself testing. I have been quite pleased with a pocket pH meter that has given accurate readings for several years. Information on soil testing laboratories and the procedure for gathering soil samples can be obtained from local agricultural agents or the nearest agricultural university.

Laurels can survive in very infertile soils but will thrive with moderate fertilization. Applications should never exceed the amounts recommended for *Rhododendron* or *Ilex* (holly). When in doubt, err on the side of too little. More laurels have been injured by excessive fertilization, especially nitrogen, than from starvation. Those who test your soil will suggest the kinds and amounts of fertilizer to apply, but nitrogen is the element most likely to be in short supply. If plant growth suggests the need for fertilizer and a soil test is not readily obtainable, then apply a fertilizer at about one-fourth the rate suggested on bags of commercially available fertilizers for acid-loving plants. For example, were you to use one of the common evergreen plant foods containing 8 percent nitrogen, 4 percent phosphorus, and 4 percent potassium (8-4-4), the recommended rate of application is 3 lbs per 100 sq ft (about 1.5 kg per 10 sq m) of ground. I recommend reducing the rate to 0.75 lbs per 100 sq ft (375 g per 10 sq m) or 300 lbs per acre (about 340 kg per hectare), but apply this rate up to three times a year: early spring, June, and August. This works out to about 1 ounce per square yard (30 g per sq m) or per established landscape plant. Sixteen percent of the 8-4-4 fertilizer is active ingredients (three macronutrients), while the remaining

84 percent is inert. Typically, one-half of the nitrogen in such fertilizers is in a slow-release form, which is very desirable but also a bit more expensive. As mentioned in the previous chapter, the nitrogen may be most effective if the readily available portion is a combination of approximately 60 percent nitrate to 40 percent ammonia nitrogen.

Cottonseed meal has an analysis of 7-3-2 and can be applied at the same rate as the 8-4-4 fertilizer. I find that an annual total of 50 to 100 lbs (22.5 to 45 kg) of actual nitrogen per acre (0.4 hectare) per year is adequate for good growth in my laurel fields. This translates to 1 to 2 lbs of nitrogen per 1000 sq ft. Two or three light applications of fertilizer at intervals are preferable to a single heavy application, especially when the nitrogen is in a readily soluble form. Even the slow-release fertilizers must be applied conservatively around laurel. In addition to nitrogen, phosphorous may be at low levels in many soils. Side dressing with superphosphate is thought to be especially valuable in encouraging the setting of flower buds. Remember, plants that are mulched and doing well in the landscape may not require any fertilizer at all. Many plants in the wild do fine just with access to nutrients recycled by Mother Nature.

Transplanting

Early autumn and early spring are the best times for transplanting laurel, although with certain precautions they can be moved any time that the ground is not frozen. Fall transplanting has some advantages over spring transplanting if the move is made early in the season. Fall plantings put in at least one month before the ground freezes will have well-established roots when spring shoot growth occurs. Despite the dormant top, the roots will remain active as long as soil temperatures are above 40°F (4°C). Nursery people and experienced gardeners have long taken advantage of this phenomenon to give their plants a head start on establishing prior to the spring growing season. To prevent frost heaving, choose a site with well-drained, porous soil and use wood chips or other mulch.

All plants suffer some degree of shock from transplanting, since no specimen, whether field or container grown, can be transplanted without some disturbance to the roots. Container-grown plants suffer less root loss, but they must adjust to a greater difference in the texture of the mix within the container and that of the soil in which they are placed. Such differences between mix and soil inhibit water exchange and root growth. To facilitate the outward growth of the roots and the assimilation of water, several shallow vertical cuts should be made in the root ball of container-grown plants before placing them in the planting hole. "Mutilate the roots!" is the headline instructions in the catalog of Oliver Nurseries, one of the premier retail nurseries in Connecticut. Action just short of this statement is a hard and fast rule when planting pot-grown plants. Failure to do so may well result in the death of the plant. Slice the roots with a knife or scratch and tease them with the fingers in order to give the roots a headstart in growing out of the container medium and into garden soil. Liberal amounts of peat moss or aged pine bark mixed with the soil should then be placed surrounding these exposed roots. Water well and you are home free.

Well, almost. The media of container-grown plants generally contains no soil, is very porous, and dries out rapidly even if the surrounding soil is moist. So the watering needs of newly transplanted container-grown plants requires more diligence than if the plants had been field grown.

Next to autumn, early spring is the best time for transplanting, although winter transplanting is possible in regions where the ground does not freeze solidly. Whenever you are transplanting, take extra care to obtain a good root ball, and never let the ball dry out. When there is a large amount of soft growth or if the roots have been severely disturbed, prune some top growth to reduce water loss through the foliage.

Root growth of plants often fluctuates in pulses, much as shoot growth may occur in flushes rather than in a straight-line continuum. This is an area of horticultural science that has not been studied in depth (pun not intended), but a few interesting facts are known. Some plants with a reputation for not transplanting well in the fall do not re-establish root growth well then, such as white pine (*Pinus strobus*) and some of the oaks (*Quercus*). It would be nice to know more about the seasonal periodicity of root growth in mountain laurel. My guess would be that in the eastern United States root growth is reduced somewhat in the summer. I base this on observations of container-grown plants transplanted to the field: root growth can be disappointing in early and mid-summer but surprisingly active in late summer and early fall.

Mulching

Native laurels usually grow where they have at least some natural mulch around them, and a good mulch is advisable for laurels in the garden. Mulches limit the growth of weeds, conserve soil moisture, reduce leaching and erosion, moderate soil temperature, and prevent compaction.

As organic mulches decompose they release nutrients to the soil. Never rake leaves out of *Kalmia* and *Rhododendron* beds; leaves are a great natural mulch and should be left under these evergreen shrubs whenever possible.

Wood chips and pine bark are also excellent mulches, but many others are usually available locally, including sugar-cane bagasse or buckwheat hulls. Peat moss is usually not satisfactory because the surface dries and mats, becoming almost waterproof; and worse, if fluffed up, it blows away. Hays and straws are good, but weed seeds in them can cause a serious nuisance. I stopped using salt marsh hay after one particularly weedy bale cost me many hours of backbreaking work. Leaves collected by ground maintenance people or municipalities are an inexpensive substitute for bark or wood chips. I have had truckloads dumped at my home in the fall; by spring they were quite usable. One drawback is that they do not last as long as chips and sometimes blow away in windy locations. If shredded, however, they have a more uniform appearance and do not blow around as readily.

As a homeowner and nurseryman, I have benefited from the closing of public landfills to organic matter. Arborists are often delighted to have a place to dump wood chips; so they give away what we used to pay for.

To be effective, mulch must be applied thick enough to cover the soil surface and keep it covered for at least one growing season. A thickness of 2 to 4 in (5 to 10 cm) is generally practical; see Table 8-1 for volumes required for different areas.

I am not particularly keen on inorganic mulches around laurel plants, but stone and gravel may be desirable in formal settings. Fresh sawdust and wood chips should be avoided, not only because the initial action of bacteria on the fresh material ties up available nitrogen, but also because plant-growth inhibitors may leach out. Fresh organic materials, such as wood chips, should first be allowed to heat up and compost before use, which may take only a few weeks in warm weather. A side dressing of nitrogen is generally advisable when using relatively fresh organic mulches. As organic mulches decay (compost), they release some of the nitrogen that was unavailable previously. To prevent anaerobic decay of mulch and the buildup of toxic materials, the piles should not be more than 6 ft (2 m) high.

Soil pH may be raised, lowered, or unaffected by mulch. The pH of sandy soils with low organic content are most easily changed. Organic mulches rich in calcium, magnesium, and potassium (such as maple, *Acer*, leaves) tend to raise pH, whereas mulches rich in tannins or other organic acids (such as oak, *Quercus*, leaves) may lower it—though my soil-scientist friends tell me that after composting, oak leaves are *not* acidic. The bottom line is that changes in pH from mulches are normally very gradual and usually can be ignored. By contrast, the leaching of calcium from masonry walls has a more significant effect on pH.

As indicated, mulches help control weeds and evaporation and they also permit more water to percolate through the soil. But despite this potential for increased leaching, organic mulches increase available nitrate nitrogen, potassium, magnesium, and phosphorus. Fungi and bacteria increase under a mulch; apparently, beneficial types prosper more than pathogenic ones. In addition, mulch protects and feeds earthworms (valuable garden allies) against freezing and desiccation. Of course, the downside is that grubs of Asiatic and Japanese beetles also do well at times under organic mulches, and they will feed on laurel roots. Moles may then come and feed on the various insect grubs and worms, but then the mice take over the mole runs and the mice can feed on laurel roots. It's not always easy!

Heavy mulch can also increase the severity of frost damage on open ground, as is explained in more detail in Chapter 10. The benefits of mulching outweigh the risks, however, so it is important to mulch despite the potential drawbacks.

Chemical Control of Weeds

Herbicides can be wonderful tools that, just like mechanical tools, have to be used judiciously and cautiously; herbicides were discussed in more detail in the previous chapter. Many commercial growers rely on herbicides for economical weed control, and certainly many professional landscape managers as well as homeowners are using them to manage their grounds efficiently.

I do not recommend chemical weed killers for all home gardeners. A good mulch can solve many of the worst weed problems, and regular—but sparing—hand weeding will complete the job. Yet, selected herbicides are virtually an economic necessity in large gardens, and commercial growers would find it difficult to continue without them. The importance of herbicides is indicated by the greater expenditure of money on herbicides than on either fungicides or insecticides. Most have extremely low mammalian toxicity and, if used properly, little impact on the environment.

If you have never used herbicides and wish to try them, start with just one, like Roundup (glyphosate). Read the instructions and labels thoroughly and try to develop an understanding of how each product works. For instance, Roundup, a chemical hoe, is nonselective and effective on anything that is green. The material is taken up through the foliage and translocated throughout the plant, including the roots. Thus if most of the foliage is sprayed, the entire plant will be killed. The active ingredient in Roundup breaks down rapidly and largely is gone within days. Roundup is generally more effective in late summer and early fall than in spring.

Simazine, in contrast to Roundup, is a residual material that remains near the soil surface. Small germinating seeds absorb the herbicide and will die. Certain plants with lots of surface roots, such as lilac (*Syringa*), are sensitive to simazine, whereas deeply rooted plants are generally tolerant. *Kalmia* is tolerant at the lighter recommended rates. If the soil surface is disturbed (tilled) after application, much of the effectiveness of the simazine is lost. Think of residual materials like simazine as almost forming a thin film on the soil surface that prevents weed germination. If application is not uniform or if the "film" is disturbed, then the herbicide is less effective.

If I could use herbicides in only one place in the home landscape, it would be on aisles and bed edges. Indeed, in over 30 years of gardening I have never edged a bed mechanically in the home grounds—that is, used a hoe, edging tool, or string trimmer. A single spring application of Roundup and simazine does the trick, possibly with a late-summer touch up of Roundup—plus, of course, a wood chip mulch applied every couple of years.

Pruning Mountain Laurel

One of the most common questions about laurel is, "My foundation planting has become leggy; how and when do I prune it?" The answer is in early spring, before growth starts. This is the best time, although some flower buds inevitably will be removed. A second choice is immediately after flowering, still early enough in the growing season to obtain at least one flush of growth subsequent to the pruning.

Pruning is an art; each plant has to be handled a bit differently, but there are some general rules. First, try to imagine what you want the plant to look like, and then prune with this design in mind. Try not to prune back to naked, unbranched stems. Pruning cuts should be made at forks and where small laterals exist as sources of additional growth (Figure 8-2). Plants with dense foliage all the way to the ground present few problems, but plants 4 to 6 ft (1.2 to 2 m) tall and lacking lower branches present a challenge. There are two approaches for these plants—neither are ideal, but each is better than cutting the tops off and leaving 2 to 3 ft (0.6 to 1 m) of naked stems. One approach is to remove the plants and replace them with smaller bushes of desired shape; this is drastic but gives immediate results.

The other approach is to cut the overgrown plants to within 2 to 3 in (5 to 7.5 cm) of the ground, best done in early spring. The plants will re-sprout and become dense and multistemmed, but it may take three to four years for them to reach flowering size again.

Judicious pruning every year is the easiest way to prevent plants from becoming leggy or too large. Since *Kalmia* foliage is attractive in flower arrangements at all times of the year—and especially so in Christmas decorations—you have excuses enough to prune the plants regularly. Thinning out or removal of odd branches can be done any time of the year with no harmful effects to the plant. Mountain laurel is normally a graceful and informally shaped plant; older plants take on an exotic character. But they are also amenable to shearing and shaping and thus can be grown in dense mounds or in formal hedges. This approach goes against my nature—and seemingly the laws of Nature!—but I admit to having seen on occasion some impressive pruned hedges and dense specimen plants. Such pruning should be done immediately after flowering to permit new shoot growth and flower bud formation for the next year. In most situations the more natural, informal appearance resulting from moderate, regular pruning is far more attractive.

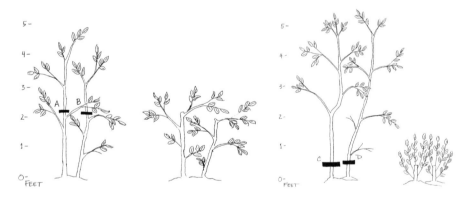

Figure 8-2. *Left*, moderate pruning cuts (A and B) are made to reduce the height of the plant and to stimulate growth nearer the ground; note that the cuts are made just above a foliaged lateral branch. *Right*, severe pruning cuts (C and D) are made to stimulate basal sprouting. Generally all branches on one plant should be pruned in a similar manner. Drawing by Andrew Brand.

Enhancing Flowering

As mentioned previously, the more sunlight the plants receive, the denser they will grow and the heavier they will bloom. We are just beginning to sort out the named cultivars as to which will do best in sun and/or full shade. A plant that does not bloom probably needs more light. Thinning and pruning the overstory trees and shrubs will allow the plants to see some sky light, even if not direct sunlight. Plants in some shade and under excellent growing conditions may produce excessive growth with few if any flower buds. A little more stress on such plants in the summer—that is, no fertilizer and less water—will likely stimulate flower bud production.

Many people become concerned with plants that have flowers covered by new growth. Although this may be a cultivar characteristic, it most often occurs on vigorously growing young plants. Reducing soil fertility and the simple aging of the plants will reduce this problem, as will transplanting. Typically, the stress of transplanting reduces new vegetative growth and enhances flower bud formation, so that plants transplanted in spring or early summer will bloom heavily the following year.

Disbudding/Deadheading

Flower buds for the following year's bloom form in August and September on the current season's growth. Hence, cultural methods that increase the number of new shoots will increase the potential for flower bud set. Flowers left on a shoot normally produce seed capsules and inhibit new growth on that shoot. Therefore, disbudding or deadheading, the removal of the flower cluster immediately after flowering, generally results in the formation of one or several new shoots, on which new flower buds may form (Figure 8-3). New growth does not guarantee flowers the next year, but without new growth there will be no flower bud set at all. The developing seed capsules not only limit new shoot growth, but evidence from work with other plants suggests that they produce a hormone which, when translocated to vegetative shoots, inhibits the formation of flower buds. Thus mountain laurel tends to produce good floral displays every other year unless the spent flowers—that is, the newly developing seed capsules—are removed to enhance the annual flowering. Deadheading is mostly of concern with mountain laurel; with the other *Kalmia* species the presence of seed capsules does not strongly inhibit flower bud formation.

Figure 8-3. The effect of deadheading. The seed capsules on the plant on the *left* were allowed to develop, and as a result there was no new growth; in the plant on the *right*, spent flowers were removed, and four new shoots grew, two of them bearing flower buds for the next year.

Sometimes a mountain laurel will have flower buds on all its shoots when transplanted, or the shock of transplanting will subsequently result in an overabundance of flower buds. When this occurs, too much of the plant's energy goes into flower and seed production and not enough into producing new growth for maintaining the plant in good condition. In this situation, at least some of the flower buds should be removed to stimulate vegetative growth. If this cannot be done in the spring, the faded flowers should be removed immediately after flowering. Removal of flowers from the lower half of the plant stimulates branching and fullness in that area. Removal of flower buds from only the top of the plant stimulates height growth. Thus, if time is limited for flower bud removal or deadheading and if plant density is important, work on the bottom half of the plant. For a discussion of chemical inhibition of seed capsules, see the end of Chapter 7.

CHAPTER 9

Landscaping

Yet, almost nothing in gardening must be done only one way. Nature offers an infinite latitude of choices. Gardeners can turn in almost any direction and still reach their goals. It is perhaps this freedom of thought, imagination, and action that makes gardening the creative, spiritually relaxing, and enormously satisfying pursuit we enjoy. (Valchar 1993)

Evolution of Landscape Design—Personal Ramblings

When you first enter a garden new to you, what do you see—individual plants, a bed of perennials or annuals, or a sense of the overall landscape and the general ambiance? As I age, I am more aware and appreciative of the latter, but my initial attention will always be drawn to individual plants. Characteristics like unusual foliage, flowers, fruit, or bark catch my eye. My guess is that most of us start out with a strong bias toward plants or design and not necessarily a balance between the two, which is not to say that such a balance should not be attempted. It is good to examine your own strong interests, which will help determine the sort of landscape you will want to develop.

Whatever your personal preferences, keep in mind what is perhaps the most significant aspect of a garden: change. Landscaping should not be looked at so much as a project to be planted and done with, but more as an ongoing relationship—a concept articulated well by Sarah Stein in *Noah's*

Garden (1993). Unfortunately, many people have failed to recognize or take advantage of the seasonal or yearly changes to gardens and landscapes. There are too many examples of yews (*Taxus*), junipers (*Juniperus*), or other shrubs that are planted around foundations and pruned several times a year so that they are little changed in size or shape 10 or 15 years later. This does not lead to a pleasing landscape in most situations, nor can it be very challenging or enjoyable gardening.

My focus on plants and plant growing goes back to my kindergarten days. As a youngster I used to delight in rescuing plants discarded by neighbors at the woodland edge that terminated our dead-end street. It mattered not whether the reject was a small arborvitae (*Thuja*) or a discarded Mother's Day azalea. If there were a few leaves and a live branch or two, it was worthy of transport to a "hospital" bed in our backyard.

I learned the care of plants largely alongside my mother and aunt. They both loved perennials, but their big gardening project was the victory vegetable garden, popular in the 1940s. Not a year has passed since without my growing at least a few vegetables.

I progressed from growing vegetables to focusing on woody plants, native and exotic (although some might question if going from food plants to ornamentals is progress). Like many gardeners, I found a certain magic and awe in watching seedlings grow, especially after determining and fulfilling the particular requirements to break seed dormancy. Then vegetative propagation came to fascinate me, as it invariably does with other gardeners at one time or another. As a 12-year-old boy, my imagination was caught by the wonder of being able to have six or more kinds of apple grafted onto a worthless seedling in the fence row. Once my dad allowed that he could graft, I could not wait to help him, and I got to cover the grafts with wax. Ever since, I have been fascinated with grafting, budding, and rooting cuttings—the collective art and science of plant propagation.

Preparation of the Landscape

When I was in college my parents took a night class to help with their struggle to improve their landscape, but my own serious thoughts of such matters were held in abeyance until my wife Sarah and I had our own land and house. Suddenly, landscaping and garden design were the concern of the moment. I could not wait to get started, but since our site contained typically rocky New England soil and old fields grown up with new forests, there was a lot to do before we could get much serious planting done.

My feelings on clearing brush and thinning the woods are articulated perfectly by Sydney Eddison in *A Patchwork Garden* (1990):

> There is nothing to beat clearing land for instant gratification. In the susceptible, it even produces a dangerous euphoria. The more you clear, the more you want to clear. In early spring or late fall when the air is cold and damp and exhilarating, it drives you on and on. Your muscles and your back moan in protest—but you can't stop. Dragging the crushed yellow roots of barberry out of the ground and seeing an expanse of open space gives you a Godlike feeling—short-lived but oh, so sweet.
>
> Although a clearing in New England is nothing but a forest waiting for you to turn your back, there is something immensely satisfying about ridding the landscape—however temporarily—of its weedy, woody burden.

My criteria for thinning trees are the same as I used with my dad when pruning apple trees in our old orchard. If you have to ask whether to cut a branch or tree, the answer is, invariably, cut. The first thinning of the overstory in the woods in preparation for underplanting with *Kalmia* and *Rhododendron* is often not enough. Once the downed trees and brush are removed and you take a fresh look, you will see additional trees to remove. It is guaranteed that within three years, you will wish you had removed twice as many. Once you start to underplant with choice plants, thinning the overstory becomes a more delicate and time-consuming operation. Besides, how are you going to find the right place for that special *Halesia*, *Stewartia*, or *Styrax* if you do not eliminate a few more of the common native trees?

In doing such work, I invariably think of the pioneers clearing the undergrowth and tall trees without the benefit of power tools, and I imagine they also felt exhilaration and self-satisfaction on completing a hard job well done. Surprisingly, I get a similar sense of euphoria from picking up all those randomly scattered stones and forming them into nice rows and columns. We have done three sides of the property now with over 1000 ft (300 m) of stone wall. The last section was the most impressive, taking parts of three years to do: 4 ft tall (1.2 m), 5 ft (1.5 m) across the base, and 200 ft (60 m) long. The size was determined by the amount of material immediately accessible: the remains of an old wall, stones from an adjacent field, and those pushed aside in making the old town road. Wall building is a job best left for the cool days of fall when the gardening and nursery business are not so pressing. The result is cleaner fields, a great backdrop for mountain laurel, and the knowledge and satisfaction that anyone can build a pyramid, even if in miniature—just have a plan and do it one stone at a time.

Design

And so with landscaping: a plan on paper or in the mind is essential to avoid a lot of grief. Major elements should be considered first: including possible future structures like another room, a deck, a shed, a swimming pool. Where will the walkways be, the vistas, a pond, etc.? For our home, initial work included the placement of stone retaining walls on slopes around the house. Roadways and paths were then established as a means to move around the property. Topography, as well as the trees and shrubs we wanted to preserve, dictated our layout, plus a desire for twists and turns to pique the interest.

Given enough room, curves are an important—if not essential—ingredient in any informal and naturalistic garden. Of course, they are not always feasible or appropriate with respect to the site, its surroundings, or the architecture, but they add a feeling of motion, depth, and intrigue to a landscape and can make an area appear larger than it really is. Curves should be bold, not weak or hesitant. Visualize a falling drop of water, swollen at one end and pointed at the other. Lay the tear drop on its side and divide it in half; on one end you have a bold outward curve, and on the other a gentle inward curve. The outward curve needs the tallest plant, the inward the shortest. Use the outward curve to enhance a view or to screen something undesirable. Trees and other tall plants should be faced or dressed down with smaller plants and groundcovers. The curves should reflect the angles on buildings; never use an outward curve on an inward corner, and vice versa. In an open or lawn area do not place outward curves opposite each other. Outward curves should in general reflect inward curves, but formal symmetry should be avoided.

So after dispensing with some of these fundamentals, then we can proceed with planting. These days it is rare to find someone whose interests are balanced between design and gardening and who also has an eclectic taste across all plant groups. Obviously, my interest focuses on the woodies—the ericaceous family as well as other trees and shrubs. Perennials, annuals, rock garden plants, dwarf conifers, meadows, and lawns all catch my eye; but to keep my two acres looking reasonably good with a minimum of upkeep, I concentrate on woodies.

Although the kalmias can and do fit in many garden styles, including formal, rock, and Japanese, I feel that they are particularly suited to an approach that involves translating the most appealing features of wild or natural landscapes into manageable and condensed forms around our homes, parks, and places of work. According to Professor Sally Taylor of Connecticut College in New London, who calls this approach a naturalistic style, it requires the following:

1. Free-flowing curves, not straight lines; asymmetrical balance, not symmetrical plant placement.
2. Knowledge of plant growth habits, so as to avoid the necessity of heavy pruning to create a desired shape; prune to tidy up only.
3. Selection of plant combinations found growing together in their natural habitat; plants that are pleasing together often grow together.
4. Appropriate groundcovers to face down and finish plantings, blending the edges of beds and lawn.
5. Consideration of the landscape value of plants at all seasons, not just the short season of floral display.

How to specifically site individual cultivars of mountain laurel or the other *Kalmia* species is beyond the scope of this discussion. With mountain laurel, *Kalmia latifolia*, especially, we are dealing with a broad-leaved evergreen that looks good all year and has exquisite blossoms in late spring. The large native plants or the cultivars can be grouped together for screening, to soften buildings or other bold structures, and to dress off the edge of wooded areas. The compact cultivars and miniature mountain laurels as well as sheep laurel, *K. angustifolia*, can perform the same function, but in a more diminutive fashion. (See Plates 97 to 105.)

The list of possible companion plants for *Kalmia* seems endless. A sampling of some of my favorites and some less commonly used shrubs and small trees are presented in the following list, giving Latin and common names and each plant's most outstanding feature. Many of these are native to the same areas as mountain laurel, and such is indicated by an asterisk (*).

Acer griseum, paperbark maple: exfoliating, cinnamon to red-brown bark

Acer pensylvanicum, striped maple or moosewood: green-and-white striped bark

Amelanchier canadensis (also *A. arborea*), shadblow or serviceberry: white flowers in early spring; smooth gray stems; delicate foliage

Cercidiphyllum japonicum, katsuratree: delicate, heart-shaped leaves; upright habit; good fall color

Chionanthus virginicus, white fringetree: white, early-summer, fleecy flowers

Clethra alnifolia, summersweet: fragrant, white, summer flowers

Cornus kousa 'Wolf Eyes', kousa dogwood: green-and-white foliage; one of many kousa cultivars

Cornus controversa 'Variegata', variegated giant (pagoda) dogwood: green-and-white foliage; layered branching

Corylopsis glabrescens (and other *Corylopsis* species), fragrant winterhazel: early, pendulous, fragrant clusters of yellow flowers

Cotinus obovatus, American smoketree: excellent fall color; upright, small tree

Fothergilla gardenii (also *F. major*), dwarf fothergilla: early, fragrant, white, bottlebrush-like flowers; excellent fall foliage color

Enkianthus campanulatas, redvein: small, white, bell-shaped flowers streaked pink; outstanding fall foliage color

Franklinia alatamaha, Franklin tree: camellia-like flowers in fall (Can this small tree be called "native" if it has not been seen in the wild since 1790?!)

Halesia carolina, Carolina silverbell: pendulous, white bells in spring

Hamamelis intermedia, Asiatic hybrid witchhazels: fragrant, mid- to late-winter blooming

Heptacodium miconioides, seven-son flower: white, fragrant, fall-flowering shrub; cinnamon bark

Hydrangea quercifolia, oakleaf hydrangea: excellent, bold fall foliage; white flowers

Ilex verticillata, winterberry: red fruit, showy from fall to mid-winter

Leucothoe recurva, redtwig leucothoe: scarlet fall foliage; little-known deciduous, multistemmed shrub

Magnolia 'Butterflies', hybrid yellow magnolia: yellow flowers before leaves

Microbiota decussata, Siberian carpet cypress: shade tolerant, spreading, juniper-like

Oxydendrum arborescens, sourwood: white, pieris-like flowers in summer; excellent fall foliage color

Pieris floribunda, mountain andromeda: early clusters of white, bell flowers; low, broad, evergreen habit

Polygala chamaebuxus var. *rhodoptera*, milkwort: small, butterfly-like flowers; evergreen subshrub

Stewartia pseudocamellia (also *S. ovata*), Korean/Japanese stewartia: camellia-like flowers in summer; attractive mottled bark

Styrax japonicus and *Styrax obassia*, Japanese snowbell and fragrant snowbell: white, fragrant, bell-like flowers

Vaccinium corymbosum, highbush blueberry: white flowers; blue edible fruit; excellent plant form and fall foliage

Everyone approaches landscape composition from a slightly different perspective. There are so many aspects to be considered that it is only over time, for most of us, that our ideas develop more complexity and depth without being confused. Fred Galle is an expert landscape gardener and author of the definitive *Azaleas* (1987). His comments on the garden are well worth contemplating.

> A well-planned garden, like a beautiful painting, has its effects on the viewer as the result of careful design and composition. Throughout the garden there should be a sense of unity and orderly arrangement of landscape features and plants in relation to their architectural surroundings. Scale in the landscape relates to the unity of the planting, tree and shrub groups, the land form, and the architectural features. The plants, as well as the architectural features, should be in scale

with one another. Throughout the garden there should be unity and harmony achieved with an understanding of the natural forms, and a repetition and dominance of plant textures. A garden does not need to be of large dimensions. It may be a small terrace, a part of a natural woodland, or it may flow into an open stretch of lawn. A garden should exist for the enjoyment of the owners and be a place for retreat from the perplexities of the day. A garden of charm has the appearance of being casually refined and well organized, but is not created without time and effort.

Texture is an important facet of the landscape and is often referred to as the subtle thread or theme running through a well-conceived design and should complement the overall texture determined by the foliage of the trees and shrubs. The texture of the evergreen leaves of Kurume azaleas would be considered fine, while many of the deciduous azaleas and many evergreens such as the Glenn Dale azaleas [and mountain laurel] would be considered as medium texture in contrast to the leaves of white oak [*Quercus alba*] or southern magnolia [*Magnolia grandiflora*], which are coarse textured. One should be able to sense the beauty of a garden at any season. Azalea [and laurel] gardens that are irresistible in the spring should display year-round beauty through a skillful blending of plants and other components of varied texture. A beautiful landscape is a tasteful blending of the ever changing seasonal forms and textures of plants.

Among the elements in a landscape plan are, then, overall design, plant composition, scale, and texture. Periods of bloom, fall color, mixes of deciduous and evergreen (needled and broad-leaved) plants, annuals and perennials, bring about both subtle and dramatic changes in the garden from season to season. Laurels are low-maintenance plants and can be an attractive major component in many gardens. Like many of their ericaceous relatives, laurels are relatively easy to transplant. So, if the initial attempts at locating them are not just right, they can be moved.

As my wife can attest, I am not the one to rely on for determining color combinations in the garden. I thought the orange azalea 'Gibralter' was a stunner when it bloomed. My mother did too, but she none too subtly insisted that it had to be removed from the nearby pink-flowered mountain laurel. It is now banished, along with similarly jaundiced relatives that bloom at the same time, to one of the few beds in our yard with no laurel.

Despite the usual admonitions of designers and those who talk and write about landscaping, I feel that as long as some of the basic elements of your landscape design are thought out, it is possible to walk around the garden with one or a few plants and set them in different locations to get a feel for where they will look and do best. As long as you have a general scheme in mind, locating individual plants can be done just as well with a shovel in hand as with pencil and paper. To be sure, a collection of specimen plants "dropped" at random is not pleasing to most of us, nor does a perfectly organized and manicured garden reflect reality for most of us. Fred Galle's garden as described above is going to be an elegant, serene composition; mine is going be less refined but will still try to capture your attention and reward you with some surprises.

If just a few American homeowners would evolve beyond the ubiquitous clipped yew and juniper phase, suburbia would become a more interesting place to live. No garden is permanent; transplanting, removal, and renewal are a part of the process. The plants grow, you try new things, and the garden evolves. You are really the only one who must be satisfied with the result. So have fun, experiment, and create what you think is best.

CHAPTER 10

Pests and Diseases

[Mountain laurels] are perfectly hardy, although in exposed
situations the foliage sometimes gets browned in winter... .
No insect attacks them, and they are subject to no diseases.
(Sprague 1871)

Despite the many merits of mountain laurel, Sprague exaggerated a bit in
the above quote! In their native habitat the laurels are relatively pest free,
but like all plants, they at times suffer from certain insects and diseases as
well as other maladies. Problems associated with all *Kalmia* species are
included here, but again the emphasis is on problems associated with
Kalmia latifolia because it is the most popular and widely grown species.

There seem to be constant changes in the availability, application, and
registration of appropriate pesticides. It is worth checking with agricultural
experts in your area for information on currently registered materials and
alternative control measures. Some pesticides are only available to licensed
applicators. Be sure to read and follow instructions on pesticide labels.

Insects and Mites

Lacebug, *Stephanitis rhododendri* and *Stephanitis pyrioides*

Adults and nymphs of the lacebug (*Stephanitis*) feed by inserting
their mouth parts and sucking sap from the undersides of the leaves
(Figure 10-1). Their feeding shows on the upper leaf surface as a mottle of
numerous whitish to bronze specks, not unlike the damage caused by

leafhoppers and mites on other plants. The undersurface of the leaf becomes brown-spotted with excrement. The lacebugs pass the winter in the form of eggs attached to the undersides of the leaves, usually near the midrib. They hatch in May and the nymphs mature in June. Eggs for the second brood are laid in June and July and hatch in August. This generation of nymphs matures late in the season; the eggs overwinter on the leaves and hatch the following spring. Mountain laurel (*Kalmia latifolia*) and sheep laurel (*K. angustifolia*) grown in full sun are most susceptible to attack. Fortunately, lacebugs are seldom as serious a problem on laurel as they are on the related Japanese andromeda, *Pieris japonica*.

These pests can be controlled by spraying both surfaces of the leaves with insecticides such as acephate (Orthene), bifenthrin (Talstar), carbaryl (Sevin), or imidacloprid (Merit), which kill both nymphs and adults. The first spraying should be in late spring shortly before mountain laurel flowers and the second in July or whenever lacebugs are observed. If Sevin is used, consider including a miticide to prevent mite buildup. Spring or late-autumn soil application of imidacloprid may be expected to provide single-treatment control of lacebugs through one year.

Figure 10-1. Lacebug on the underside of a *Kalmia angustifolia* leaf. Excrement spots are a characteristic of lacebug infestations.

Blackvine and Strawberry Weevils, *Otiorhynchus sulcatus* and *Otiorhynchus ovatus*

Blackvine weevil (*Otiorhynchus*) is certainly one of the most devastating pests in gardens and nurseries of the eastern United States. One problem is that once damage by the larvae is observed it is too late for control measures to be effective. Blackvine weevil larvae are present in the soil for much of the year, devouring small roots and gnawing the bark of larger roots, often girdling them and ultimately killing the plant. Adult weevils, developing from overwintering larvae, start emerging from the soil in late May and continue to emerge through most of the summer. They spend daylight hours resting around the bases of plants in loose soil and plant litter, but at night they climb to the foliage where they chew notches in leaf margins (Figures 10-2, 10-3). Large populations can cause notches to coalesce, and the leaves will take on a very ragged appearance. The serious damage, however, is done by the grub or larvae stage.

Control of this pest is concentrated almost entirely on reducing adult populations before eggs are laid. Adults must feed for at least three weeks before laying eggs. Therefore an effective method of control is to spray

Figure 10-2. Blackvine weevil adult, the maker of notches in leaves. Photo by Richard Cowles.

Figure 10-3. The characteristic notching caused by the nocturnal feeding of adult blackvine weevils.

foliage, branches, and stems and to soak litter directly under plants where the adults seek refuge during the day. In southern New England the first spray is normally applied in early June and, depending on the insecticide, may have to be repeated at three-week intervals throughout August. Adult weevils may live more than one year. Overwintering adults may emerge earlier and lay more eggs than those that develop from overwintering larvae and pupae. If overwintering adults are present, then sprays directed against them should be initiated three weeks following their emergence. June and July applications are the most critical, since most egg production takes place during these two months. Acephate (Orthene), bendiocarb (Dycarb, Turcam), and chloropyrifos (Dursban) have been used for control of blackvine weevil adults. Orthene works best if applied in late afternoon or early evening.

To determine if adults are present, plants can be examined for fresh feeding notches during the day, or shaken over a tarp at night for direct counts. Another technique is to fold burlap around the base of plants. If weevils are present they will hide in the burlap during the day, where their presence can be readily checked.

White Grubs

The white grubs include the larvae of Japanese beetle (*Popillia japonica*), Asiatic garden beetle (*Autoserica castanea*), and Oriental beetle (*Anomala orientalis*). These can be a notable problem on young plants especially. Typically, the adults lay their eggs in the soil in early summer—they hatch and the larvae feed in late summer, fall, and spring. The larvae feed on the roots and may girdle small plants at the soil line. The presence of grubs can be determined by digging in the soil. If two or more grubs are detected in a spade full of soil, treatment may be warranted. Chloropyrifos (Dursban) has been used for control, as has the relatively new insecticide imidacloprid (Merit). The latter is very promising because of its effectiveness at low rates and its low toxicity to mammals. Unfortunately, imidacloprid is not effective on the larvae of the blackvine weevil.

Mulberry Whitefly, *Tetraleurodes mori*

The mulberry whitefly (*Tetraleurodes mori*) attacks mountain laurel as well as numerous other species and genera, including mulberry (*Morus*). The oval nymphs or larvae appear on the undersides of the leaves and are dark brown or black, fringed with a whitish border composed of a waxy secretion. In the wild they may become so numerous that they are a nuisance when you are walking in laurel patches, but the plants seem to suffer little from their presence. The extent of damage by these insects usually does not warrant control measures. They can be destroyed with a spray application of cyfluthrin (Tempo), imidacloprid (Merit), or a synthetic pyrethrin (SBP-1382, Resmethrin).

Cankerworms, Gypsy Moths, and Other Leaf Eaters

When entomologists list the preferred foods for caterpillars, including inchworms, cankerworms, gypsy moths (*Lymantria dispar*), and elm spanworms (*Ennomos subsignaria*), *Kalmia* foliage appears way down on the list. Dietary preferences go out the window, however, when populations of these insects reach epidemic levels. Laurels growing under trees that have been defoliated by the larvae of these pests are soon attacked. Control is possible with sprays of acephate (Orthene), bifenthrin (Talstar), carbaryl (Sevin), methoxychlor, or the bacterium Bt (*Bacillus thuringiensis*, Dipel and other trade names) at 10-day intervals when the larvae are present. Bt products always work best when directed against young caterpillars.

Rhododendron Borer, *Synanthedon rhododendri*

The borer *Synanthedon rhododendri* prefers rhododendrons but also attacks mountain laurel. The larvae bore under the bark on main stems, leaving scars and sometimes girdling or weakening branches. The day-flying moths resemble wasps, with clear wings spreading about 0.5 in (12 mm). They appear in May and June, when the females lay their eggs on the twigs. Injured stems should be removed and burned. Additional control measures usually are not required. To prevent damage, however, the larger stems can be sprayed or painted with the insecticide lindane or chloropyrifos (Dursban) at 20-day intervals starting in mid-May; apply two or three treatments. The activity of adult moths can be controlled with traps using sex-attracting pheromones specific for clear-wing moths.

Leaf Rollers or Leaftiers, *Archips* species

The larvae of *Archips* species roll the young leaves of plants around themselves, hold the leaf in place with webbing, and then proceed to feed on it. They also enter the flower buds and eat pollen from the anthers, disfiguring the flowers and making them shorter-lived. This has been a particularly vexing pest for me when attempting to cross-pollinate and finding nearly every bud injured and the pollen eaten. The same preventative measures listed for cankerworms and other leaf eaters will control these insects as well. Apply spray several days before the flowers open so that flower- visiting bumblebees will not be affected. Bt is nontoxic to bumblebees.

Seed Eaters and Other Insects

In addition to the leaf roller that thrives on the pollen of laurel flowers, another larva or later generation of the same leaf roller is a notable feeder on the seeds in developing capsules—a particularly cursed beast for the plant breeder. Occasional dustings of the developing seed capsules with an insecticide such as malathion (Cythion) controls the damage.

Aphids, *Neoamphorophora kalmiae* and Others

Aphids are sucking insects and generally are only a problem on succulent new foliage. If large numbers of the insects are present, they stunt and deform new growth. I have observed them on young greenhouse-grown plants of bog laurel and on young mountain laurel in shaded beds. They can be controlled with acephate (Orthene), bifenthrin (Talstar), endosulfan (Thiodan), or malathion (Cythion) applied as a spray or with the systemic imidacloprid (Merit) applied as a spray or drench.

European Red Mite, *Metatetranychus ulmi*

Mites are not usually a problem on mountain laurel, but they do occur regularly on western laurel (*Kalmia microphylla*) and eastern bog laurel (*K. polifolia*) cultivated in the eastern United States. I have occasionally experienced serious problems on cuttings of mountain laurel placed in polyethylene-covered propagation cases. Since extremely humid conditions are not normally associated with mite infestations, their buildup in propagation beds might be explained by the lack of natural predators.

Mature mites are extremely small and are best seen using a magnifier (Figure 10-4). The adult female European red mite is dark red with white spots. Mites feed by sucking plant juices. They pass the winter in the egg stage on bark. Several generations develop each summer, with peak infestations usually occurring in mid- to late summer. Mites have tremendous reproductive abilities and can rapidly reach epidemic proportions. In four weeks at 80°F (27°C), a female mite is capable of giving rise to well over 13 million offspring. Infested foliage takes on a mottled, bronze cast, and affected leaves may drop prematurely. Several miticides, including bifenthrin (Talstar), dicofol (Kelthane), or oxythioquinox (Joust, Morestan), can be applied as a spray.

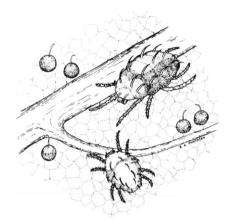

Figure 10-4. Mites and eggs on the underside of a leaf. The adults are about the size of the period at the end of this sentence and often go unnoticed until the leaves become discolored. Drawing by Rita Sorensen-Leonard.

Rhododendron Tip Midge, *Clinodiplosis rhododendri*

The rhododendron tip midge, also known as the rhododendron gall midge, has become a serious pest on rhododendrons and occasionally on mountain laurels in the northeastern United States in recent years. The midge spends the winter as a pupa in the soil beneath the plant, where it fed as a larva. Adults emerge in the spring and lay their eggs on expanding buds and shoots. Once the eggs hatch, the larvae feed on the new growth, causing it to become distorted. Appearance, growth, and vigor of affected plants is diminished. Insecticidal sprays can be effective if applied at this early stage of growth. This is an extremely busy time in nurseries, however, and also a period when plants are likely to be handled, thus increasing the risk of contact with any applied insecticides. Tests at the Connecticut Agricultural Experiment Station in the 1980s demonstrated that applying chloropyrifos (Dursban 2E) to the soil surface before bud break prevented adults from emerging and laying eggs. Timing was not critical and only the soil beneath infested plants required treatment. Diazinon and dimethoate have also been labeled for control of this insect.

Miscellaneous

Other insects and mites may cause problems from time to time. For instance, one year we observed major defoliation on two young *Kalmia latifolia* plants in late summer, and the larva of a large cecropia moth was found feeding on one of the plants. Since then there has been no recurrence of this insect. Local agricultural agents will help in identifying unknown pests and in suggesting controls.

Diseases

Leafspot and Leafblight

Fungal infections on foliage of *Kalmia latifolia* have typically been separated into leafspots or leafblights based on the symptoms that they produce. Leafspots are typically discrete, often small circular spots with distinct margins, whereas leafblights are zonate circular areas that become irregular, coalesce, and appear blotchy. Davis and Mix (1993) conducted an extensive survey of native mountain laurel in Pennsylvania and other states and found that there was no consistent association between the morphology of the leafspot and the genera of fungi isolated. Different genera of fungi were isolated from leafspots that looked alike; conversely, the same genera of fungi were isolated from different types of leafspot. This discussion, therefore, combines the diseases often treated separately as leafspot and leafblight.

Symptoms generally appear as yellow, brown, or reddish spots on the leaves, which may display concentric zones as they increase in size. The affected areas may remain round or become irregular and even spread to large portions of the leaf and affect portions of the stem (Figure 10-5). In light to mild infections the main effect is unsightly foliage. In more severe cases there is foliage loss and stem dieback. Death of plants from leafspot infections is rare unless the plants are extremely weak from other causes.

Leafspots and blights are most commonly observed on plants that are crowded or shaded—conditions under which humidity is high and moisture from dew or rain is retained on the foliage for long periods. Similar conditions may exist in blocks of container plants that are close together and irrigated from overhead sprinklers.

Figure 10-5. Leafspot and leafblight on *Kalmia latifolia* caused by fungal infections.

Fungi commonly associated with leafspots on mountain laurel include *Mycosphaerella colorata* (conidial stage *Phyllosticta kalmicola*) and *Diapothe kalmiae* (conidial stage *Phomopsis kalmiae*). Numerous other fungi can cause spotting and blighting of laurel foliage. These include *Cercospora kalmiae*, *Cercospora sprasa*, *Septoria angustifolia*, *Septoria kalmicola*, *Venturia kalmiae*, *Physalospora kalmiae*, and *Pestalotia* species. *Pestalotia* has been found on petioles and leaves of sandhill laurel cuttings kept in a humidity case.

Davis and Mix (1993) reported that *Cercospora* (probably *Cercospora kalmiae*) was the genus most commonly associated with leafspots on native mountain laurel. Less prevalent but also common were *Phomopsis* and *Colletrotrichum*. *Pestalotia* was also prevalent but was often associated with other pathogens and is considered a secondary pathogen.

Leafspot infections occur during or just after leaf expansion. By the time the disease symptoms appear, it is too late for control measures. To reduce the incidence and severity of future infections it is often recommended for homeowners to collect all fallen and infected leaves and burn or remove them from the area. However, I have yet to see or read any scientific evidence to suggest that this is either practical or effective. When possible, give the affected plants more light and air circulation by removing competing vegetation, thinning the overstory, and increasing the spacing between plants. If using overhead irrigation, plants should be watered in early morning so that the foliage is dry for as many hours as possible each day.

Fungicide sprays have been effective, with applications made when new growth is half developed and again when the leaves are fully developed. Materials registered for use include chlorothalonil (Daconil 2787, Ortho Multipurpose Fungicide), mancozeb (Dithane, Fore, Mancozeb), thiophanate methyl (Domain, Cleary's 3336, FungoFlo), and triadimefon (Bayleton).

Petal Blight

Primarily a disease of azaleas, petal blight occasionally attacks mountain laurel flowers during warm, humid flowering seasons. The fungus, *Ovulinia azalea*, attacks the flower corolla. The symptoms are tiny pale or whitish rust-colored spots on the corolla. These enlarge rapidly and the corolla becomes limp within two to three days, at which time it is often covered by the frost-like bloom of the fungal spores. Control measures are not necessary unless the season is abnormally wet. The same materials used for leafspot are effective in preventing petal blight when sprayed at the time flower buds have expanded and during flowering.

Phytophthora Root Rot or Wilt

Phytophthora root rot, a serious, widespread fungal disease caused by *Phytophthora cinnamomi* is difficult to control. It is soil-borne and affects a wide range of plants including *Rhododendron*, *Castanea* (chestnut), *Cornus* (dogwood), *Leucothoe*, *Pieris*, *Pinus* (pine), *Taxus* (yew), and *Kalmia*. The most noticeable symptom is wilted foliage, which is easiest to detect in the early morning when healthy plants are turgid. Foliage becomes discolored and acquires an olive-green cast. One or two branches may first show symptoms, but they eventually appear on the entire plant. Tissue of the stem near the ground level will be dead and brown. By scraping the bark along the stem, a characteristic reddish band traveling up the vascular tissue may be evident. The band may be either threadlike or up to 0.5 in (12 mm) across. Phytophthora wilt is almost always fatal to infected plants. This disease can occur on seedlings in the cutting bench and in older plants grown in containers or in the field.

The disease is most active in warm weather and is common in cases where aeration of the roots is poor and soil pH is high. Although mountain laurel grows best at pH 5.5, the fungus can be combated by increasing acidity to pH 4.5. Roots that have been killed or damaged by water-logging, transplanting, or other means are most susceptible to infection. Container-grown plants allowed to sit in puddles of water suffer not only from insufficient drainage but are susceptible to the motile spore stage of the fungus, which travels through the water from diseased to healthy plants.

Infected plants should be removed and destroyed. Soil, benches in greenhouses, and containers such as pots or flats should be fumigated routinely or heat-sterilized before planting or use. Freezing of the soil apparently reduces the amount of overwintering inoculum since the fungus does not appear to survive well in the absence of host plants. Therefore, diseased plants should be removed and destroyed and infected fields should be left fallow over winter. In the landscape, selecting a site with good soil drainage and aeration is very important. In heavy soils, incorporate pine bark and raise the planting area several inches to increase drainage. For container plants it is best to avoid growing on black plastic. The likelihood of disease is also minimized by placing containers on several inches of coarse gravel or rock.

Phytophthora is widespread and attacks many different plant genera. Therefore, in areas where plants have died from root rot, it is best to replant with plants resistant to the disease. Selection of resistant varieties may be one of the best long-term solutions. We still have much to learn about the susceptibility of laurel selections to *Phytophthora* and about the means of developing resistant cultivars.

Preventative applications of fungicides such as fosetyl-Al (Aliette) and metalaxyl (Subdue) may reduce the incidence of disease, but they are effective only on a preventative basis. There is evidence of *Phytophthora* strains resistant to Subdue.

Damping-Off and Root Rot

The fungus *Rhizoctonia solani* (*Pellicularia filamentosa*) causes stem rot at the ground line. This disease is most serious on young seedlings, especially when they are planted in mixes containing soil. Symptoms are commonly referred to as damping-off, as seedlings topple over and lesions are visible on stems at the soil line. Larger plants are also susceptible, especially where soil aeration is poor and when overwatering has occurred. Symptoms are similar to those of *Phytophthora* and include general decline and dieback of twigs and branches. Roots are destroyed, but the reddish vascular streaks beneath the bark associated with *Phytophthora* are not present. As with wilt and some other soil-borne pathogens, *Rhizoctonia* is associated with soils or mixes having a relatively high pH. If damping-off or other diseases are a problem, the pH should be maintained at 5.0 or lower. The disease may be controlled by drenching the soil with fungicides such as etridiazole (Terrazole and Truban). To a large extent this disease can be avoided through the use of soilless mixes containing milled sphagnum and/or peat moss. These mixes contain natural antibiotic-like compounds that prevent or limit the growth of the fungus.

Pythium is another fungus that attacks young seedlings and causes damping-off symptoms. This disease frequently occurs on seedlings grown in closed humid chambers where they have been overwatered. Aeration and a drier medium will help check its spread. Control with fungicides may be necessary, but they should be applied sparingly on the young seedlings.

My two serious experiences with damping-off fungi in transplant beds occurred during rainy periods several weeks in duration and with soils that did not drain as well as they should have. I am convinced that *Kalmia* has fewer disease problems if the soil is allowed to dry—almost to the point of wilting—every few weeks.

Other Fungal Diseases

Other fungi may attack laurel roots and cause symptoms similar to those of *Phytophthora* and *Rhizoctonia*; one such example is shoestring root rot, *Armillaria mellea*. Although most of the fungi are fairly common soil inhabitants, diseases occur most frequently on roots that have been injured by poor growing conditions such as overfertilization, winter injury, overwatering, and lack of aeration.

Crown Gall and Tissue Culture Proliferation (TP)

The common denominator of the crown gall and tissue culture proliferation (TP) diseases is the swelling and calluslike growths of tissue at or slightly below the soil line. Fortunately, crown gall, caused by the bacterium *Agrobacterium tumefaciens*, has been seen only rarely on *Kalmia*. This bacterium requires wounds to cause infections, so careful handling and cultivating can minimize disease occurrence. Sanitation is also important; start with disease-free plants. There are no effective chemical controls, but some success has been reported using the biocontrol agent *Agrobacterium radiobacter* (strain 84, Galltrol).

TP looks like crown gall, but to date no causal organism has been identified. It appears to be the result of a physiological imbalance and most often has been associated with plants started in tissue culture. Rarely encountered with *Kalmia*, it is more common with certain micropropagated *Rhododendron* cultivars.

Twig Blight

This twig dieback disease, caused by *Botryosphaeria dothidea*, is most often associated with plants under stress and commonly occurs in landscape plantings. Symptoms can appear on large branches of established plants or new transplants, and it is likely the most common affliction of recently moved mountain laurel. Leaves on infected twigs first appear gray-green and wilted, and they eventually turn brown but remain attached to the twigs (Plate 106). A reddish brown discoloration of the wood under the bark can often be found on one side of dying branches. This distinctive discoloration may extend a few or many inches along the stem.

From 1993 to 1995 mountain laurel in central Pennsylvania experienced a high level of mortality. According to Don Davis, pathologist at Pennsylvania State University in University Park, Pennsylvania, several factors seem to have been involved. There were some very severe droughts; gypsy moth defoliation was heavy for several years; and the winter of 1993–1994 was very cold, with lows of −30°F (−35°C). Perhaps 10 to 20 percent of the plants showed some twig dieback, and *Botryosphaeria* was isolated consistently from these plants.

Fungicides are of little value in treating this disease. Prune out infected branches and perform cultural practices—such as watering, fertilizing, and removing competing vegetation—to restore plants to good health. In most cases the plants recover and grow well the next year.

Necrotic Ringspot

Necrotic ringspot is thought to be one of the few viral diseases of *Kalmia*. The causal agent has not yet been identified, but flexuous rodlike particles have been observed consistently in tissues bearing symptoms of the disease. The disease is identified by distinctive necrotic, reddish brown concentric rings on the leaves. In some cases, symptomatic leaves turn entirely red and drop prematurely. Symptoms do not occur on the current season's growth but rather on two-year-old leaves. Symptom severity has been associated with light intensity: the more light, the more symptoms. It is not a common problem but has been reported on cultivated plants in England, the Pacific Northwest, and in the eastern United States. Disease is spread primarily through vegetative propagation and grafting. Mechanical transmission is very infrequent and difficult to reproduce, and orthropod insect vectors have not yet been identified. Economic losses due to the disease have been minimal, so it does not presently pose a serious threat. In rhododendrons the problem is associated with progeny of *Rhododendron campylocarpum* and *Rhododendron griffithianum*. In *Kalmia* it may also be associated with certain cultivars, such as 'Olympic Fire'.

Miscellaneous Afflictions

Winter Injury

Winter injury is a nonparasitic disease characterized by browning of the leaves at the tips and around the edges (Figure 10-6). When severe, entire leaves and even branches may be killed. Affected foliage first changes from the normal dark green to a light, dull green and then to brown. Severe damage occurs when the roots are frozen and strong freezing winds desiccate the leaves. Injury is not confined to the coldest periods in mid-winter but often occurs after warm periods in March when the ground is still frozen. One of the best preventative measures is good mulch applied over the roots in November to insulate the soil. Avoid using windswept locations as planting sites. They can be identified easily as snow-free patches after a blustery snowstorm. Plants in areas exposed to buffeting winter winds should be protected with snow fencing, pine boughs, burlap, or other means. Killed and injured portions of winter-damaged plants should be pruned or removed. If in doubt as to how much to prune off, wait until the new growth begins in the spring and then prune back to the new shoots.

Native plants of southern origin grown in the harsher northern climates are particularly susceptible to damage from hard freezes in late fall and to injury in winter. When temperatures drop below freezing, these plants are also more prone to drooping and even curling of the leaves than is the native laurel, since they are adapted to mild winters.

When well-watered and kept warm and humid, container-grown plants in unheated, plastic overwintering structures may, like *Rhododendron*, suffer from water soaking of the leaves. Symptoms often appear as water-soaked or dead patches along the midvein; plants in this condition are particularly susceptible to damage by freezing. Good aeration around the plants during warm spells in the fall and conservative watering are the two best preventatives.

Figure 10-6. Winter injury is characterized by browning of the leaf tips and edges, as seen on the leaves of this *Kalmia latifolia* plant.

Salt Damage

Salt damage occurs both on plants along highways where road salt is used in winter and also on plants in containers or landscapes that are over fertilized. Symptoms are similar to those of winter injury and are associated with salt damage to the roots as well as excessive uptake and accumulation in the leaves. Leaf tips and edges turn brown. Prevention is the best cure. Once damage is observed, it is likely that the high soil salts have already been leached or diluted. Leaching with water may be worthwhile, however, especially for container plants.

Drought

Young plants, container-grown plants, or new transplants will simply wilt, discolor, and die if deprived of water for long periods of time. Established plants and especially large plants may also wilt and drop older foliage, but this usually occurs before they suffer dieback and death. In either case, individual branches may die, and the symptoms are much like those described for twig blight disease. Once plants receive adequate water, the dieback stops, although it is not uncommon for symptoms to appear long after the period of drought—even up to one year later. To maintain overall health, dead branches should be pruned out.

Decline and Dieback of Old Established Plants

Plants that once thrived may lose foliage, become leggy, suffer from dieback, and eventually die. Twig blight, described earlier, may well be present in such plants. Most often when I have observed such declining plants the surrounding trees and shrubs had grown and the laurel became heavily shaded. In addition to receiving less light as a result of the surrounding overstory plants, the laurel received less moisture and nutrients because of increased tree root competition. Mountain laurel is shade tolerant, but when conditions approach that of an unthinned forest, the plants will decline. The solution is to remove trees and to remove lower branches from those remaining. Adding an organic mulch, if one is not present, is advised as well as at least an annual spring application of fertilizer.

Sunscald

Sunscald typically occurs on either newly transplanted or established plants acclimated to shade and then exposed to full sun and an inadequate water supply. Several rainy and overcast days followed by a bright, sunny day also may cause sunscald on field-grown plants during the period when new shoot growth is expanding. Symptoms include bleaching of the chlorophyll on the upper surface of exposed leaves and eventual browning. Cultivars vary in their susceptibility to sunscald; 'Pink Frost' has proved to be susceptible in the eastern United States. Acclimation through gradual exposure of shaded plants to full sun is one preventative measure; another is intermittent irrigation during the hottest part of the day. Highly susceptible plants should be planted in light shade. Affected leaves and branches should be pruned.

Frost Damage

Unusually low temperatures in the spring or fall may damage plants. A hard frost in early fall will injure plants that have continued growing and have failed to harden off. The shorter days and cool weather of autumn normally signal plants to stop growth and prepare for winter. However, a moist, rich soil and mild fall weather, especially after a hot, dry summer, may delay normal dormancy and promote plant growth. Overfertilization in late summer or early fall also contributes to delayed hardening of plant growth. Mulched, field-grown plants in low areas are particularly susceptible to frost because the mulch slows the heat and water loss from the ground and helps maintain root growth. As previously noted, cold air on still nights flows down the slopes to the low areas. Thus the normally beneficial effects of a mulch are detrimental on a clear, still, frosty night. The air above the mulch supercools, because heat from the ground is trapped by the mulch. A similar problem occurs in the spring, as was illustrated dramatically to me a few years ago. A field of tomatoes was planted adjacent to my field of established mountain laurel mulched with wood chips. On a clear evening late in May, the weather station recorded a low of 35°F (2°C). The tomatoes in bare soil came through the night with no damage, while new growth on most of the mountain laurel was killed. The heat rapidly radiated off the wood chips and the air actually cooled to the freezing point, causing the laurel shoots to freeze. The air around the tomatoes over the bare, moist soil, however, was kept warmer by a constant supply of heat escaping upward from the soil.

The moral of this story is that heavy organic mulches may lead to frost injury in low pockets with poor air drainage. Frost damage seldom occurs under a tree canopy (evergreen, or even deciduous) because the canopy reflects radiated heat back to the ground. Damage is much more prevalent on plants growing in open locations without a protective canopy.

An early, hard fall freeze not only destroys succulent branch tips but also may actually split the bark on stems and kill the plant to the ground. This type of damage is often not noticeable until the following spring, when the top of the plant dries up. Fortunately, laurel plants are much less susceptible to this kind of damage than are evergreen azaleas. Measures to acclimate plants in autumn include removal of heavy mulch until after a hard freeze, and reduction of fertilizer and watering in late summer and early fall.

Yellow Leaves (Chlorosis)

The sudden onset of yellow leaves in the fall is often viewed as a sign of severe plant stress and cause for immediate action; however, it is most likely merely the onset of the annual loss of the previous year's foliage (Plate 107). If the yellow leaves show up at about the time the leaves on hardwood trees are turning color, and if the yellowing is confined to older foliage, despair not. Given a little wind, rain, and a week or two, they will be gone and forgotten.

On the other hand, if chlorosis (yellowing) occurs on the *current* year's leaves it is probably a sign of one of the most common troubles encountered with laurels: improper soil pH. The symptoms appear first on the youngest leaves; leaf veins typically remain green, but the main body of the leaf turns yellow (Figure 10-7). On severely affected plants the leaves may turn white before drying up. The problem is often caused by soil with a pH of 6.0 or higher. At these pH levels, iron is converted into a form that is unavailable to the plant. This condition can be remedied quite simply by lowering the pH with ferrous sulfate or aluminum sulfate (see Chapter 7).

Figure 10-7. Chlorosis is characterized by yellow foliage with green veins, especially on branch terminals. It results from root injury, heavy or wet soils, or neutral or alkaline soils.

Chlorotic symptoms can also result from causes other than high pH, including fertilizer root burn resulting from too much nitrogen; winter injury to roots; heavy, poorly drained soils; and even blackvine weevil root damage. Immediate reversal of symptoms can often be achieved by applying iron in the chelated form (such as Sequestrene) either as a drench or foliage spray. The actual cause of the chlorosis should be determined by examining the growing site and the plant and by testing the soil in order to determine if additional corrective measures are necessary.

Moles, Rabbits, and Deer

Moles are insectivorous (non-vegetarian) and are commonly believed to cause no garden problems. Wrong! They love grubs and earthworms and can wreak havoc in beds of small plants. Their apparently random, subterranean tunnels lift plants, exposing the roots to air and desiccation. Their presence around older plants is less objectionable unless the tunnels are taken over by voles and mice. These latter invaders also have a habit of eating bark from plants during the dormant season, when their populations are high and food is scarce. Beds of small plants can be treated with materials such as Diazinon, Dursban, or Oftanol to eliminate the food source (grubs) of the moles. Lacking a food source, the moles will search and dig elsewhere for food.

If rabbits and woodchucks were given a choice of food, most *Kalmia* species would rank very low. As is described in Chapter 12, laurel foliage is quite toxic to domestic animals. Rabbits will, however, seek out foliage of the bog laurels, *Kalmia polifolia* and *K. microphylla*. If young plants of the other species are in their pathways, rabbits will clip them and leave the shoots. For a small plant this may result in "pruning" right to the ground. Several potential methods exist to control these animals, such as repellents, fencing, and shooting, but all are fraught with difficulties. If damage is serious, check with neighbors and local game authorities for control means effective in your area.

Deer have become a nuisance and a prime cause of damage to nursery stock and ornamental plantings in many areas. *Kalmia* foliage is not among their preferred foods, but they will browse on it, as do rabbits. Check with state agricultural and game officials for assistance in determining practical control measures. Reduction of herd size should be an overall goal. Repellents, including human hair, fragrant soap bars, compounds containing rotten eggs (such as Big Game Repellent, BGR), and special formulations of the fungicide thiram (Thiram 42-S, Chew-Not, Bonide Rabbit-Deer Repellent) have some value but must be renewed regularly. In addition, the effectiveness of these methods is reduced as herd size and food requirements increase. One deer needs to consume the equivalent of 500 to 800 ft (150 to 240 m) of apple (*Malus*) wood per day just to maintain its weight in winter. That translates into all the new growth on 10 to 20 moderate-sized apple trees per deer per day. If deer are a persistent problem, fencing may be required. A fence is one of the best solutions, and several schemes are available, including electric and staggered, multistrand configurations. I have been very pleased with the results of a seven-strand, high-tensile, high-voltage electric fence that is 5 ft (1.5 m) high. Clearly deer have the ability to jump the fence, but apparently, once resident deer touch it, they stay away. Local dogs also quickly learn to respect the fence.

Despite the preceding discussion of a multitude of problems and pests, be assured that they are not often serious in the case of *Kalmia*. Awareness of potential problems and their control, however, is important in limiting serious depredation.

CHAPTER 11

Burls, Boughs, and Bouquets

Its beauty, combined with its utility, causes [mountain laurel] to be much sought after. Hundreds of tons of its foliage are used at Christmas. It is the most abundant of all holiday "greens." In early summer, florist's shops are full of its magnificent pale pink blooms, collected usually from wild plants, and week-end parties returning from the country come back laden with great clusters of its beautiful flowers. Naturally there is a great demand for entire plants for use in garden and estate planting. Finally, the wood itself has value, when it reaches sufficient size, for rustic work and for the manufacture of imitation brier pipes. (Buttrick 1924)

There is a group of people who hate mountain laurel. We who promote its esthetic beauty in the natural as well as managed landscape generally ignore, remain aloof, and just dismiss these unappreciative scoundrels! In actual fact, foresters and loggers can be excused for their disdain of what they call "ivy thickets" or "laurel hells." Not only do these tangles of mountain laurel make it difficult to nearly impossible for people and machinery to operate in such woods, the presence of masses of mountain laurel (*Kalmia latifolia*) and great bay rhododendron (*Rhododendron maximum*) shade out and prevent regeneration of trees. Thus not only is the harvest of timber made difficult, but the re-establishment of new trees is prohibited. So any harvesting of laurel in forests would likely be considered a blessing by those most concerned with managing and harvesting trees. With laurel occurring on millions of acres of land in the eastern United States, there is certainly no current threat to its survival.

With a bit of irony played out by Mother Nature, foresters may have to accept some of the blame for those laurel hells. It is generally agreed that up through the 17th and 18th centuries the forests of the eastern United States had much less undergrowth than they do now, fire being much more common then. It is presumed that in earlier times the Native Americans started fires regularly to keep the woods free of underbrush for better movement and hunting. Such recurrent fires typically were not so hot as to kill the overstory trees, but understory plants, including mountain laurel, might be killed or at least killed back, only to re-sprout from the base. The advent of fire control in the early 1900s by state and federal foresters, however, changed the ecology of the forest, and one aspect of that change was bigger thickets of laurel.

Another factor in the proliferation of laurel is that most states prohibit pruning and digging of laurel on state lands and public right-of-ways. Laurel is specifically protected in the laws of Pennsylvania, New Jersey, and North Carolina and is covered by more general statutes in other states. Connecticut repealed some of the laws protecting specific plants, including *Kalmia latifolia*, not so they would be less protected, but to get the word out that all plants on public lands should be respected. By designating specially protected plants, it is implied that the other plants are available for cutting and collecting. In contrast to the situation on public lands, the cutting of mountain laurel or the digging of plants on private land is generally allowed, given permission of the landowner.

Burls

Many ericaceous plants, mountain laurel included, produce swellings at or below the soil line called burls (lignotubers). These are specialized organs that appear to have survival value when plants are stressed from events such as fire, drought, and defoliation. Peter Del Tredici, at the Arnold Arboretum, Jamaica Plain, Massachusetts, is to be given credit for drawing attention to and delving into the function of burls on *Kalmia* and *Rhododendron* as well as some other plants, like *Ginkgo*. Burls are certainly not universal features on all woody plants, but when they occur they are often associated with species adapted to sporadic burning ("fire species"). In addition to a swelling, burls are characterized by many dormant buds.

Young seedlings have little if any swelling but do have multiple dormant buds. It is these buds that are capable of growing new shoots if the plant is severely stressed.

Plants grown from normal cuttings or from micropropagated cuttings apparently do not form burls. Del Tredici (1992) suggests that such vegetatively propagated plants may, therefore, not have the same survival characteristics under extreme environmental conditions as seed-grown plants—an interesting and seemingly valid theory that needs to be tested. For instance, will there be a difference in survival of seedling-grown plants compared to vegetatively propagated ones when they are drought stressed to the point of death, when they are cut to the ground, or when the tops are killed by fire?

Some micropropagated rhododendrons and, rarely, mountain laurels produce abnormal, calluslike growths near the soil line, referred to as tissue proliferation (TP; see Chapter 10). Del Tredici proposes that TP may be a burl-like response in these laboratory-produced plants resulting, in part, from the growth regulators in the tissue culture medium. It is generally agreed that these TP growths are abnormal and not actual lignotubers.

Tobacco (*Nicotiana*) is another North American plant whose use in pipes likely goes back to mound-building aborigines and was later prevalent among the Native American peoples. Pipes for smoking tobacco have been constructed from many substances, including clay, gourds, and corn cobs (*Zea mays*); but wood has been most popular in this century—especially wood burls of the Mediterranean brier (*Erica arborea*). During the First and Second World Wars, however, shortages of Mediterranean brier wood in the United States necessitated that burls of mountain laurel (*Kalmia latifolia*) and great bay rhododendron (*Rhododendron maximum*) be harvested. Burls of the two species are similar to brier in density and are also beautifully figured. Sporadic attempts to substitute brier with mountain laurel burls had begun at least as early as 1910. A more sustained effort occurred briefly from 1918 to 1920 and then again 20 years later (Barrett 1941).

By 1941, seven pipe-block plants were in operation in North Carolina and eastern Tennessee. They used mostly mountain laurel burls, and the seven processing plants required 196 tons per week (Figure 11-1). They averaged 900 blocks per ton; hence, they produced about 176,000 blocks weekly. Barrett (1941) estimated that if the processing plants operated 46 weeks of the year, their production would be just in excess of 8,000,000 blocks annually, or about one-fourth of the entire United States' needs.

Figure 11-1. *Top*, large burls dug from the Pisgah National Forest, North Carolina, and ready to be taken to a mill. *Bottom*, burls cut into blocks and ready to be processed into pipes. United States Forest Service photos, c. 1940 (Barrett 1941).

Unfortunately for those employed in this effort, the burl-processing industry failed to be self-sustaining after the war. Apparently the quality and price of Mediterranean brier could not be matched by the American plants.

In his discussion of the United States pipe-burl industry, Barrett presents some interesting facts. The total area on which these burl-producing plants occur can be measured in millions of acres. But in an area as large as one acre (0.4 hectares) there may be only a dozen or fewer burls of adequate size to dig. These harvestable clumps also are not uniformly spread but occur within an area of a size from a few acres to a maximum of 200 or 300 acres (80 to 120 hectares). The minimum size of burls harvested is generally 25 to 30 lbs (12 to 14 kg) and commonly weigh an average of 100 to 200 lbs (45 to 90 kg); the largest weighed 600 lbs (270 kg). Plants with harvestable burls are generally between 80 and 200 years old. Because of the patchwork nature by which the plants were dug, Barrett claims that the gaps in vegetation created by the harvesting of laurel quickly re-vegetate and that the visual effects are all but unnoticeable within a short period of time.

Boughs and Bouquets

In the 1920s Buttrick estimated that 20 million pounds (9 million kilograms) of laurel foliage were used annually in the United States for decorations during the holiday season. Since the estimated average yield per acre (0.4 hectares) was as low as one-quarter ton, nearly 40,000 acres (16,000 hectares) were cut over annually for laurel foliage. A new crop could be harvested from the same land every five years. Thus, a total of 120,000 acres (48,000 hectares) would grow indefinitely all the laurel required by the trade. Obviously this is but a small fraction of the total area where laurel is presently growing.

In 1924 Buttrick wrote,

> The growing of laurel for the sale of its foliage would be quite different from its cultivation for ornamental use in gardens. Its production for market could best take place in woodland, [where] advantage would be taken of its sprouting power. No attempt would be made to grow it from seed or produce large and handsome clumps.
>
> The cutting of laurel so that it will sprout satisfactorily and produce further crops is quite simple. Ordinarily collectors cut or break it off at about 18 inches [45 cm] back from the tips of the branches. Inferior branches are apt to be left growing. A good second growth seldom follows such a cutting. To secure a good second crop the cut should be made close to the root and those parts of the plant not useful for decorating purposes should be discarded.

I take exception to some of Buttrick's observations. Plants growing in sunny locations could certainly be harvested more often than every five years. In exposed locations, such as on the edge of woods or under power lines, it could be harvested every two to three years. Furthermore, regrowth is quite thrifty when 18-in (45-cm) branches are taken from large, established plants. Management of native laurel stands for greens is something that a few landowners might wish to consider. Other than harvesting, labor would be required to remove competing vegetation. In some situations the spraying of foliage with a fungicide for control of leafspot might be considered, although the more sun received by the plants, the less likely would be leafspot problems.

Mountain laurel wreaths, roping (garland), and swags are still produced for winter holiday decorations. For example, Jim Gildea of Mountain Greenery, Bernardston, Massachusetts, specializes in laurel wreaths and roping and has found that demand exceeds the production capacity of his small, family operation. We make wreaths at Broken Arrow Nursery and have always found a demand for laurel wreaths. The evergreen branches are also useful to decorate conifer wreaths. As with holly (*Ilex*) and other broad-leaved evergreens, however, laurel wreaths hold up best when used outdoors, where they do not dry as rapidly as they do indoors. With the tendency to leave decorations and Christmas trees up longer and longer, there has been a shift to materials that desiccate more slowly, such as white pine and true firs.

No statistics are available, but mountain laurel greens are still used extensively in florists' arrangements throughout the year. In the southern Appalachians, collectors of laurel are called "ivy breakers," derived from the local name for the plant, ivy bush. The trade in laurel foliage appears to have diminished considerably since Buttrick's time, in large part because of high labor costs for harvesting, and certainly due to restrictive and misunderstood state laws. Since most collection was from woodland, the quality of the material must have varied greatly. Markets today would require a reliable and consistent supply of high-quality material. Selected plants of mountain laurel with thick, glossy, deep green leaves would be perfect for the collection of decorative boughs. Because of the cost of propagating such plants and their slow growth, however, it is not likely to be economically feasible at this time to establish plantings for this purpose.

Other Uses of Laurel

In the 19th century in England, mountain laurel was forced in the greenhouse as a pot plant. There is no reason why the several species, their hybrids, and the newer selections should not be considered for pot culture today and possibly forced for cut flowers. For mountain laurel, however, a means to shorten the cold dormancy requirement of approximately 100 to 120 days at 45°F (7°C) is likely needed for commercially acceptable forcing. Exhibitors in the Boston and Philadelphia spring flower shows (held in March and April, respectively) often have mountain laurel in bloom. Such plants are usually brought into a cool enclosure in late fall and, after at least two months, are gradually exposed to increasingly higher temperatures over a period of many weeks. Without adequate chilling, they do not break dormancy. I have found it best to leave plants cold until approximately the first of February. Then plants can be forced into bloom in six to eight weeks (Plate 108). Daytime forcing temperatures have to be high, but cool night temperatures are required to maintain the pink and red colors in the flowers. Like many other plants that bloom in late spring, laurel is not easy to force into flower in the winter.

As mentioned earlier in Chapter 3, the vernacular name spoonwood was derived from the use of the wood of *Kalmia latifolia* for utensils by the early European settlers in America. The dense, hard, fine grain served well for small implements. These same characteristics were valuable in weavers' shuttles and other small devices before iron and steel parts became readily and cheaply available. Laurel wood is still valued today, especially by rural craftsmen. I prize a beautiful bowl turned from a South Carolina laurel burl and a spoon carved from the limb of a Pennsylvania plant (Plate 109). I have even seen a sturdy, rustic chair in Georgia crafted from laurel branches. Mountain laurel is underutilized today for novelty and native crafts; it rarely is depicted on mugs, plates, shirts, cards, or calendars, for instance, and it is rare to find any wooden hand-crafted items, even in Connecticut and Pennsylvania where *Kalmia* is the state flower.

Rules of the National Council of State Garden Clubs once added to the mystique and taboo surrounding laurel use, for they stipulated that mountain laurel flowers and foliage could not be used by their members in arrangements entered for competitive judging. Fortunately, in recognition of the cultivated varieties now available—that is, the domestication of laurel—this rule was dropped. What better, more pleasing way to appreciate and enjoy this handsome plant than to use the foliage and flowers for decorative purposes, whether from cultivated plants or from native plants on one's own property.

CHAPTER 12

Toxicity, Medicinal Uses, and Allelopathy

John E. Ebinger, Professor Emeritus, Botany Department,
Eastern Illinois University

From Pehr Kalm's entries in his journal, which he started publishing in 1753, we know of many early uses of the mountain laurel, most of which the settlers learned from the Indians. When Kalm was in America, the laurel was already being grown in colonial gardens as an ornamental. The evergreen branches of this shrub were used as church decorations at Christmas and New Year's Day. Its usefulness was the primary reason for its importance, however. The strong wood was carved into weaver's shuttles, pulleys, and spoons and trowels. The early common name spoonwood indicates this usefulness for tools. The leaves also were valued for their supposed medicinal powers, especially when prepared as a wash for skin diseases. (Holmes 1956)

Toxicity of Laurel

Mark Catesby was, in 1743, one of the first Europeans to report the poisonous properties of *Kalmia latifolia*. He found that, when deprived of better forage, cattle and sheep died from eating the leaves of this species. Later, Peter Kalm wrote an extensive, interesting account of the appearance, habit, and poisonous properties of both mountain laurel and sheep laurel, *K. angustifolia*. In this travelog of 1770 Kalm mentioned that young sheep were killed by eating only small portions of the leaves of mountain laurel, whereas older sheep became very sick and recovered with great difficulty. He also observed that after eating the foliage, calves swelled, foamed at the mouth, and had difficulty standing. They could usually be cured by giving them gunpowder and other medicines. He reported that larger animals were also affected, but usually recovered.

It is now known that many members of the family Ericaceae contain toxic substances. The related chemicals, grayanotoxins (formerly called andromedotoxins and discussed in more detail later in this chapter), have been isolated from some members of the family, including some species of *Kalmia*. Though the grayanotoxins differ slightly in their chemical structure, all produce similar symptoms in domesticated animals. Most cases of laurel poisoning have occurred in upland pastures of eastern North America and in the mountain ranges and coastal regions of the West, areas where *Kalmia* species are common. Since the species of this genus are extremely common, grow in habitats readily accessible to livestock, and are available at times when other food is scarce due to their evergreen foliage, some cases of poisoning have been attributed to them.

Cases of laurel poisoning occur most frequently among sheep; cattle poisoning is less common. In the eastern United States poisoning is usually caused by mountain or sheep laurel. The eastern bog laurel, *Kalmia polifolia*, is also poisonous but, owing to its bog habitat, is seldom encountered by livestock. Some experimental work has been done to determine the dosage, symptoms, and treatment for poisoning by these species. One of the first studies was made by Thomas Wood in 1883. He fed boiled extract of sheep laurel leaves to a sheep, and he concluded that extremely small quantities would not harm animals but that large quantities caused sickness and death.

Recent studies confirm the poisonous properties of both mountain laurel and sheep laurel. In all experiments, both species were found to be poisonous, producing almost identical symptoms. The major variable is the time from ingestion to the appearance of the first symptoms. Symptoms usually appear in six hours, depending on the amount of foliage consumed. The symptoms, in order of appearance, are lack of appetite, repeated swallowing, copious salivation, dullness, depression, and nausea. As the poisoning progresses, the animal becomes weak, is unable to coordinate voluntary muscular movements, and falls to the ground. Vomiting and bloating are also common. In fatal cases death is preceded by coma and occurs from a few hours to a week after the first symptoms appear.

Observations suggest that sheep laurel is about twice as toxic as mountain laurel. The minimum toxic dose for mountain laurel fed to sheep is 0.35 percent of the animal's weight, while for sheep laurel the minimum toxic dose is only 0.15 percent. Similar results were found with other animal species tested. The minimum toxic dose of mountain laurel fed to cattle and goats is 0.4 percent of the animal's weight, while for sheep laurel the minimum toxic dose is 0.25 percent for goats and 0.2 percent for cattle.

At present, no antidote for laurel poisoning is known, although lard or oil hinders absorption of the poison while also acting as a purgative. This practice, used since colonial times, still gives the best results. The recommended dosage is 4 fl oz (120 ml) of linseed oil administered every two to three hours. In a recent experiment, six sheep were given lethal doses of mountain laurel foliage, and all recovered after being treated with linseed oil.

Like its eastern relatives, the western laurel, *Kalmia microphylla*, is also poisonous. Because of its alpine habitat, this species is rarely encountered by livestock. Moreover, livestock will rarely eat it, but instances of sickness and death among lambs have been reported when they were admitted to the high range too early in the spring. Experiments with western alpine laurel revealed that both cattle and sheep could be poisoned; in fact, as little as 1 oz (30 ml) of fresh leaves made sheep sick. Studies by A. B. Clawson (1933) show that sheep are affected by eating as little as 0.3 percent of their weight of alpine laurel foliage, but they may consume as much as 2 percent without being fatally poisoned. In all studies the symptoms are similar to those reported for livestock poisoning with other *Kalmia* species.

While there is now no doubt that most species of *Kalmia* are poisonous, fortunately the number of domestic animals killed by these plants is very small—in spite of the fact that the laurel species are extremely common and grow in areas where livestock graze. As pointed out earlier, losses are small because the laurels are not very palatable and are therefore eaten only when other vegetation is scarce, as occurs when pastures have been overgrazed or in the spring after animals are turned into pastures in which grasses have not had time to grow.

Other cases of laurel poisoning have resulted from the animals accidentally being fed the foliage or eating decorations made of mountain laurel leaves. For example, some cows were poisoned when they ate laurel wreaths thrown into their pasture from a nearby cemetery. During Christmas week in 1894, six trained goats on exhibit at the Philadelphia Dime Museum died after browsing on laurel leaves that were being used for stage decorations. Both Angora goats and a monkey were poisoned at the National Zoological Park in Washington, D.C., when they were fed mountain laurel leaves and flowers by visitors.

Reports from 18th-century colonial America note that although mountain laurel is poisonous to most domestic livestock, many wild animals, particularly deer, can eat the leaves with impunity. Recent studies confirm that mountain laurel and rosebay, *Rhododendron maximum*, are sometimes eaten by deer, particularly in times of food shortages. In experiments, confined deer rejected both mountain laurel and rosebay, and when provided alternatives, they ate very little of either of the former. Furthermore, when restricted to a diet of these two species for 45 days, the deer did not eat enough of either to maintain their weight. They all became thin and weak, suffered from the cold, and developed a mild case of rickets. None of the deer, however, showed the typical symptoms of laurel poisoning. In related experiments, deer exhibited the typical symptoms of laurel poisoning and died when force-fed 1.75 percent of their live weight of laurel leaves. Clearly the toxic principle of both mountain laurel and rosebay is poisonous to deer, but they normally will not eat enough of either plant to exceed their tolerance for them.

Most species of *Kalmia* are probably poisonous to humans, but no deaths have been attributed directly to this genus. The first detailed study of human poisoning from mountain laurel was conducted by George C. Thomas in 1802. He found that after eating very small quantities (0.5 to 1 g) of dried mountain laurel leaves, unpleasant symptoms resulted: rapid pulse, headache, throbbing at the temples, nausea, vomiting, and dilation of the pupils. Other cases have been reported in which a strong decoction (boiled extract) of leaves caused vertigo, dimness of sight, reduction in heartbeat, and cold extremities. In each instance the decoction was being used in an experiment to determine its effect on humans, or it was being used as a medicine. It is unlikely that anyone would eat the leaves under normal conditions, because they are tough and bitter. There are reports, however, that the Delaware Indians used a decoction of mountain laurel leaves to commit suicide.

In 1974 R. Darnley Gibbs reported that sheep laurel contained cyanogenic glycosides. Though the glycoside was not identified, it was capable of liberating hydrogen cyanide when the leaves were crushed. Though not common in the Ericaceae, where only a few species have been found to produce hydrogen cyanide, many plants synthesize compounds capable of liberating hydrogen cyanide upon hydrolysis. Cyanogenesis has been reported from bacteria, fungi, lichens, ferns, fern-allies, gymnosperms, and at least 2650 species representing more than 130 families of flowering plants. Depending on the concentration, hydrogen cyanide may be poisonous to both humans and livestock. A recent unpublished study by me (Ebinger) of more than 50 sheep laurel (*Kalmia angustifolia*) plants indicated that cyanogenesis is not common in this species, finding no individuals that produced hydrogen cyanide. However, sheep laurel may be polymorphic with respect to cyanogenic glycosides in the few individuals in which the compound is present. It is also possible that hydrogen cyanide production only occurs under certain environmental conditions.

Occasionally, humans and other animals have become sick from eating birds whose crops contained the leaves and buds of mountain laurel. As a result, the common belief during the last century was that the flesh of birds feeding on mountain laurel is poisonous. In all cases, however, the reported symptoms were identical to those associated with food poisoning, so the probable cause of the discomfort was decompositon of the bird itself before it was cooked. There is no evidence that the flesh of any animal is itself inedible by virtue of that animal eating any part of *Kalmia* species.

A great deal of anecdotal evidence indicates that when honeybees work certain members of the family Ericaceae, they produce a honey that is poisonous to humans. Xenophon reported that his soldiers suffered from honey poisoning while they were camped at Trebizond on the shores of the Black Sea in 400 BC. He noted that those who had eaten small amounts of honey were merely intoxicated, whereas those who had eaten a great deal became mad. Within 24 hours, all the soldiers recovered.

It is presently believed that Xenophon's men were poisoned with honey derived from the flowers of *Rhododendron ponticum*. This species of azalea is extremely common in the mountains of the eastern Black Sea area of Turkey. Ingestion of honey from this species causes profound hypotension and brachycardia. It is known locally as "mad honey." From 1984 to 1986, 16 patients with honey intoxication were examined at the Hospital of Karadeniz University in Trabzon, Turkey. All had eaten honey that contained pollen from *Rhododendron* species. The patients became sick within one hour after eating the honey and all complained of dizziness, weakness, excessive perspiration, nausea, and vomiting. In an average of 24 hours, all patients recovered and their clinical findings and blood pressures and electrocardiograms returned to normal.

In the western United States there are occasional reports of individuals becoming sick from eating toxic honey. Western species of azalea are probably responsible, but the western laurel, *Kalmia microphylla*, does occur in the area. People who obtain honey from individual hives are at particular risk because in commercial processing the pooling of honey from many hives dilutes any toxic substances.

In eastern North America individuals have occasionally become sick from eating grayanotoxin-contaminated honey as well. In 1802 American botanist Benjamin S. Barton observed that honey from sheep laurel is poisonous to humans. He reported that late in the 18th century a group of young men moved their beehives to the savannas of New Jersey at the time *Kalmia angustifolia* flowered. On eating the honey produced, the men became intoxicated. Since this early incident, subsequent cases have been reported from the Great Smoky Mountain region of Tennessee and North Carolina northward to New Jersey, in New England, and in eastern Canada. Most of these cases are presumed to result from toxic honey derived from the nectar of members of the family Ericaceae. Though members of the genus *Rhododendron* are sometimes responsible, mountain laurel and sheep laurel probably are the most important sources of this toxin. In all reported cases, the honey acts as an extremely distressing narcotic, varying in its effect in proportion to the quantity eaten. The usual symptoms are nausea and vomiting, and in extreme cases, prostration and almost complete loss of voluntary muscle function. Since the honey produced is slightly bitter and astringent, it is hard to imagine fatal amounts being eaten.

Some authors have expressed doubt that members of the genus *Kalmia* are responsible for poisonous honey, for in none of the reported cases of poison honey is the source of the honey known for certain. Since many of these species are extremely common, contaminated honey might be expected more often than is reported. On the other hand, honeybees are rarely found on laurels. I have observed that when a honeybee lands on a mountain laurel flower, the elastic stamens—which are bent backward under tension—are released, striking the bee with considerable force. Though bumblebees are not as adversely effected, honeybees commonly leave the plant, declining to visit other mountain laurel flowers. In contrast, the smaller flowers of sheep laurel have stamens that are not under as much tension and do not appear to strike the bees as hard. Again, however, after many hours of observation I rarely found honeybees on sheep laurel. Real and Rathcke (1991) have shown that nectar production varies greatly among mountain laurel plants and that plants with the most nectar receive the most visits by pollinators. Perhaps such variation and a unique set of environmental conditions are required to induce honeybees to use laurel flowers.

Chemical studies of the "poison principle" (not necessarily the same as the substance hindering root growth) in genera of the Ericaceae have been undertaken. The first detailed analysis was made by Johan F. Eykman in 1882 using extracts from the Japanese andromeda, *Pieris japonica*. The physiologically active substance was named asebotoxin after the Japanese name of the plant. At about the same time, the German chemist P. C. Plugge found the same substance in some species of *Andromeda*, *Pieris*, and *Rhododendron* as well as in the non-green, herbaceous Indian pipe (*Monotropa uniflora*) and in sheep laurel. The list has since been expanded to include western alpine laurel, eastern bog laurel, and mountain laurel, and some members of the genera *Chamaedaphne*, *Leucothoe*, *Lyonia*, and *Pernettya*. Interestingly, some species of *Rhododendron*, *Lyonia*, and *Leucothoe* lack these toxic substances, as does sandhill laurel, *Kalmia hirsuta*.

There is now general agreement on the structure and the properties of the poisonous substance found in many members of the Ericaceae. In addition to the names andromedotoxin and asebotoxin, other designations of the substance include rhodotoxin (from *Rhododendron hymenanthes*), acetyl-andromedol (from *Rhododendron maximum*), and grayanotoxin I (from *Leucothoe grayana*). These poisonous substances, now commonly referred to as grayanotoxins in the literature, are andromedane diterpenes, which are polyhydroxylated cyclic hydrocarbons that do not contain nitrogen; the chemical composition of grayanotoxin I is $C_{22}H_{36}O_7$. The specific grayanotoxin varies with the plant species; presently at least 16 have been isolated from various members of the Ericaceae. In 1990 Jocelyn Burke and Raymond Doskotch found three different grayanotoxins from the southern sheep laurel, *Kalmia angustifolia* var. *caroliniana*, whereas previously ten were obtained from mountain laurel. It seems that at least some of these grayanotoxins from mountain laurel inhibit feeding by gypsy moth larvae (*Lymantria dispar*), a serious defoliator that has become established in the northeastern United States.

Presently grayanotoxins have been obtained only from species in the Ericaceae, and not all are toxic. The harmful effects of most of these compounds result from their ability to bind sodium channels, increasing the permeability of sodium ions in cell membranes. As a result, the excitable cells (particularly nerve and muscle cells) are maintained in a state of depolarization, during which time the entry of calcium into the cells may be facilitated. Recent studies, which have shown that the physiologically active compounds extracted from many of the species have similar physical and chemical properties, do not preclude the presence of other compounds with characteristics similar to grayanotoxins.

Medicinal Uses of Laurel

Notwithstanding the aforementioned hazards, extracts from species of *Kalmia* were used as medicine for as long as from the 17th century until well into the 19th century. The leaves of mountain laurel (*Kalmia latifolia*) were occasionally found in drug stores, principally as a remedy for diarrhea. A decoction was made by softening 2 oz (56 g) of dried leaves in 1 pint (0.5 liter) of alcohol, letting it stand for a week, and then straining. The dosage customarily administered to an adult was 30 drops four times a day; stronger dosages caused vertigo. This preparation has also been used as a wash to relieve itching and skin infections and was recommended for use as a sedative, as well as a cure for syphilis and fever. Furthermore, a powder of the dried leaves was popular as snuff.

Other species of *Kalmia* have also been used as medicine. Sheep laurel, *Kalmia angustifolia*, was used by the Cree Indians of the Hudson Bay region as a bitter tea both for the treatment of bowel complaints and as a tonic. The sandhill laurel, *K. hirsuta*, has been used in the southeastern United States as a cure for itching and mange in dogs. Treatment consisted of applying a strong, warm decoction to the affected area, a single application sufficient to effect a cure. There are no reports of medicinal uses of other species of the genus, although most of them also contain grayanotoxins.

Grayanotoxins are not presently being used as drugs, although experiments indicate that they have potent hypotensive action. These studies demonstrate that intravenous injections of small quantities into normal dogs cause blood-pressure reductions of 20 to 40 percent.

Renewed interest in grayanotoxin I has led to the development of more exacting, although not technically difficult, methods of isolating the compound. In one study 200 lbs (90 kg) of fresh rosebay (*Rhododendron maximum*) leaves were used to produce 0.25 oz (7 g) of grayanotoxin I. Southern sheep laurel (*Kalmia angustifolia* var. *caroliniana*) is an even richer source of grayanotoxin I. Large-scale isolation experiments show that 100 lbs (45 kg) of leaves of this species yields 1 oz (30 g) of grayanotoxin. Thus, southern sheep laurel yields 0.06 to 0.09 percent of the fresh weight or about 10 times the amount obtained from rosebay. Small amounts of grayanotoxin can be extracted fairly simply with basic laboratory equipment.

Some of the other compounds in the sap of *Kalmia latifolia* are of special interest because of their therapeutic potential. Susan Mancini and John Edwards (1979) at the School of Pharmacy, University of Connecticut, reported finding an active, anti-cancer compound in the sap that was not identified. A more recent letter from Professor Edwards states that the findings are reproducible and definite, but that the compound has not yet been identified.

Allelopathy

Allelopathy is the growth inhibition of one plant by another. A long- and well-known example is the growth inhibition effect of black walnut (*Juglans nigra*) trees on several plants, including tomatoes (*Lycopersicon*) and rhododendrons. In addition to their toxic foliage and honey, some members of the family Ericaceae are allelopathic. In particular, ericaceous species associated with heathland conditions seem to be responsible for slowing conifer regeneration and growth. In the boreal forests of North America, members of the genera *Gaultheria*, *Kalmia*, *Ledum*, and *Vaccinium* dominate cutover areas and poor-quality sites, with the aggressive northern sheep laurel (*Kalmia angustifolia* var. *angustifolia*) dominating extensive areas of eastern Canada and northern New England. Following disturbances such as logging and fire, sheep laurel spreads rapidly by rhizomes, impeding the successful regeneration of commercial softwood species, especially black spruce, *Picea mariana* (Plates 110 and 111). On these sites, black spruce as well as some other conifers have extremely low germination rates, and their seedlings exhibit nutrient deficiency symptoms and slow growth. This is a serious economic problem that has been intensively researched by

Canadian foresters in an effort to develop sound ecological means to re-establish the black spruce stands (Titus et al. 1995).

In 1990 Louise de Montigny and Gordon Weetman reported that erica-ceous plants, including sheep laurel, have been found to be associated with water-soluble phenolic compounds that are phytotoxic. These compounds hinder primary root development and prevent mycorrhizal inoculation of black spruce by destroying root epidermal and cortical cells. Sheep laurel is also more efficient than black spruce at accumulating soil nutrients, partic-ularly nitrogen, and the leaves are slow to decay, increasing the amount of humus on a site. This increase in humus, the lack of nutrients, and the allelopathic effects of the phenolic compounds effectively slow regeneration of black spruce.

Part II
Breeding Better Laurel

Introduction to the Last Four Chapters

Gardeners have developed many interesting and beautiful varieties of rhododendrons by breeding and grafting. It would seem as though there would be an equal field for this with the mountain laurel, yet it does not appear to have attracted their attention in this respect. (Buttrick 1924)

Growing plants from seed is the tried and true means of obtaining improved selections. The use of controlled crosses—that is, selecting both the seed and pollen parent—is the most efficient approach, but next best is growing seedlings from open-pollinated seed taken from selected plants. More *Kalmia* seedlings need to be grown by more people. Perhaps a few of those growing azalea and rhododendron hybrids will fancy devoting a bit of space and time to laurels—they will be fascinated and amazed by their offspring!

Plant lovers, whether nursery people, amateurs, or academics, often brag that one of the side benefits of their (a)vocation is the warm and delightful people they meet. Regardless of disparate temperaments and widely different social, political, and religious backgrounds, the common interest in plants typically eliminates differences that are in other settings so often barriers to communication and friendship. It is always fascinating at a

Rhododendron Society meeting to see, say, a retired surgeon getting point-ers from a machinist who lives across town on how to propagate a new hybrid or even proposing in detail a cross of two complex hybrids to pro-duce that elusive hardy yellow.

The diverse backgrounds of plant lovers is no news to most of us, but it needs to be pointed out to the newly converted. Do not let the plant names and scientific terms bewilder and discourage you. Enjoy the plants and the people and choose a niche that will not be overwhelming. Become a laurel expert and breeder instead of an orchid or rhododendron specialist! The latter two plant groups each involve hundreds of species and thousands of hybrids—great intellectual challenges that need to be approached cautious-ly by the innocent beginner.

It is sometimes shocking to find that so many people whose lives are consumed with plants have had little or no horticultural training. It is as if formal training in high school, college, or graduate school is irrelevant. Certainly many of us have completed our formal schooling years before experiencing the rewards of working with plants.

The breeding and selection of improved laurel is of recent vintage. No literature on laurel breeding existed prior to 1968. By contrast, the litera-ture on breeding azaleas and rhododendrons is extensive. Fewer than 100 *Kalmia* cultivars have been named, but hybridizers and growers of azaleas have named over 6000 cultivars in 160 years, and that is to say nothing of the even more extensive hybridizing and selection done within the rhodo-dendron section of the same genus. Though there are many fewer *Kalmia* species than *Rhododendron* species, their variation is great, and therefore their potential for improvement by breeding is considerable.

To be a plant breeder one has to be optimistic. Not everything has been done; we just need a little more imagination to expand the horizons. If most of the named mountain laurel cultivars have come from growing approximately 250,000 plants from selected parents, what can we expect if we collectively grow at least as many plants again, but this time are even more critical in choosing the parent plants? More people growing more seedlings from controlled crosses cannot help but produce a continuing spectrum of new outstanding *Kalmia* cultivars. Consider the tremendous advances, made largely by amateurs, with *Hemerocallis*, the daylilies.

Kalmia-phile Jon Weirether of Pennsylvania puts it this way:

> I would encourage enthusiasts to go out and look for
> enhancements in the wild. I believe that with the relative
> newness of interest in *Kalmia latifolia* and by sheer numbers
> of plants in the wild, there has to be a myriad of interesting
> habit and flower variation waiting to be discovered. In just
> one spring of hiking in the wilderness over a limited area, I
> found at least three plants that expressed potential
> enhancements in the aesthetic value or physical vigor of
> mountain laurel. Even if not a single new discovery were
> made, the beauty of the search would make it worthwhile.

Jon finished a recent letter with, "it may be nothing—but last spring I found a plant in the woods that had an unusual flower. At first glance the flower looked typical, but closer inspection revealed that all the filaments were deep red. It appeared as if each flower contained a red-legged spider." This is just one of many subtle variations to add to the library of traits useful in developing new cultivars. Join the fun and help produce an ever broader array of beautiful, flourishing laurels for the landscape.

CHAPTER 13

Plant Breeding Principles

The woods, plains, mountains and deserts of North America
are an immense reservoir of exciting plant material awaiting
the hand of the plant breeder who has the vision and desire to
explore the unknown. (Viehmeyer 1974)

Plants are propagated by either asexual or sexual means. As has already
been discussed, cultivars are almost universally reproduced by such methods of asexual propagation as cutting, grafting, layering, or tissue culture.
On the other hand, new cultivars are usually discovered and selected from
large populations of plants grown from seed, that is, from sexual reproduction. Each seed produces a completely unique individual, differing to a
greater or lesser degree from all others. The frequency and kind of variations in a population of seedlings depends on the parents. The more similar
the parents, the more uniform the progeny. The plant breeder controls the
traits expressed in the offspring not only by selecting the seed parent but
also by selecting the pollen parent.

Pollination and Fertilization

Each seed results from the union of a male gamete (contained in a
pollen grain) with a female gamete, the egg (contained in the ovule of the
pistil) (Figure 13-1). Pollination of *Kalmia* is usually carried out by bumblebees that bring the two gametes together. The union of sperm and egg in
the ovary is called fertilization. The male and female gametes contribute
equally to the genetic content of the resulting seed and the next generation,
although it is recognized that the storage tissue of the seed (endosperm) is

triploid with a two-thirds contribution from the seed parent. Thus in a cross between any two plants it does not matter which one is used as the female parent, since the reciprocal crosses are identical. (Reciprocal refers to reversing the parents or direction of the cross-pollination.) Exceptions to this rule occur only rarely. In laurel, only albino and yellow sectoring in the foliage are suspected of being dependent on maternal inheritance. Reciprocal crosses are sometimes not equally successful in producing seed, however, because pollen tube inhibition may exist in the pistils of one plant. Some examples are cited in the next chapter.

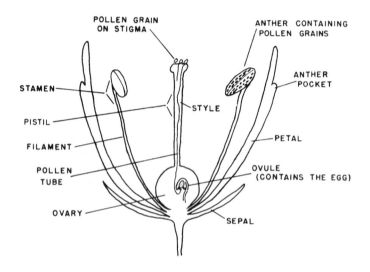

Figure 13-1. Stylized section through a *Kalmia* flower. The ovary actually contains many ovules, which, after fertilization, develop into seed. The pollen grains are four-celled, as is typical of plants in the family Ericaceae. Each grain is capable of producing four pollen tubes and of fertilizing four eggs.

Self-Fertilization and Cross-Fertilization—Inbreeding and Outbreeding

If the male and female gametes both come from the same plant or clone, the union is called self-fertilization or inbreeding; if from different clones, cross-fertilization or outbreeding. In nature, the laurels, like many woody plants, are predominantly outbreeders (outcrossers). The mechanism limiting self-fertilization in laurel has not been identified, but it may be a result of inhibition of pollen tube growth in the style or, as my studies indicate, from inhibition at a later stage.

Inbreeding clearly causes a decrease in vigor. A 50 percent reduction in height growth of *Kalmia angustifolia*, *K. latifolia*, and *K. polifolia* after one generation was observed in inbred plants as compared to outbred ones. Self-pollination also often results in greatly reduced flowering and seed set in *K. angustifolia* and *K. latifolia*.

The reduced vigor associated with inbreeding is caused by the expression of recessive traits which are normally masked by outbreeding. True-breeding *Kalmia* lines, completely uniform from generation to generation as a result of selfing, are difficult to develop due to both inbreeding depression and reduction in seed set.

Inbreeding uncovers recessive traits that may or may not have ornamental value. In natural outbreeding populations of laurel these recessive traits are normally hidden, occasionally unmasked only by chance recombination. It should be noted, however, that inbreeding, particularly of mountain laurel, may result in compact-growing forms of ornamental value (Plate 112). Such forms could be propagated vegetatively or by sibling crosses.

Hybrid Vigor

A cross between two species or even between two plants within a species may produce offspring more vigorous than the parents. This phenomenon is called hybrid vigor. Crosses between eastern bog laurel and western laurel (*Kalmia polifolia* × *K. microphylla*) sometimes, for example, show hybrid vigor, usually expressed not as increased height growth but as a general thriftiness or well-being.

Cultivar or Variety Selection

Cultivars (cultivated varieties) of woody plants usually have been selected from wild populations or from seedlings grown in the garden. Such selected materials are commonly used to start breeding programs to develop improved cultivars. The plants judged to be the best garden forms are those named, propagated, and introduced into the nursery trade. Sometimes unusual plants are designated as botanical forms, which may or may not have horticultural value (see Chapter 2). Feather petal (form *polypetala*) and banded (form *fuscata*) mountain laurel and white-flowered (form *candida*) sheep laurel are examples of such botanical forms. Several banded selections have received cultivar names.

The first deeply pigmented, rich pink and red-budded laurels were not directly selected from the wild or from controlled crosses, but from a more gradual one-parent selection process. Charles O. Dexter of Sandwich, Massachusetts, presumably started with one or more of the best pinks available from the wild. He took seed from these plants and grew several successive generations of seedlings; from each generation he gathered the seed of those plants that exhibited the deepest flower color. This method of selection in gardens and nurseries has been effective (notably at Weston Nurseries, Hopkinton, Massachusetts), but it can also be somewhat inefficient because, while the seed parent is known, the pollen parent is not. With controlled crosses both seed and pollen parents are known, so it is possible to determine how particular traits are inherited (Plates 113–115). This knowledge is valuable in planning the development of new cultivars and in reproducing desirable kinds from seed. Specific examples of gene inheritance are presented in the following chapters; guidelines for naming plants appear in Chapter 3.

Species Hybridization

It is difficult to overemphasize the point that variation is the key to plant breeding and selection. The greater the variation between plants to be crossed, the greater the likelihood that diverse, improved cultivars can be developed. When the desired characteristics occur in related species, the breeder can resort to species hybridization. For example, it would be wonderful if one could develop a mountain laurel hybrid possessing the general mountain laurel traits plus the solid, deep wine-colored flowers of sheep laurel and the easy-rooting characteristic of eastern bog laurel. Unfortunately, interspecific hybrids in *Kalmia* are difficult to create and, when successful, are often sterile—a disappointment, but not a total surprise since genetic barriers between species are the norm, if not the rule. Crosses above the species level, that is, between genera, are seldom successful. As one might predict, crosses of *Kalmia* with the genera *Rhododendron* and *Kalmiopsis* have all failed, with one possible exception: *Kalmia latifolia* × *Rhododendron williamsianum* (see Chapter 14).

First- and Second-Generation Crosses

The seedlings of a cross between two different plants or clones are referred to as first-generation, or F_1, hybrids. ("F" is for filial, pertaining to a son or daughter.) When two of these F_1 hybrids are then crossed, the off-spring are called second-generation, or F_2, hybrids. To obtain the desired expression and recombination of characters, the breeder usually must select from among offspring of the second or later generations (Plate 116). For example, the traits in mountain laurel for red flower buds and petaled corollas are known to be controlled by recessive traits; therefore, in a cross of these two types, the F_1 would be expected to have normally colored and shaped flowers. A cross of two of these F_1 hybrids should then produce a small proportion of seedlings exhibiting the unique combination of flowers with red buds and petaled corollas. The actual proportion of such plants depends on the number of genes controlling these two traits.

The odds of recovering the desired recombinant in the F_2 generation depends on the number of traits being selected for and on the number and nature of the genes involved—that is, whether the controlling genes are dominant, recessive, or additive. Additive genes are those for which expression is neither dominant nor recessive but rather is dose dependent; the more genes, the more strongly the expression of the trait. (For details on segregation of genes and on selection, consult a basic genetics or breeding text, such as those used in teaching general genetics; some specific references are given at the end of this chapter.)

Since the effectiveness of selection decreases as the number of desired traits increases, we can express this relationship mathematically. If n traits are selected for, the effectiveness of selection for any one alone drops to $\sqrt[n]{v}$, where v is the size of the population from which one is selecting. Stated another way, the same degree of selection is exerted for one trait in a population of ten as in a population of ten thousand, if in the latter case four traits are selected for simultaneously.

If the desired recombinant characteristic does not appear in the F_2, and if it seems that a very large number of plants will have to be grown to produce the desired trait, then third- and fourth-generation seedlings must be grown. Thus if the breeder is selecting for a mountain laurel recombinant that is to be dwarf, red-bud, and petaled, it may not be practical to grow enough F_2 seedlings to recombine all three traits in one plant. Therefore, among the F_2 seedlings, the breeder must select two plants that express separately all the desired traits, and these are crossed to produce an F_3; for example, a dwarf/petaled crossed with a dwarf/red-bud. By going to the F_3 and successive generations, the odds of recovering the long-desired recombination of the original traits are dramatically increased and fewer plants need to be grown, although more time is needed to grow the successive generations.

The trade-off then, when selecting for many traits, is whether to grow a vast second generation or to grow smaller populations and go through more subsequent generations, thus taking more time. For most of us with limited facilities, the long-term approach is the more practical one.

Backcross

The term backcross refers to the crossing an F_1 hybrid with one of the original parents. A backcross is used to maintain the identity of one parent (species) and to incorporate a particular trait from a second parent (species). The best strategy is to cross the F_1 hybrid back to the parent possessing the most desirable traits. Two or more generations of backcrossing may be necessary, but this is practical only if the characteristic sought is expressed in the F_1.

If a breeder wants to develop a cultivar possessing the small size and rooting ease of sandhill laurel (*Kalmia hirsuta*) but resembling mountain laurel (*K. latifolia*) in other characteristics, he/she should backcross small, well-statured plants of the F_1 hybrid to a good mountain laurel plant (possible, of course, only if the F_1 is fertile and practical only if cuttings of the selected F_1 plants root readily).

Chromosomes

Strandlike structures called *chromosomes* are present in all living cells and contain within them the hereditary determinants called *genes*. Chromosomes are visible with a high-powered microscope and are most easily seen in properly stained dividing cells. The number of chromosomes in a plant cell is constant and usually the same for all plants in one species. Thus for any plant, all the cells of the cambium, stems, roots, and leaves (somatic tissue) will have the same number of chromosomes. The chromosomes of each cell can be matched into pairs by size and shape, and if their origin could be traced, we would find that one chromosome of a pair was derived from the pollen parent and the other from the seed parent.

The number of chromosomes in a gamete (sex cell of pollen or ovary) is half the normal somatic or diploid number. A single set of chromosomes is referred to as the haploid number. If four sets of chromosomes are present it is called a tetraploid. The somatic chromosome numbers typical of the laurel species are 24 for *Kalmia angustifolia*, *K. cuneata*, *K. hirsuta*, *K. latifolia*, and *K. microphylla*; 48 for *K. polifolia*; and unknown for *K. ericoides*.

I have introduced the subject of chromosome number and chromosome structure because this information is useful in planning and predicting the results of breeding experiments. In addition, unusual crossing results can sometimes be explained by investigating chromosome number and behavior. Unfortunately, gaining this knowledge is not easy; the chromosomes of most woody plants are small, about 0.0001 in (0.0004 mm) long. As a result, chromosome study of the laurels and their relatives has been insignificant compared with that of the many herbaceous plants and even some insects, which have considerably larger chromosomes. Indeed, since I first reported the number of chromosomes of some of the *Kalmia* species in 1969, no additional publications on the subject have emerged.

Polyploids

A polyploid is an individual with more than one set of chromosomes. The eastern bog laurel (*Kalmia polifolia*), with 48 rather than 24 chromosomes, is a natural polyploid. Polyploid species result from a multiplication of the chromosome number of an existing species, or from the hybridization of two species, followed by chromosome multiplication.

Triploid and tetraploid plants (one and two extra chromosome sets, respectively) are valued for their large, heavy leaves and their flowers, which often have more body and are longer lasting. The greatest value of the polyploids, however, may be as breeding stock. Related species that do not cross or whose hybrids are sterile may often produce fertile offspring if the chromosome numbers are doubled. The extra sets of chromosomes allows normal pairing to occur during the reduction division prior to pollen and egg formation.

Artificial Production of Polyploids

The chromosome number in plants can be artificially doubled through the use of colchicine, an extract from the autumn crocus (*Colchicum autumnale*). This substance affects spindle formation in dividing cells so that the chromosomes, but not the cells, divide. (If you decide to use colchicine, please read and follow the label precautions.)

In the numerous papers on the use of colchicine by plant breeders, ericaceous plants have received little attention. Dr. August Kehr, however, formerly with the U.S. Department of Agriculture and now living in Hendersonville, North Carolina, successfully doubled chromosomes of azalea and rhododendron. Others have used colchicine successfully on blueberries (*Vaccinium*).

I have treated seedlings and buds of mountain laurel (*Kalmia latifolia*) and sheep laurel (*K. angustifolia*) to produce polyploids. My most successful technique in the past used newly germinated seedlings picked as soon as the cotyledons (seed leaves) spread. The seedlings were then inverted on filter paper saturated with a 1.0 percent solution of colchicine in a small covered dish for 8 to 24 hours. By having the roots in the air, this technique exposes the developing shoot, but not the more sensitive roots, to the chemical. The method has worked well on plants as diverse as tomato (*Lycopersicon*) and African violets (*Saintpaulia*). In my hands, however, it has not proved to be very efficient or effective.

A greatly improved method, developed by Dr. Kehr, radically increases the success of obtaining almost unlimited numbers of polyploid plants. In fact, with *Magnolia* one can produce polyploid plants with nearly 100 percent success by this new and extremely simple method. I thank Augie Kehr for supplying me with the following information on the technique.

The improved method starts with making a 0.5 percent stock solution by dissolving 0.5 grams of colchicine in 100 cubic centimeters (cc) (3.25 oz) of water. Making a stock solution and later diluting it enables one to make very accurate concentrations without the need for analytical scales. The stock solution can be kept for years in the refrigerator. Pharmacists are often willing to weigh small amounts on their scales.

The stock solution is diluted by using 180 cc (5.8 oz) of water and 20 cc (0.7 oz) of stock solution to make a 0.025 percent solution, to which is added 1 cc (0.2 tsp) dimethyl sulfoxide (commonly called DMSO) and one-tenth of a drop of surfactant (dishwashing liquid). This fraction of a drop is obtained by diluting the dishwashing liquid 1 to 10 in water, and then using one drop of the resulting dilution. Young leaves are very sensitive to dishwashing liquid and are killed by too great a concentration. The DMSO drastically increases the permeability of cell walls and thereby increases the amount of colchicine solution entering the dividing cells, while the dishwashing liquid "wets" the surface of the cell walls and thereby increases the overall effectiveness of the solution.

The laurel seeds (as well as any other seeds one wishes to treat) are then planted in the normal way in the normal substrate. When the cotyledons of the germinating seedlings are well developed—but before the first true leaves appear—the mixture of colchicine, DMSO, and dishwashing liquid is finely misted on the developing seedlings until a minute amount of the solution collects in the crevices between the two cotyledons. The seedlings are then misted daily for 7 to 10 days, or until the true leaves are visible.

The method is most effective when done in a shallow, boxlike structure covered with clear polyethylene film to maintain a constant, high relative humidity, and placed under cool-white fluorescent lights for 18 hours per day. The high humidity keeps the aqueous solution from evaporating, and the tiny seedlings are therefore kept wet for most of the 24 hours between treatments.

The improved method maintains healthy and normal growth of the roots and avoids the difficulties of planting wet seedlings from filter paper. Of course, the polyploid plants derived by this method will have roots that are not doubled in their chromosome numbers, so one must propagate only from the polyploid shoots or from seed grown from the polyploid shoots. When seedlings grown from polyploid shoots are self- or cross-pollinated with other polyploid plants, they will produce 100 percent polyploid offspring.

Perhaps the most difficult problem for inexperienced breeders is recognizing the polyploid seedlings. In general, the cotyledons and new leaves of polyploid seedlings are darker green and fatter than those of unaffected seedlings. Also, the first true leaves may be somewhat abnormal or ragged in appearance and are broader and heavier in texture.

Colchicine in the crystalline form is expensive and sold in small quantities. Kehr remarks that he has found it difficult to get all the material out of the small bottles. Consequently, he now buys the desired quantity and dilutes all the contents of the bottle to make the stock solution. In this way, an accurate stock solution is made without the use of scales to weigh out the powder and none of the expensive chemical is left in the bottle.

Artificially produced tetraploids, if fertile, might conceivably be crossed with the naturally tetraploid bog laurel to produce new, fertile, interspecific hybrids. Tetraploids offer the possibility of getting around the present barriers between most of the species, but achieving them can be challenging. My attempts to double the chromosome number of developing buds on plants of F_1 hybrids of mountain and sandhill laurel to restore fertility were unsuccessful. The attempt was made by immersing a growing shoot for eight hours in a 1.0 percent solution of colchicine. I did not use seedlings in this case due to the difficulty in obtaining interspecific hybrid seedlings, and because they are often weak and would have difficulty surviving the treatment. When tetraploid plants of both mountain and sandhill laurel species become available, the cross should be repeated. Seedlings from such a cross should be tetraploid and fertile. If fertile tetraploids of all the *Kalmia* species were available, repeating all the interspecific crosses would be well worth the effort.

Manipulation of ploidy level in *Kalmia* has been difficult, and the few plants I produced were slow to flower and/or were sterile. Perhaps Dr. Kehr's technique will open up some new avenues in *Kalmia* breeding. As he said at a meeting of the American Magnolia Society, "It is surprising to me that in a period of over a half a century no one has come up with this simple method. How was it possible to have missed it for so long?"

It appears that some of the significant advances in producing polyploids will be done by micropropagation laboratories. Briggs Nursery of Olympia, Washington, began research on producing polyploid *Rhododendron* cultivars in 1987, and they have used some of the techniques suggested by August Kehr on their young plants propagated from tissue culture. Promising results were obtained with the *Rhododendron* cultivars 'Jean Marie de Montague', 'Nancy Evans', 'Nova Zembla', and a compact selection of 'PJM'. The nursery plans to release several of these new selections.

According to Steve McCulloch, Vice President of Research and Tissue Culture at Briggs Nursery, the treated plants were first screened by evaluating morphological traits. They found that the polyploids generally exhibited leaves that were thicker and wider and flowers that were larger in size, had greater substance, and lasted longer. These suspected polyploids were then confirmed with a more sophisticated technique that actually measures the nuclear and chromosomal mass.

The efforts at Briggs Nursery to produce polyploid *Kalmia* are more recent and include not only doubling chromosomes of mountain laurel cultivars, but also the production of fertile, intergeneric hybrid "bridges" between several genera, including *Kalmia* and *Rhododendron*. McCulloch says that with the use of these bridges, plant breeders will certainly be able to produce novel and valuable new hybrids.

Radiation, Other Mutagens, and Gene Splicing

The use of radiation and chemicals to cause the sudden genetic change known as mutation has caught the imagination of both amateur and professional plant breeders. Unfortunately, more than 99 percent of the mutations so induced are of no value. This is because a very low rate of mutation occurs under natural conditions, and most of the beneficial mutations, such as those leading to increased vigor or seed production, have been selected for and incorporated into the native species. Where mutation breeding has been especially useful is in grain crops, where millions of individuals can be screened in a single mutation experiment.

No doubt mutation breeding could play an important role in developing improved *Kalmia*, but efficient screening techniques would have to be devised so that large numbers of individuals could be handled at the seedling size or in tissue culture vessels. In this way, the need to grow large populations of plants beyond this early stage would be eliminated. At present, however, breeders have so much variation available that there is little need to become deeply involved with alternative techniques of questionable merit to produce more variation.

Molecular geneticists are now doing wondrous things with genes of viruses and bacteria and can literally transfer single genes or chromosome segments into higher plants. We can thus visualize the time when, for example, unique traits not found in the genus could be introduced into mountain laurel to produce, say, yellow or blue flowers. Although such schemes are moving from the theoretical to the practical, I suspect it will be a long time before they will become economically viable for a plant like mountain laurel. Major economic crops are receiving attention first. As in the race between the turtle and hare, we turtles may accomplish a lot before the hare even shows up.

Objectives

The plant breeder should have definite, attainable objectives in mind before undertaking any breeding activity, for it is a waste of effort to make unplanned crosses of whatever happens to be in bloom. Acquiring the knowledge to make intelligent planning is half the fun of plant breeding.

The amateur plant breeder should begin with a small-scale program lest he/she be overwhelmed and lose interest. The project can be expanded as interest, experience, and resources develop.

Improvements are usually sought in one or more of the following:

1. Flowering characteristics—color, size, shape, abundance, and pigment pattern
2. Seed capsule appearance and retention—seed-sterile plants require no deadheading and would grow faster
3. Foliage characteristics—size, shape, color, and retention (density)
4. Shrub form and size
5. Ease of rooting cuttings
6. Hardiness, including ability to withstand neglect, rough handling, and heavy or alkaline soils
7. Disease and insect resistance
8. Heat and drought tolerance

In setting objectives, remember that the greater the number of traits being targeted at one time, the lower the chances of recovering the desired recombination in the offspring. A straight-forward and time-tested, practical approach is to cross cultivars—that is, to recombine the best traits of the best plants available.

The next two chapters review the crosses between and within species to record what has been done to date and, perhaps more importantly, to suggest rewarding areas for additional work.

For more on the principles of plant breeding and genetics, a handbook such as *Breeding Plants for Home and Garden*, published by the Brooklyn Botanic Garden (New York, 1974), is suggested for beginners. One of the older, interesting, and still-relevant reviews can be found in the 1937 *Yearbook of Agriculture*, published by the U.S. Department of Agriculture. A more contemporary book on plant breeding and genetics is *Flower and Vegetable Plant Breeding* by L. Watts (Grower Books, London, 1980), although as the title indicates, there are few examples or illustrations dealing with woody plants.

Regardless of approach or objectives, the breeder has to be careful not to become too attached to his or her offspring. No more than a few plants should be kept from each cross; mediocre material must be eliminated. It is important to do what may seem like ruthless culling; otherwise space, time, and resources become limited. Public institutions often find destruction of material to be most efficient in the long run. Of course, nursery people and amateurs need not destroy good plants, for they can be sold or given away. However, it is not always easy to give plants away. Sometimes the plants are little valued because they were free or people complain because they got none, not enough, or not as good plants. When research institutions start selling, they are notoriously inefficient, and talented researchers and their assistants end up spending valuable time to oversee, dig, and sell plants that often return less money than the time invested. Phil Savage, eminent magnolia breeder, says he keeps only the one best plant in a batch of seedlings and he "brush piles" the rest. One has to be hardhearted to be a plant or animal breeder.

CHAPTER 14

Hybrids Between Species and Across Genera

> So the hybridizer, the seedsman who's got his eye cocked toward the future, has got to take risks, to use his imagination to dream up something new, and then work his tail off trying to make it a reality. (Claude Hope, in Lacy 1986)

One of the most fascinating aspects of breeding is the potential for making hybrids between species of the same genus. There are barriers to such crosses, but the occasional successes make the attempts well worth the effort and uncertainty. The variation within each of the seven *Kalmia* species is considerable, but it could be greatly increased through interspecific crosses. Appropriate crosses between *Kalmia latifolia* and the other species could, in theory, produce plants like mountain laurel with deeply colored flowers, compact growth, and stem cuttings that root readily—for all these traits are available in the other species.

I have crossed six of the laurel species (*Kalmia ericoides* is the exception) in all possible combinations, including reciprocals. For each species combination, at least two plants of each species and a minimum of 20 flowers were used. The average number of flowers pollinated for each of the 30 species combinations was 200. For one of the most difficult and yet occasionally successful combinations—*Kalmia angustifolia* × *K. latifolia*—more than 1300 flowers were emasculated and pollinated, involving over 20 different plants of each species. In selecting the plants of each species, individuals were chosen that differed in flower color, growth habit, and geographic origin, so that failure or success would not be dependent on idiosyncrasies peculiar to a single plant.

Unfortunately, only a few of the crosses produced hybrid plants, and only the crosses between the two bog laurel species, *Kalmia microphylla* and *K. polifolia*, were easy to complete. The relative success of the F_1 crosses is summarized in Figure 14-1. The success rate from the crosses between species was extremely low. The amount of seed set and survival of seedlings averaged less than 1 percent of that obtained from crosses within species.

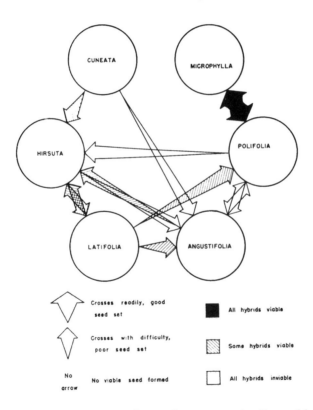

Figure 14-1. The crossing ability of six *Kalmia* species in all possible first-generation combinations.

Following are some observations on the F_1 hybrids that survived more than one year. The female parent is listed first for each cross. Only three of these combinations have any ornamental or horticultural potential. The least valuable ones are discussed first.

Kalmia hirsuta × Kalmia angustifolia

From 800 hybrid seeds, only 18 seedlings grew from crosses of *Kalmia hirsuta* × *K. angustifolia*; all but four of these seedlings were weak, yellow-green plants that died within one year. *Kalmia hirsuta* has alternately arranged leaves, and *K. angustifolia* has leaves in whorls of three. In the hybrids, whorled and alternate leaves sometimes occurred on the same plant (Plate 117). The reciprocal cross produced no viable seedlings.

Kalmia hirsuta × Kalmia cuneata

Most of the seedlings produced from *Kalmia hirsuta* × *K. cuneata* were weak and produced at least sectors of albino or yellow-green tissue. One plant did flower, but it was leggy and had no particular merit as a garden plant.

Kalmia polifolia × Kalmia angustifolia

Only one of 17 combinations of *Kalmia polifolia* × *K. angustifolia* produced viable seedlings. They were weak, yellow-green, and all died within three years. In the reciprocal cross, pollen tube growth was abnormal in the style, resulting in little seed production and no viable seedlings.

Kalmia polifolia × Kalmia latifolia

About 4 percent of the 3000 seeds from crosses of eastern bog laurel and mountain laurel (*Kalmia polifolia* × *K. latifolia*) germinated. The seedlings were extremely variable, ranging from weak and miniature to comparatively vigorous, large plants. The hybrids resembled the female parent, *K. polifolia*, more than the male parent. This was expected, however, because eastern bog laurel is a natural tetraploid with 48 chromosomes; it contributes two sets of chromosomes to the hybrid, while mountain laurel contributes but one. The hybrid should therefore be triploid with 36 chromosomes. This was not confirmed, but the hybrids were pollen- and seed-sterile, as is expected of a triploid. To obtain more-vigorous and possibly fertile hybrids, the cross should be repeated using a tetraploid mountain laurel. (Tetraploid *K. latifolia* plants have not been verified, but a few selections with heavy, broad leaves, such as 'Silver Dollar', are likely candidates.) The reciprocal cross, *K. latifolia* × *K. polifolia*, resulted in no seed set, apparently due to an inability of the pollen of *K. polifolia* to grow down the style of *K. latifolia*.

Kalmia latifolia × *Kalmia hirsuta*

The F_1 offspring of reciprocal crosses of *Kalmia latifolia* and *K. hirsuta* were the same, although the seed of *K. hirsuta* can be difficult to germinate, and hence, it is more convenient to use *K. latifolia* as the seed parent. The more than 200 hybrid seedlings produced from this cross were highly variable in vigor, habit, leaf shape, and flower color (Plate 118). Plants with leaves sectored green and white, or yellow (chlorophyll deficiencies), were common.

Sandhill laurel is not reliably hardy in Connecticut; likewise, the hybrids are generally not as hardy as mountain laurel but will survive in zone 6. Cuttings of the hybrid root more readily than those of mountain laurel. The more compact, multibranched seedlings have horticultural promise, but none has been selected for naming and release.

Fifty or more of the F_1 hybrids flowered, but none was fertile except for one of several plants grown from a stem cutting of one of the hybrids. Why this one plant became fertile after initial sterility is not known. The seeds harvested from this one fertile plant were grown; the offspring were apparently the product of a backcross to mountain laurel, which they resembled. Some of these plants have been sib-crossed (intercrossed), and some plants resembling mountain laurel, but smaller in leaf size and stature, were selected from the offspring. Because of that one single fertile F_1 it has been possible to produce third- and fourth-generation hybrids of mountain laurel and sandhill laurel.

Tom Dodd, Jr., and Tom Dodd, III, of Semmes, Alabama, have successfully grown second- and third-generation hybrids of *Kalmia latifolia* × *K. hirsuta*. These plants have been sold in the southern United States through nurseries such as Woodlanders, a mail-order nursery in Aiken, South Carolina. The Dodds have selected and tentatively named one 'Sandy Mountain', which has large, light pink flowers and foliage and growth habit resembling that of mountain laurel. The name refers to the two parent species as well as to Sand Mountain in Alabama. Selections from this cross should be more tolerant of the high humidity and heat of the South, although plants apparently still have to be grown there in light shade.

Using these two species, there is an opportunity to develop outstanding laurel selections, especially for warmer climates. More sandhill laurel × mountain laurel hybrids need to be grown, either open-pollinated seedlings or crosses among the better hybrids—or even backcrosses to the parent species. The great variation in the two species and their offspring is a store of untapped potential.

Kalmia angustifolia × *Kalmia latifolia*

Of the more than 2000 seedlings germinated from nearly 10,000 seeds sown of the cross *Kalmia angustifolia* × *K. latifolia*, the vast majority were yellow-green and weak and eventually died. However, when the *K. angustifolia* parent was the pure white-flowered form *candida*, the cross produced more seeds per pollinated flower, and many of the seedlings survived. The hybrids are intermediate between the parents in appearance (Plates 119 and 120); they are, however, somewhat more tender than either parent and are slow to produce flowers. They have little ornamental value in the garden, except that the foliage of new growth is white to yellow initially and then turns green. The flowers have little substance and are a pale pink and pollen- and seed-sterile. Stem cuttings root more readily than those of *K. latifolia*. Interestingly, the reciprocal cross failed completely. Microscopic studies using fluorescent stain show that the pollen tubes of *K. angustifolia* fail to grow down the styles of *K. latifolia*.

Kalmia polifolia × *Kalmia microphylla*

Kalmia polifolia × *K. microphylla* is the only species cross that is easy to make and consistently gives healthy green seedlings (Plate 121); reciprocal crosses give the same result. Because the chromosome numbers of the two species are different (somatic numbers of 48 and 24, respectively) the hybrids are usually triploids and sterile. Some of these hybrids have horticultural merit; one released for test (356h) was named 'Rocky Top' (Plate 92). Their value lies in their greater tolerance of the hot summers and open (snowless) winters in the northeastern United States as compared to the western *Kalmia microphylla* and also in their more compact habit relative to that of the eastern *Kalmia polifolia*.

Unfortunately, rabbits find the shoots of this hybrid tasty; they also enjoy the parent species. The rabbits' fondness for bog laurel is nothing new. In 1882 an anonymous writer (Alpha) reported in an English horticultural magazine that "rabbits are very fond of [bog laurel] and will crop it close to the ground." The toxic effects of the hybrids on rabbits are not known. Another pest of the hybrid is spider mites, but these are readily controlled by spraying. Despite the relative ease of controlling these two problems, neither the species nor the hybrids are long-lived in most gardens of the northeastern United States. Two notable exceptions are plants of 'Rocky Top': one has survived and done reasonably well for years at the Arnold Arboretum, Jamaica Plain, Massachusetts; the other is Polly Hill's, grown on Martha's Vineyard, Massachusetts.

The only species that I have not crossed with the other kalmias is Cuban laurel, *Kalmia ericoides*. *Kalmia ericoides* is closely related morphologically to the sandhill laurel, *K. hirsuta*, and hence, it may cross with that species, but I would not expect it to hybridize with *K. latifolia*, a species that will cross with *K. hirsuta*. There is, however, only one way to find out, and that requires live, flowering plants or at least pollen to make the cross-pollinations.

These many attempts to hybridize laurel species show conclusively that genetic barriers to gene flow between *Kalmia* species are well developed. Natural hybrids among the species have not been reported, and the results of experimental crosses suggest that such natural hybrids are unlikely ever to be found. The genetic barriers between species limit the prospects of fully utilizing the variation found among the species, unless other techniques, such as breeding at the polyploid level, prove successful.

A few of the F_1 hybrids do have horticultural merit. Yet all the hybrids that have flowered are pollen- and seed-sterile with two exceptions: a few of the western laurel and eastern bog laurel hybrids, in which only partial seed and pollen fertility was observed on only a few plants; and one first-generation hybrid of mountain laurel and sandhill laurel and the offspring of this one plant. This latter exception is leading us to some compact laurels adapted to the southeastern United States. As for future progress, the fertility of other F_1 hybrids might be restored by doubling the chromosome number with colchicine (see Chapter 13). So far, however, the development of improved laurel cultivars has relied most heavily on variation within species rather than on variation between species, because of the problems with sterility.

Intergeneric Crosses

Based on these observations with crosses between *Kalmia* species, I assumed that crosses at the next level, between genera, would be impossible. Well, almost! My own attempts to cross *Rhododendron* species or *Kalmiopsis leachiana* with several of the kalmias have been unsuccessful. Yet a plant does exist at the U.S. National Arboretum that may be a natural hybrid between *Rhododendron maximum* (rosebay) and *Kalmia latifolia*. It is indeed an unusual plant, but most likely it is only an aberrant form of *Rhododendron maximum*. A chromosome count would shed some light on the matter, because mountain laurel has 24 somatic chromosomes and rosebay has 26. An F_1 hybrid between the two would be expected to have 25. The chromosomes of this reputed hybrid have yet to be examined, due to the technical difficulty in preparing adequate slides for counting.

The late Halfdan Lem of Seattle, Washington, is attributed with a successful intergeneric cross between *Kalmia latifolia*, which was the seed parent, and *Rhododendron williamsianum* (Plate 122). This cross came to the attention of horticulturists when a color photograph of the plant appeared in the January 1974 *Quarterly Bulletin of the American Rhododendron Society*, and again in the fall of 1994 in the same publication, but now called *Journal, American Rhododendron Society*. The plant has been named 'No Suchianum', which may be prophetic. Although it was claimed that mountain laurel was the seed parent, the overall characteristics of the putative hybrid are that of a rhododendron. The stamens number more than 10, there is no evidence of pouches in the corolla, and the ovary shape is elongate rather than globose. Again, chromosome counts of the hybrid would be helpful in shedding some light.

The science of genetics and plant systematics helps to predict the success or failure of a cross, but the science is not developed to the point where it can predict the exceptional, successful intergeneric cross such as that purportedly performed by Lem. The usual failure of wide crosses is reason enough to not devote all one's effort to them, although the occasional and unexpected success may tempt even the conservative breeder to try a few.

Recent taxonomic studies by Kathleen Kron and Jennifer King, Wake Forest University, North Carolina, and Peter Stevens and Nancy Gift, Harvard University, Cambridge, Massachusetts, suggest that *Leiophyllum buxifolium*, sand myrtle, and *Loiseleuria procumbens*, mountain azalea, are closely related to *Kalmia*. These two species, therefore, might cross with one or more *Kalmia* species and should be included in future *Kalmia* breeding.

An Observation on the Successful Interspecific Crosses

The offspring of the few successful crosses between *Kalmia* species demonstrate tremendous variability among the F_1 generation, especially from the cross of *Kalmia latifolia* × *K. hirsuta*. It is generally assumed and observed that variation between species is vastly greater than that within species, and that offspring from a cross of two species are quite uniform in the first generation. This is clearly not true with *Kalmia*. These variable first-generation offspring indicate great variability within each of the parent species, and it may also be telling us other things about genetic control in these plants. I leave it to others to speculate about these matters and to delve into them further.

CHAPTER 15

Techniques for Controlling Crosses

The art of plant breeding has been practiced continually since
primitive man gave up nomadic food gathering to settle in
permanent settlements around dependable sources of food.... .
Plant breeding continued to be largely based on empirical
knowledge until the "discovery" of Gregor Mendel's great
1865 paper on inheritance which gave rise to the science we
know today as genetics. (Moore and Janick 1975)

Controlled crosses are pointless unless there is the intention of planting the
seed and nurturing the seedlings until they flower. Occasionally, desired
characteristics can be determined in the seedling stage, and then only such
selected seedlings need be grown. The advantage of selecting both the seed
and the pollen parents lies in the tremendous increase in odds of recovering desired types in the offspring and in the ability to repeat the cross
exactly. Crosses between individual plants of mountain laurel (*Kalmia latifolia*) are not difficult to make because the flowers are relatively large; more
dexterity is needed, however, in handling the small flowers of sheep laurel
(*K. angustifolia*).

The principles of the crossing technique are simple. Before the flowers
open, remove the male parts from the seed parent. When the stigma
becomes receptive (when it is viscid and moist), apply pollen from the
selected male parent. Prevent contamination of pollen from other plants.
If the cross is successful, the resulting seed will produce hybrid seedlings.
Crosses can be made in a greenhouse or outdoors, or even between distant
plants. Geographically distant plants, as well as plants that flower at

different times, can be cross-bred by the techniques of storing and shipping pollen, discussed later in the chapter.

Isolation by Emasculation

Flowers to be used as female parents should be selected before they have opened, otherwise there is no way to tell if they have already been pollinated. Use the largest tight buds. Small buds fail to develop after emasculation. To emasculate, use tweezers (forceps) to remove the corolla and the 10 anthers (Figure 15-1; see Figure 13-1 for flower parts). In this way, not only are the anther sacs and pollen removed to prevent self-pollination, but by removing the corolla the visual attractant and landing platform for insects are also eliminated. In addition, all flower buds within 1 ft (30 cm) of the emasculated buds should be removed to decrease insect activity in the area and thereby reduce chances for contamination of the emasculated flowers by selfing or outcrossing.

As described in Chapter 2, laurels are insect-pollinated. Because of the spring-loaded anthers and the powdery pollen of some of the species, we were curious about airborne pollen distribution. We placed glass slides greased with petroleum jelly on stakes 1 ft (30 cm) high and 1 ft (30 cm) apart in a line from east to west among flowering sheep laurel and in another test line among flowering mountain laurel. The results are shown in Figure 15-2. Pollen blew downwind, but most of it fell within 2 ft (60 cm) of the plant. These experiments demonstrate that pollen can in fact be

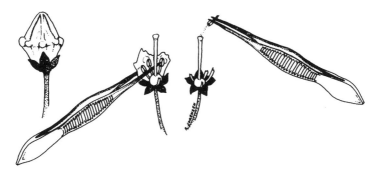

Figure 15-1. Steps in the process of emasculation and pollination: *left*, flower bud at proper stage for emasculation; *center*, removal of the anthers and corolla; *right*, pollination, usually carried out one day after emasculation. Drawing by Rita Sorensen-Leonard.

airborne for short distances, but that it is not widely distributed in air. The hybridizer should thus take heed; when using large plants for crosses—and when it is impractical to remove all the flowers—use flowers near the top to reduce the chance of pollen contamination from above. These simple precautions make bagging unnecessary, and accidental outcrossing is rare.

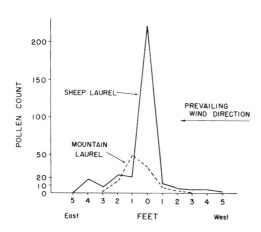

Figure 15-2. Distribution of airborne pollen from mountain laurel (*Kalmia latifolia*) and sheep laurel (*Kalmia angustifolia*), caught on petroleum-jelly-coated slides and counted after 24 hours of exposure. The results support other evidence that the pollen is not primarily airborne. Of the two species used here, sheep laurel has pollen which is loose and free as it comes from the anther, whereas pollen of mountain laurel clings together.

Pollination

Although some of the stigmas may be receptive at the time of emasculation, wait to apply the pollen until the next day. During very cool or rainy weather it may be necessary to wait two to three days. The pollen of mountain laurel, *Kalmia latifolia*, and sandhill laurel, *K. hirsuta*, clump together, so with these species the whole anther can be transferred to the stigma. There it can be gently tapped or teased with the forceps to release pollen onto the stigmatic surface. If the pore end of the anther is placed against the stigma, the sticky surface will catch a mass of pollen from the anther. This method also works with sheep laurel, *K. angustifolia*, and white wicky, *K. cuneata*, but their pollen readily scatters. To avoid this difficulty, collect anthers from about-to-open or newly opened flowers where the anthers are still held in the anther pockets. To remove the anthers without losing the pollen, pinch the filament with tweezers just below the anther sacs and place the anther along with others in a vial. The pollen will collect at the bottom of the vial and can be picked up on a slightly moistened small artist's brush and applied to the stigmas.

Pollen Storage

Pollen will remain viable for at least one week when stored at normal room temperature and humidity and out of direct sunlight. To ship pollen, place the anthers removed from the flowers in gelatin capsules (available from druggists). To guard against high humidity and mold during shipment, put the capsules in a larger container with a drying agent such as silica gel or calcium chloride.

Long-term storage is possible by drying and refrigerating the pollen. To do this, place the pollen in a small open vial or in a gelatin capsule and place inside a larger closed vial containing a drying agent, such as is illustrated in Figure 15-3. Label the container clearly with the pollen source and the date collected. In four to eight hours, when the pollen has dried, place the closed vial in a freezer at 0 to −20°F (−18 to −30°C). Laurel pollen stored in this manner has been used successfully in crosses one year later. Pollen storage is invaluable when the flowering times of the parent plants are different.

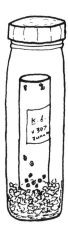

Figure 15-3. Storing pollen in a vial within a sealed container.

Caging (The Lazy Way to Produce Hybrid Seed)

Emasculation and pollination of individual flowers are tedious tasks, especially if large quantities of seed are desired from the crosses. Comparative hand-pollination tests have shown that seed from cross-pollination of mountain and sheep laurel is 85 percent more successful than seed set from self-pollination. This led me to experiment with two plants of the same species placed in a cage with bumblebees. This scheme has worked well—selfing is minimal, and hybrid seed is produced in quantity.

The plants to be crossed were planted next to each other in the spring. The cage, made of cube-shaped wooden frames covered with aluminum screening on four sides and the top (Figure 15-4), was placed over the plants just prior to flowering and sealed around the lower edge with 2 in (5 cm) of soil. When the flowers began to open on both plants, a bumblebee was released under one edge of the cage by temporarily removing some soil with a trowel. The cage also prevents other pollinating insects from entering.

Catching the bees was a challenge. Our first attempts with nets were hazardous at best. To reach black locust (*Robinia pseudoacacia*) flowers, where bees are plentiful, we would drive under a tree and, standing on the van's roof, operate a long-handled insect net. Securing a bee in the net was only half the problem; getting it into a jar proved fully as risky! These difficulties, however, soon led to our devising a better technique. The net was discarded, and the bees were collected directly in quart jars from a variety of flowers. They were easiest to catch from shrubs with deep-throated flowers, such as *Weigela*, to which our approach could be made while the bee remained busy within the flower.

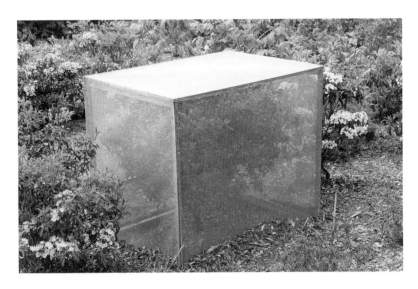

Figure 15-4. A cage for controlled cross-pollinations using bumblebees.

In the first caging experiments we even washed the bees in lukewarm water on the chance that they might be carrying some laurel pollen. Bathing a bee sounds tricky but was accomplished simply by placing two jars together, the lower one with the water and the upper one with the bee and a piece of cardboard between them. When the cardboard was slid out, the bee landed in the water. After a quick rinse, the water was drained and the wet and befuddled bee taken to the caged plants. In subsequent experiments we decided that the washing was unnecessary as long as the bees were collected several hundred feet from flowering laurel.

The cages were checked every day or two. If the bee had died, a fresh one was put in. After all the flowers had faded, the cages were removed.

The amount of seed obtained depends on the number of flowers, the cross involved, and weather. For example, the 1972 flowering season in Connecticut was so wet that many flowers collapsed (molded) without setting any seed. A few of the plants, including some of the near red-flowered selections, have shown partial pollen sterility and low seed set. To maximize seed set from controlled crosses, avoid such infertile plants and, if possible, cage several plants together to increase cross-fertilization and seed set.

Be careful with insecticides when bees are used. If you must combat leaf rollers or other insects on the caged laurel, spray them several days before the plants flower with a short-residual spray like pyrethrin, or delay the spraying until after flowering.

Honeybees are neither effective pollinators of laurel flowers nor do they survive for more than a day away from the hive. Bumblebees, however, can survive in the cages if enough flowers are open to provide nectar and pollen for the entire flowering period of two weeks.

I have used cages successfully to obtain seeds for red-budded and white-flowered mountain laurel and for white-flowered sheep laurel. A cage of six flowering miniature plants (form *myrtifolia*) in 1976 produced enough seed to distribute to seed exchanges and individuals over a period of 18 years; and better yet, 'Elf' was selected from this cross. In the 20th year the seed was still good and producing 99 percent miniature mountain laurel—a good test of the longevity of mountain laurel seed. True-breeding seed of other types of laurel can also be produced by the same method (see next chapter).

The bee cages worked even with the interspecific cross of sheep laurel and mountain laurel. I estimate that one cage over a sheep laurel and a mountain laurel plant saved two to three workdays that would have been needed to emasculate the more than 1500 flowers by hand. In addition, the rate of seed set was probably higher from the bees than we could have achieved with hand emasculation and pollination. Bumblebees are more successful because of their light touch and because they visit each flower many times.

There is no reason why bumblebees could not be used advantageously in making controlled crosses of other ornamentals, such as azaleas and rhododendrons, especially where large quantities of hybrid seed are desired. Bee cages can be used to obtain large quantities of seed of known parentage, and it allows certain color or foliage forms to be reproduced in quantity from seed as opposed to from stem cuttings or tissue culture. The use of bee cages is not high-tech like gene splicing, but it is an efficient means to obtain bulk seed from controlled crosses without having to hand-pollinate.

Isolation of Plants to Control Crosses

Another non-intensive means to produce large quantities of seed from crosses between selected plants is to isolate those plants several hundred feet away from other flowering laurels of the same species. I planted clusters of three to eight plants each of white, deep pink, and red-budded mountain laurel. Each group was isolated from one another and from other flowering mountain laurel by at least 350 feet (110 m). Seed collected from these plants produced seedlings that were virtually as true-to-type for flower color as would be expected from hand-pollination or bee-caging. This, then, is another means of obtaining hybrid seed without having to emasculate and hand-pollinate. Since this method works with color forms of mountain laurel, it also will surely be successful with other traits, such as miniature size, that we know will breed true.

The reason such isolated clusters of plants will be intercrossed among themselves has to do with the habits of the pollinating bumblebees. The bees tend to work plants within small areas rather than moving back and forth over long distances. Some "outcrossing" with plants beyond a cluster is likely to occur, but this likelihood is small compared to intercrossing among neighboring plants.

CHAPTER 16

Inheritance of Flower and Foliage Traits, and Some Unique Unnamed Selections

[S]election is a major part of horticultural plant breeding, even when the most sophisticated modern techniques and knowledge are used. To be able to carry out effective selection it is essential for the breeder to know and to have a "feeling" for the crop being worked. The person who knows plants may "pick a winner" without having a scientific background, but the scientist who has no feeling for plants has little hope of becoming a successful plant breeder. Genetics are not synonymous with plant breeding but a knowledge of genetics is essential if a breeder is to achieve his or her full potential. (North 1979)

Data on inheritance of specific traits accumulate slowly with a plant like mountain laurel, *Kalmia latifolia*, whose generation time (the period from seed to flower) is five years. The following information is based largely on more than 1500 controlled crosses I have made since 1961. Not all of the crosses were successful. Many crosses between species produced no seed, and even crosses among mountain laurel plants occasionally failed in a given year. Reliable inheritance data have been obtained for several striking foliage and flower traits, but much remains to be learned.

At least 40 dissimilar flower, foliage, and physiological traits of mountain laurel have been identified, and many are enumerated in the list below with representative named cultivars for each trait. Of these, inheritance data are available for about 12. The full extent of natural variation is less well known in the other species, and there is also a corresponding lack of information on the inheritance of specific traits. This chapter enumerates those traits for which we have some information on heritability, followed by a brief discussion of other traits for which we lack genetic data. Chapter 3 describes in more detail those cultivars and forms exhibiting the specific traits. These following groupings are not definitive; other variations and intermediates exist.

Flower types
  Bud color
      white ('Stillwood', 'Snowdrift')
      pink ('Alpine Pink', 'Pink Surprise')
      pink tip/white base (none named)
      red ('Olympic Fire', 'Ostbo Red')
  Corolla, inside ground color
      white ('Snowdrift')
      pink ('Bridesmaid', 'Pink Charm', 'Sarah')—a broad spectrum of
        variation exists in the pinks
      candy stripe ('Peppermint')
  Pigment distribution on inside of corolla
      no spots at anther pockets ('Pristine')
      spots at anther pockets ('Silver Dollar', 'Splendens')
      interrupted band (*fuscata* forms, 'Freckles')
      continuous narrow band (*fuscata* forms, 'Star Cluster', 'Yankee
        Doodle')
      broad, continuous band virtually filling corolla (*fuscata* forms,
        'Bullseye', 'Kaleidoscope', 'Minuet')
      no pigmented circle at base of corolla ('Snowdrift')
      heavily pigmented circle at base of corolla ('Sarah', 'Silver Dollar')
      heavily pigmented circle with five radiating points, star-ring types
        ('Peppermint')
  Color of anther filaments
      clear or white (normal for the species)

      red (none named)
  Corolla shape
      normal, with five rounded to pointed lobes (most)
      multilobed, up to nine lobes instead of five (expression often variable)
      doubled or hose-in-hose ('Madeline')
      five deeply cut lobes that reflex ('Comet', 'Galaxy', 'Shooting Star')
      lobes completely cut, five petals usually straplike (*polypetala* forms)
      corolla fails to open ('Tightwad', 'Tightwad Too')
      reduced corolla ('Bettina')
      no corolla (apetala)
  Flower size
      normal (most)
      large ('Silver Dollar')
  Flower distribution
      loose inflorescence (most)
      tight ball-shaped inflorescence ('Hearts Desire', 'Pink Globe')
  Time of flowering
      normal (most)
      early (none at present)
      late ('Comet', 'Shooting Star', 'Tightwad', 'Tightwad Too')
Foliage and plant habit
  Growth habit
      normal (most)
      compact (*obtusata* forms; 'Carol' and 'Nathan Hale' are semicompact)
      miniature, small leaved (*myrtifolia* forms, 'Elf', 'Little Linda', 'Minuet')
      tiny (hybrids of miniature × willow-leaved)
      procumbens or prostrate (none named)
  Leaf shape
      normal (most)
      willow leaved (*angustata* forms, 'Willowcrest', 'Willowood')
      ovate or obtuse (*obtusata* forms)
      wavy or strongly undulate ('Raspberry Swirl')
      large ('Big Boy', 'Silver Dollar')
  Leaf color
      all green (most)
      new leaves yellow, maturing to green ('Golden Flush')

variegated (sectored, mottled, or margined with white, yellow, or
yellow-green) (none named)
Stem color of new shoots
yellow-green ('Snowdrift')
reddish bronze ('Bullseye', 'Kaleidoscope', 'Raspberry Glow',
'Sarah')
Rooting ability
Difficult (most)
Can be rooted ('Carousel', 'Nipmuck', 'Pink Charm', 'Pink Surprise')
Hardiness or tolerance
Cold ('Eloise Butler')
Heat ('Pristine', 'Willowood', possibly *Kalmia latifolia* × *K. hirsuta*
hybrids such as 'Sandy Mountain')
Drought (not determined)
Heavy soils/high pH (possibly 'Star Cluster')
Disease Resistance
Leafspot (see Chapter 3, cultivar list)
Phytophthora (unknown)

Kalmia latifolia, Mountain Laurel

White Bud and Corolla Color

Pure white flowers are rare. I have never been able to find a pure white
(anthocyanin-less) mountain laurel in the wild, although others have. In
1977 Tony Dove, formerly horticulturist with London Town Publik House
and Gardens, Edgewater, Maryland, sent material from a plant with pure
white flowers; in 1980 Clarence Towe sent cuttings from a pure white-
flowered plant found earlier by Henry Wright in the Carolina mountains;
and more recently, Walter Sutcliff of Glen Head, New York, discovered a
plant in the landscape on Long Island. I grafted cuttings of the Wright and
Dove plants, and when both selections flowered a few years later, I crossed
them. Virtually all the seedlings lacked red pigment (anthocyanin) in the
foliage and were pure white in flower. New growth on these plants was yellow-green, but the color deepened to the normal dark green as the foliage
matured. Thus, pure white-flowered plants appear to breed true, or nearly
so, when intercrossed. The few plants with pigment, less than 5 percent,
may have resulted from outcrossing (contamination). Inheritance for the

presence of red pigment is probably the same as described for sheep laurel, *Kalmia angustifolia*, discussed at the end of this chapter.

Crosses between plants with *nearly* pure white flowers, such as 'Stillwood' (Plate 80), produce all light-colored or white-flowered plants (Plate 123). A plant like 'Stillwood' is white flowered for all practical purposes, but when grown in full sun it produces an occasional fleck of light pink in the corolla and a faint pinkish ring near the corolla base. Crosses of deep pink and white result in seedlings with a variable, intermediate pink color. The purer the white parent, the less likely is pink to be strongly expressed in the offspring. Seedlings of 'Stillwood', a good white, seldom have much pink color even when the other parent is a strong pink or red budded, because white is usually dominant (Plate 124).

Pink Bud and Corolla Color

Numerous shades and patterns of pink exist, and crosses of pink parents generally produce a range of pink types. This near continuum from light to dark pink and subtle variations in the patterns of distribution are complex enough that actual inheritance patterns of specific genes have not been worked out. Apparently several major and modifying genes affect the expression of pink flower color. The results of crosses between the deepest pinks demonstrate that a true-breeding line can be developed. One of my better crosses between two deep pink-flowered plants produced 35 seedlings, all with richly colored flowers; 30 flowered in the fourth growing season, and the rest the following year. A cross of 'Pink Charm' (Plate 63) and 'Pink Globe' (Plate 60), or plants of similar flower color, would be expected to produce offspring all with deep pink flowers.

Among the crosses of deep pink-flowered and red-budded plants, a low frequency of dwarf seedlings with purplish foliage may appear. Although the seedlings are fairly vigorous at first, they grow slowly and are difficult to raise to maturity (Plate 125). I have one such compact plant that has normal-sized foliage but only grows 0.5 in (about 1 cm) a year, and after 30 years it is less than 1 ft (30 cm) tall. The flowers are deep pink. The plant would be almost impossible to propagate vegetatively because there would be so few cuttings and the stems would be extremely short.

Red Bud Color

Although no mountain laurel with a solid red corolla is known, plants with brilliant red buds can be bred true from seed (Plate 126). These red-buds are often almost iridescent, and some are so intensely pigmented that they have a purplish black hue. However, only plants grown in some sunlight fully express this trait. Red is recessive relative to both white and the normal light pink flower bud color, but pigmentation on the inside of the corolla is under separate genetic control and may be white or various shades of pink in color. Because the red-bud character is recessive, such plants breed true when intercrossed and can be mass-produced from seed using caged bees as described in Chapter 15. Lack of vigor noted in some of these red-bud crosses may be due to inbreeding that inadvertently resulted from the intense selection pressure exerted in developing these vibrantly colored plants.

As indicated, red-bud seedlings are distinctive as a class yet variable among themselves (Plates 127 and 128). Plants with lighter colored red buds may be difficult to distinguish from those with deep pink buds. 'Ostbo Red' (Plate 59), selected from seedlings grown in the northwestern United States, was the first red-bud clone to be named and vegetatively propagated. Several others have since been named for their ease of propagation and/or improved habit and foliage, including 'Sarah' (Plates 72 and 73) and 'Olympic Fire' (Plate 57). The latter is an offspring of 'Ostbo Red' with somewhat less intensely colored flower buds.

Table 16-1. *Kalmia* Traits Under Single Gene Control.

Trait	Gene symbol
Kalmia latifolia	
fuscata (banded)	*B*
star-ring	*Sr*
angustata (willow-leaved)	*w*
apetala (no corolla)	*ap*
bettina (reduced corolla)	*be*
compact	*c*
myrtifolia (miniature)	*m*
obtusata (broad leaves/compact plant)	*ob*
polypetala (petals)	*p*
shooting star (cut corolla)	*s*
Kalmia angustifolia	
anthocyanin (red pigment)	*A*

uppercase letter = dominant; lowercase = recessive

Banded (f. *fuscata*)

The banded mountain laurels form a distinct class, but considerable variation exists in the width, continuity, and hue of the band. Presence of the band itself is controlled by a single dominant gene (*B*) (see Table 16-1), but other genes control size and color modifications. One unusual plant was discovered in our plantings in 1973. All the flowers on the plant were characterized by a narrow band, except for one cluster on one branch that had flowers with an intense, broad band. I have not observed this distinct a chimera since. Instability of the banded trait has been observed, however, especially in micropropagated plants.

The genetic basis for the tremendous variation in band width has not been determined, but it appears that there are different forms (alleles) of the gene for banding that control interrupted, narrow, and broad bands as well as other modifying genes. Plants with the double dominant (*BB*) are rare. I had one plant that, whether used as pollen or seed parent, always yielded offspring with banded flowers. Unfortunately, by the time the offspring had flowered, the parent plant had been lost. Such a double-dominant banded plant is quite valuable since all the offspring will have banded flowers no matter what other plants are crossed with it. But even the common heterozygous banded plants yield high percentages of seedlings with bands: 50 percent banded when outcrossed to normal natives, and as high as 75 percent banded when crossed with another banded.

Several newly named cultivars resulting from controlled crosses combine the banding character with other traits, for instance 'Minuet' (banded/miniature) and 'Kaleidoscope', 'Keepsake', and 'Yankee Doodle' (banded/red-bud).

Star-Ring

The star-ring flower characteristic was first observed by the late Edmund Mezitt in one of his plants at Weston Nurseries in Massachusetts, and it was first pointed out to me in 1968. Star-ring is distinguished from the normal type by the greater prominence of the inner pigmented ring and especially by the five radiating points that travel up the creases of the corolla to the margin of the flower. Such plants are rare in the wild. The star-ring plant was crossed with three other plants having prominent, but not starred, inner rings. Of 45 flowering seedlings, just over 50 percent had the star-ring trait. Thus the star-ring appears to be under the control of a single dominant gene (*Sr*). Subsequent crosses confirmed this conclusion.

If the pigmentation and width of this star pattern could be enhanced, it would make a striking ornamental selection. I have intercrossed star-ring plants to obtain the homozygous dominant; a few of those plants have flowered and have a bold star-ring. One will likely be named if it proves to have good habit and be a good grower. Crosses of star-ring plants with selections having an interrupted band, such as 'Freckles' (Plate 40), have also yielded some unique and attractively pigmented flowers (Plates 129 and 130). One has been released with the name 'Peppermint' (Plate 61), and others may be named.

Stem and Foliage Color

As previously noted, mountain laurels with pure white flowers produce no red pigment, and hence the stems and leaves are green. Indeed, new flushes of growth on such plants are typically yellow-green, but they darken as they mature. Plants with deep pink and red flowers often—but not always—have purplish red stems and reddish bronze new foliage. Plants in the normal flower color range may have either red or green stems, although the red stems are generally found on plants bearing darker flowers.

Feather Petal (f. *polypetala*)

The form *polypetala* was first described in 1871 in Massachusetts (Plate 17). A great deal of variation exists in expression of the trait, from partially to fully cut corollas. Most feather petal type plants have narrow, strap-shaped petals. I have grown numerous feather petal seedlings, but as of yet none have had flowers of the apple blossom type with good vigor and plant habit. Analysis of several first- and second-generation crosses indicates that this character is controlled by a single recessive gene (*p*). The corolla types of 'Shooting Star' (partially cut; Plate 75) and 'Bettina' (reduced) are under control of genes other than feather petal (full cut), so each could be considered a different botanical form. The genes for the 'Shooting Star' flower type (*s*) and the 'Bettina' flower type (*be*) are recessive and apparently not linked. All three variant types have a tendency to lack vigor and vitality. Offspring of 'Shooting Star', bearing the parent's flower type, have also proved to be somewhat weak growers, but I keep making more crosses and growing more seedlings, and many have merit (Plates 131 and 132). 'Comet' (Plate 38) is a new release that promises to be a denser growing plant with better foliage than 'Shooting Star' and still have the same attractive flowers with deeply cut lobes.

When the trait for the reduced corolla of 'Bettina' is combined with the near-petaled character of 'Shooting Star', the result is a "ministar" flower (Plate 133). These small flowers have the added feature of lasting one or more weeks beyond the normal bloom period.

Apetala

Plants of the apetala form lack a corolla, but they have functional anthers and pistils (Plates 18 and 134). As with the polypetala types, the apetalous character is apparently under the control of a single recessive gene *(ap)*. When apetala plants are crossed with normal mountain laurel, all the offspring are normal; but when these F_1's are backcrossed to the apetala parent, the resulting seedlings segregate, with 50 percent being apetalous. To meet the small demand for apetala plants, I have found it most practical to intercross such plants and grow the seedlings, rather than trying to root cuttings or to micropropagate the plant. When both parents are apetalous, all the offspring will be as well.

Miniature, Small Leaved (f. *myrtifolia*)

In the field of horticulture, the terms used to designate plants reduced in size can be misleading, and so it is with miniature mountain laurel. We should probably call these plants semidwarf or just small-leaved mountain laurel. They generally have leaves and internodes reduced one-third to one-half normal size, although the flowers are often somewhat less reduced in size. "Miniature" as used here does not mean "midget." Under nursery conditions miniature plants can easily produce two flushes of growth in one growing season and have an annual increase in height of 5 in (12 cm) or more. My oldest and largest plant is about 5 ft (1.5 m) tall after 20 years, for an average height increase of 3 in (7.5 cm) per year. The Royal Horticultural Society Garden in Wisley, England, has a much older plant that is at least 6 ft (2 m) tall. A plant found by the late Henry Wright and planted in his garden in North Carolina grew to 8 ft (2.5 m) tall in shade. Of course, assuming it was at least 50 years old, that is an average of only 2 in (5 cm) or less per year.

Although the miniature laurel has been in cultivation since 1840, it has been largely unknown and unavailable. It is extremely rare in the wild. The most recent find was a plant discovered in 1984 by Glenn Dreyer of Connecticut College, growing near the Connecticut River in New London, Connecticut. This plant is very dwarf and slow growing. If propagated and released, it will be called Connecticut College Miniature.

Plants grown from seed obtained from open-pollinated *myrtifolia* specimens are usually normal in appearance, unless they happen to self-pollinate. If the normal-looking seedlings of *myrtifolia* parentage are inter-crossed, 25 percent of the seedlings will be miniature. The form is under the control of a single recessive gene (*m*); therefore, miniature crossed with miniature breed true for this character.

I have crossed plants of the miniature form with banded, deep pink, and red-budded plants of normal growth habit. Some second- and third-generation crosses have bloomed, and the results are exciting. We are seeing miniature plants with banded, deep pink, or red-budded flowers and, most recently, one that is similar to 'Shooting Star' with near petals (Plate 135). Heretofore, miniature plants bore only normal flower color: light pink in bud and white open, such as 'Elf' (Plate 39). Now a range of types are becoming available. After 'Elf', the first to be named was 'Minuet', a banded-miniature (Plate 54). Subsequently, 'Little Linda' (Plate 52), 'Tiddlywinks' (Plate 82), and 'Tinkerbell' (Plate 85) were named. As always, the task of identifying the best selections has not been simple, for there are numerous striking as well as subtle variations from which to choose. There are still many opportunities to produce an assortment of new plants from the miniatures that are well suited for today's landscapes

Willow-Leaved (f. *angustata*)

The form *angustata*, with strap-shaped leaves, is also rare in the wild. As with the miniatures, Henry Wright collected one in the southern Appalachians of the United States. I later named it 'Willowcrest' (Plate 86). There are only three other reports of willow-leaved laurel plants ever being found in the wild. The most recent introduction of a plant of this form is 'Willowood' from Aiken, South Carolina (Plate 87). The flowers of both selections are sometimes sterile; the styles may be misshapen (fasciated) so that seed set does not occur. Yet this is not always the case, for I have successfully crossed 'Willowcrest'. The willow-leaved trait is inherited as a single recessive gene (*w*).

One of the more interesting crosses achieved with mountain laurel was between miniature and willow-leaved plants. All the first-generation seedlings had normal growth habit. In the second generation, however, four types of plants segregated: (1) normal foliage and habit, (2) miniature, (3) willow-leaved, and (4) miniature/willow-leaved. They segregated in the ratio expected for two independent recessive genes (9:3:3:1). The miniature/

willow-leaved laurel, the one with both recessive genes and only appearing in about 1 of every 16 plants in the second generation, is of potential value for rock garden use (Plate 136). The plants are handsome and slow growing, but difficult to propagate, even though both parent types have been micropropagated. All attempts to propagate the hybrids in tissue culture have resulted in contamination—presumably because the densely packed leaves and glandular stems and leaf surfaces are difficult to free of fungi and bacteria. At Broken Arrow Nursery we have had the best success propagating these miniature/willow-leaved plants from summer cuttings placed in fog.

Compact and Obtusata

The compact mountain laurel type is distinguished by shortened internodes and closely packed leaves. Although a sparse bloomer, it makes an attractive compact plant (Plates 137 and 138). When it does bloom, the flowers are buried in the foliage. The foliage is characteristically somewhat chlorotic in appearance, especially in the fall and winter. Like the form *myrtifolia*, the compact trait is apparently under the control of a single recessive gene (*c*). I have propagated plants from seed as well as from cuttings.

The form *obtusata* can be distinguished from the compact form by the large, thick, and bluntly tipped leaves and thicker stems. It is also under the control of a single recessive gene (*ob*).

Variegated Foliage

Plants with variegated foliage have leaves and whole shoots that are sectored green and white or yellow. Several reciprocal crosses indicate that this trait is not transmitted through the pollen (male parent) but only through the egg (female parent); a factor in the cytoplasm (extra-chromosomal material) may be responsible. Other types of sectoring and chlorophyll mottling have been observed, and certainly the different kinds may be under different sorts of genetic control. The attractive and unusual foliage color pattern give these forms good ornamental potential, but to date no attractive, stable, and strongly growing plant has been introduced. One of the most interesting recent finds is a plant with a mottled pattern of variegation found by the Ammons brothers, Tuckasegee, North Carolina (Plate 139).

Albino Seedlings

Albino seedlings usually occur in about 1 percent of newly germinated seedlings. Lacking chlorophyll and the ability to manufacture food, they soon die. A much higher proportion of albino seedlings occurs among crosses of some of the banded (f. *fuscata*) plants. The percentage varies widely from 14 to 65 percent, but it is generally about 25 percent, suggesting that the cause may be a single recessive gene. The reason for the wide variation in frequency of albinos from the different crosses is not understood.

Flower Buds that Fail to Open ('Tightwad' types)

Several plants have been discovered in the wild that characteristically do not open their flower buds. The first of these named was 'Tightwad', a plant found in the southern Appalachians; another was found in Wilton, Connecticut, and I named it 'Tightwad Too' (Plates 83 and 84). In addition, Tom Dilatush found a similar plant in Virginia, Denton Shriver sent me cuttings from a plant he found in New York, and Douglas MacLise found one growing locally in Connecticut. Each of these plants seems to be the result of a single gene mutation and therefore could well be considered collectively a botanical form. Each plant is different from the other, but they all have the characteristic of flower buds that swell but do not fully open. The inheritance of the trait is unknown and may be difficult to determine because the plants are usually seed- and pollen-sterile.

Double Flowers

Hose-in-hose or double-flower forms have been virtually unknown in *Kalmia* until recently. Clarence Towe was perhaps the first to discover a native *Kalmia latifolia*, found in the southern Appalachians, with a tendency toward double blossoms, in which some of the stamens were converted to petals so that some flowers had almost double corollas. The cultivar 'Madeline' (Plate 53) appears to be the first with fully double flowers. The fertility of these plants and the inheritance of the trait in mountain laurel remains to be determined.

This past growing season at the nursery we noted two young, compact plants flowering in August (two months late), and both had double flowers much like those of 'Madeline'. It remains to be seen if they will remain double in future growing seasons. I suspect that the strange bloom time was weather related and that bloom time, at least, will revert back to normal.

Abnormal flower form in mountain laurels that bloom out of season is not unknown; sometimes unusual stresses on plants may bring out hidden genetic traits. For instance, I have seen *myrtifolia* plants (siblings of 'Elf') forced for an early-spring flower show produce petaled flowers. When the plants were returned to the landscape, they grew normal flowers in subsequent years.

Other Traits

To date there has been little plant selection or breeding designed to extend the length of the flowering season. Variations occur in the species, but the normal flowering season for *Kalmia latifolia* lasts about three weeks. It may be possible to breed or select plants that flower a week earlier with those that bloom two weeks later, and thus effectively double the length of the blooming season.

The age at which seedlings flower varies from plant to plant, as does the number of flowers. Such variation occurs among different mountain laurel crosses and sister seedlings as well. Often the most precocious seedlings are also those that continue to produce flowers in successive years. Thus, breeding plants that flower at a young age and flower profusely each year should not be difficult. 'Bridesmaid' and possibly 'Minuet' are of this sort.

Other traits for which we know little about their genetic control include plants with a weeping or prostrate habit; those with ovate leaves or leaves with a notch rather than a point at the apex; remontant plants (that is, reblooming late in the season); or plants that produce multiple branches from a growing point and thus are dense and require little pruning. Additional foliage and habit characteristics can be identified, such as ones exhibiting slow growth, thick stems, and leaves that are thick and wavy. Inheritance patterns of physiological traits, such as tolerance of cold, heat, and drought, ease-of-rooting, and resistance to diseases and insects, all merit more attention for purposes of breeding. Thus there are an abundance of tasks for the stout-hearted to undertake.

Many of the named cultivars have not been used in controlled crosses, but I have had considerable experience with a few. 'Carol', 'Nathan Hale', and 'Sharon Rose' have been excellent parents when crossed with one another or with other red-budded or deep pink-flowering plants. The offspring, in addition to having red or deep pink flowers, typically have attractive foliage and a dense growth habit as well. 'Sarah' and 'Sunset' can be good parents, but a portion of their offspring often have dusty gray foliage instead of being dark glossy green. When 'Sunset' was crossed with 'Nathan Hale', approximately one-fourth of the seedling offspring had crinkled, small, unattractive foliage (Plate 140).

Kalmia angustifolia, Sheep Laurel

White Flowers

Sheep laurel plants bearing white flowers lack the red pigment anthocyanin. As young seedlings, they can be recognized by the lack of red pigment in the stems and leaves. White-flowered sheep laurel plants are rare in the wild, but they are not difficult to reproduce from seed. The presence of color is governed by a single dominant gene (A); hence, white-flowered plants are homozygous recessives (aa). When two white-flowered forms are intercrossed, all the seedlings are white-flowered. I have demonstrated that the bee-caging technique described in Chapter 15 can be readily used to mass-produce seed of white-flowered sheep laurel.

One of the interesting findings in studies of the white-flowered forms is that although white-flowered plants are seldom found in nature, the recessive gene is present in a high frequency in some populations. Among 300 flowering, colored plants in Madison, Connecticut, it was determined that approximately 24 percent carried a single recessive gene for white (Jaynes 1971b). While no white-flowered plants were found in the wild, they did occur among seedlings grown from collected native seed.

Future Breeding

I have indicated many goals for the improvement of mountain laurel as well as possibilities within and between the other species. Combining unique traits, such as those listed earlier in this chapter, could lead to many new attractive cultivars. The following are some combinations already achieved from controlled breeding:

Cross	Example
Red-bud/banded	'Kaleidoscope'
Banded/miniature	'Minuet'
Deep pink/miniature	'Tinkerbell'
Red-bud/miniature	'Little Linda'
'Shooting Star' type/banded	'Galaxy'
Willow-leaved/miniature	none named

Many other combinations await the efforts of plant breeders. Chuck Molnar, an amateur plant breeder from Connecticut, suggests combining the 'Shooting Star' flower form with each of the following: willow leaf, compact, red flower, deep pink flower, and double flower. Chuck, incidentally, made the original first-generation cross of 'Shooting Star' and banded. There are still additional possibilities in combining unique and attractive flower types on plants with miniature or compact foliage, such as using the 'Peppermint' pattern of pigmentation or the double-flowered form of 'Madeline'.

The discovery and development of many new cultivars in the last 20 years certainly suggests that there are some surprises and unique cultivars to come in the years ahead. The domestication of *Kalmia* will continue. Do join in.

Research Needs

The following are some of the more obvious areas where additional information and research are needed if we are to continue making progress in breeding and domesticating *Kalmia*, especially *Kalmia latifolia*.

New cultivars. Continue the quest for the perfect plant: stunning flower, lush foliage, dense plant growth, ease of propagation and growing, and wide adaptability to garden sites and climates. Develop cultivars that bloom when young and annually thereafter.

Breed and select plants in the more extreme southern or northern limits of the native range as well as at other locations where *Kalmia* is marginally adapted. Screening large seedling populations in these areas is a good means to obtain locally adapted selections.

Define/determine for existing cultivars: heat and cold tolerance, shade tolerance, annual blooming, leafspot resistance, deer resistance, and other traits. Obtaining this information will not be easy; in some cases it might be obtained in the laboratory. For instance, leaf and twig samples of cultivars can be subjected to freezing temperatures in a laboratory freezer, thereby determining the critical low temperature that causes injury—Paul Cappiello is working on this with his students at the University of Maine, Orono. The same procedure may be attempted for roots as well.

Screen mountain laurel cultivars and seedling populations for tolerance of heavy soil and/or high pH. Could this be done efficiently in the laboratory in sterile culture?

Determine inheritance of many of the traits mentioned above as well as resistance to specific pests and diseases.

Flower color. With colorimeters and spectrophotometers to read and analyze color, as well as the analytical means to determine the cell chemistry responsible for color, much could be done to define the flower color of current cultivars and suggest means for breeding additional variations.

Obtain the Cuban laurel, *Kalmia ericoides*. Test the seed to see if it has special dormancy requirements similar to those of *K. hirsuta*. Determine if *K. ericoides* will cross with the other *Kalmia* species and, if it is compatible, then develop hybrid selections for warm climates.

Determine why the first-generation crosses between *Kalmia* species are so variable. Common wisdom suggests that they should be uniform.

Grow more seedlings from hybrid plants derived from *Kalmia latifolia* and *K. hirsuta* to develop dense-growing, small-leaved plants for warm climates.

Attempt intergeneric crosses between the several *Kalmia* species and both *Loiseleuria procumbens* and *Leiophyllum buxifolium*. Taxonomic studies suggest a close relationship among these three genera.

Polyploid breeding. If vigorous polyploids of the *Kalmia* species can be produced, they may be a means of successfully completing many of the interspecific crosses and thus increase the gene pool for developing a wider range of garden plants. Polyploid breeding within species could also be useful in producing plants with heavy foliage and large, long-lasting flowers.

Chromosome counts or other tests need to be developed to identify putative interspecific or intergeneric hybrids and polyploid plants, such as 'No Suchianum' and 'Silver Dollar'.

Plant growth regulators (PGR). Continue efforts to determine how best to use these compounds to induce early flowering and to improve growth habit, so as to avoid mechanical pruning in commercial production.

Induce female sterility (temporarily) to prevent seed capsule formation and to obtain more vegetative growth. Ethephon has worked on *Pyrus* and *Liquidambar* and shows promise with *Kalmia latifolia*.

Develop genetically seed-sterile plants for better vegetative growth, annual blooming, and no seed capsules, which are considered unsightly by some; chemical sprays (see preceding) would then not be required.

What is the seasonal periodicity of mountain laurel root growth? Does it come in "flushes," like shoot growth? Such information could be important in the timing of potting and transplanting.

Develop fast-growing mountain laurel for cooler climates, where it is hardy but grows slowly. Growth can be enhanced by raising the temperature, such as growing the plants in enclosed, polyethylene-covered hoop houses. What are the most practical means to maximize growth in regions with a cool growing season?

Rooting cuttings. Improve techniques for reliable rooting of *Kalmia latifolia* and select more cultivars for the ease of rooting cuttings.

Forcing mountain laurel. Are there ways to shorten the dormancy requirement to enhance growth of greenhouse-grown plants in winter, to speed the forcing of flowers on pot plants as well as on plants for early-spring flower shows?

Day-length effect. Are long days needed, or at least helpful, to keep young mountain laurel plants growing in the winter?

Mycorrhiza. Much needs to be learned about these root-fungal associates and their necessity and management in growing laurel, as well as other ericaceous plants.

Why do some soils with apparently proper drainage, acidity, and nutrients not support good growth of mountain laurel?

Burls/lignotubers. Is there a real difference in survival of mountain laurel seedlings (with lignotubers) compared to rooted cuttings and micro-propagated plants (no lignotubers) when severely stressed?

Learn how to educate homeowners, caretakers, and others to grow a greater variety of plants in ways that feature the plants' natural appearance and growth habits, with less reliance on heavy shearing that produces stiff, unchanging geometric forms.

Gardens with Kalmia Collections

Open to the public; appointments may be necessary.

United States

Connecticut

Bartlett Arboretum of the University of Connecticut, Stamford
Broken Arrow Nursery, Hamden
Connecticut College Arboretum, New London
Highstead Arboretum, Redding
University of Connecticut, Plant Science Department, Storrs

Delaware

Mt. Cuba Center for the Study of Piedmont Flora, Greenville

Georgia

Callaway Gardens, Pine Mountain

Maine

University of Maine, Plant, Soil and Environmental Sciences, Orono

Massachusetts

Arnold Arboretum of Harvard University, Jamaica Plain

Garden in the Woods, New England Wildflower Society, Framingham

New Jersey

Skylands Association, New Jersey State Botanical Garden, Ringwood

New York

Brooklyn Botanic Garden, Brooklyn
Planting Fields Arboretum, Oyster Bay, Long Island

North Carolina

Mountain Horticultural Crops Research and Extension Center, North
   Carolina State University, Fletcher
North Carolina Arboretum of the University of North Carolina, Asheville
North Carolina Botanical Garden, University of North Carolina, Chapel Hill
Susie Harwood Garden, University of North Carolina, Charlotte

Ohio

Holden Arboretum, Mentor

Washington, D.C.

United States National Arboretum

United Kingdom and Europe

Kalmthout Arboretum, Kalmthout, Belgium
Harold Hillier Gardens and Arboretum, Hampshire, England
Royal Horticultural Society Gardens (Wisley), Woking, Surrey, England
Secretts Garden Centre, National Collection of *Kalmia latifolia*, Surrey,
   England
Sheffield Park, Uckfield, Sussex, England
Glendoick Gardens, National Collection of *Kalmia*, Glendoick, Perth,
   Scotland
Royal Botanic Garden, Edinburgh, Scotland

Laboratories, Mail-Order Nurseries, and Growers of Kalmia

This is not intended to be an all-inclusive list of *Kalmia* sources. It is more of a starting point for contacts with firms, laboratories, and individuals who have had extensive experience with *Kalmia*. Whether the outfit is involved in micropropagation, mail-order sales, retail sales, or wholesale is indicated for each.

Apalachee Nursery
1333 Kimsey Dairy Road
Turtletown, Tennessee 37391, U.S.A.
Keith Kilpatrick
(615) 496 7246
wholesale

Bioplant in Vitro SA
Rue Eysden Mines 43A
B-6698 Brand-Halleux, Belgium
micropropagation laboratory

Briggs Nursery
4407 Henderson Boulevard
Olympia, Washington 98502, U.S.A.
Joe Blue
(206) 352 5405
micropropagation laboratory;
    wholesale

Brown's Kalmia and Azalea Nursery
8527 Semiahmoo Drive
Blaine, Washington 98230, U.S.A.
Ed and Barbara Brown
(206) 371 2489
mail order; retail

Broken Arrow Nursery
13 Broken Arrow Road
Hamden, Connecticut 06518, U.S.A.
Dick Jaynes and Andy Brand
(203) 288 1026
mail order; retail

Buds & Blooms Nursery
7501 U.S. Highway 29 North
Brown Summit, North Carolina
    27214, U.S.A.
Doug Torn
(919) 656 7819
wholesale

Clark's Greenhouse and Nursery
344 Rattlesnake Ledge Road
Salem, Connecticut 06420, U.S.A.
Hendrick Clark
(203) 859 3330
wholesale

Clay's Nurseries & Laboratories
3666 224th Street
Langley, British Columbia V2Z 2G7,
    Canada
Les Clay
(604) 530 5188
micropropagation laboratory;
    wholesale

Cummins Garden
22 Robertsville Road
Marlboro, New Jersey 07746, U.S.A.
Elizabeth Cummins
(908) 536 2591
mail order; retail

Dowling Road Tree Farm
P. O. Box 878
Sandy, Oregon 97055, U.S.A.
Nancy Stachosky
(503) 668 5012
wholesale

Duncan and Davies Nurseries
P. O. Box 340, Waitara Road
New Plymouth, New Zealand
(064 0 6) 754 8789
wholesale

Elliotts Wholesale Nursery
234 Withells Road
Christchurch 4, New Zealand
Jeff Elliott
(064) 584 210
wholesale

Fairweather Gardens
P. O. Box
Greenwich, New Jersey 08323, U.S.A.
Robert Hoffman and Robert Popham
(609) 451 6261
mail order

Firma Esveld
Rijneveld 72
2771 XS, Boskoop, The Netherlands
D. M. van Gelderen
(031) 1727 13289
wholesale

Flora Lan
7940 N.W. Kansas City Road
Forest Grove, Oregon 97116, U.S.A.
Larry Lauder
(503) 357 8386
wholesale

Forest Farm
990 Tetherow Road
Williams, Oregon 97544, U.S.A.
Ray and Peg Prag
(541) 846 6963
mail order

Glendoick Gardens
Glencarse, Perth, Scotland PH2 7NS
Peter A. Cox
(073 886) 205
mail order; retail

Greer Gardens
1280 Goodpasture Island Road
Eugene, Oregon 97401, U.S.A.
Harold Greer
(541) 686 8266
mail order

Heritage Laurels
13313 Fillmore Street
West Olive, Michigan 49460, U.S.A.
Jeri and Wayne Kiel
(616) 842 4407
retail; wholesale

Herman Losely & Son Nursery
3410 Shepard Road
Perry, Ohio 44081, U.S.A.
Edward H. Losely
(216) 259 2725
micropropagation laboratory;
    wholesale

Historylands Nursery
Route 1, Box 485
Montross, Virginia 22520, U.S.A.
Tom Huggins
(804) 493 8442
wholesale

Knight Hollow Nursery
3333 Adam Road
Madison, Wisconsin 53705, U.S.A.
Deborah McCown
(608) 831 5570
micropropagation laboratory

Lakedale Nurseries
P. O. Box 247
Sicklerville, New Jersey 08081, U.S.A.
Jim Gianaris
(609) 768 0400
wholesale

Laurel Springs Nursery
401 Regal Street
Hendersonville, North Carolina
    28792, U.S.A.
Wes Burlingame
(704) 891 1264
retail; wholesale

Liss Forest Nursery
Petersfield Road
Greatham, Hampshire, England
    GU33 6EX
Peter Catt
(044 1 4) 207 620
wholesale

Medford Nursery
Eayrestown Red Lion Road
Medford, New Jersey 08055, U.S.A.
Ernie Raraha
(609) 267 8100
wholesale

North Cascade Nursery
8895 Weidkamp Road
Lynden, Washington 98264, U.S.A.
Al Reimer
(206) 354 6592
wholesale

Oakover Nurseries
Calchill, The Lecon, Charing
Ashford, Kent, England GU33 6BS
Tom Wood
(44 1 233) 713 016
wholesale

Plane View Nursery
770 Wapping Road
Portsmouth, Rhode Island 02871,
    U.S.A.
Michael Medeiros
(401) 849 2464
micropropagation laboratory;
    wholesale

Plants Unlimited
State Route 798, Route 3, Box 350
Afton, Virginia 22920, U.S.A.
Cheryl Borgman
(703) 456 6554
micropropagation laboratory

Prides Corner Farms
Waterman Road
Lebanon, Connecticut 06249, U.S.A.
Mark Sellew
(203) 642 7535
micropropagation laboratory;
    wholesale

Roslyn Nursery
211 Burrs Lane
Dix Hills, New York 11746, U.S.A.
Phillip Waldman
(516) 643 9347
mail order; retail

Saunders Brothers Nursery
Route 1, Box 26-A
Piney River, Virginia 22964, U.S.A.
Tom Saunders
(804) 277 5455
wholesale

Summer Hill Nursery
888 Summer Hill Road
Madison, Connecticut 06443, U.S.A.
Mike Johnson
(203) 421 3055
wholesale

Stoneboro Nurseries
88 Barbour Road
Stoneboro, Pennsylvania 16153,
    U.S.A.
William Barbour
(814) 786 7991
micropropagation laboratory;
    wholesale

Tom Dodd Nurseries
P. O. Drawer 45, U.S. Highway 98
Semmes, Alabama 36575, U.S.A.
Tom Dodd, Jr.
(205) 649 1960
wholesale

Transplant Nursery
1586 Parkertown Road
Lavonia, Georgia 30553, U.S.A.
Jeff Beasley
(706) 356 8947
mail order; retail; wholesale

Vineland Nurseries
Box 98, Martin Road
Vineland Station, Ontario L0R 2E0,
    Canada
Jim Lounsbery
retail

Wales Nurseries
Peck Road, P. O. Box 158
Wales, Massachusetts 01081, U.S.A.
Jeffrey Nissenbaum
(413) 267 4706
micropropagation laboratory;
    wholesale

Wayside Gardens
Hodges, South Carolina 29695, U.S.A.
(800) 845 1124
mail order

Weston Nurseries
East Main Street (Route 135)
Hopkinton, Massachusetts 01748,
    U.S.A.
Wayne Mezitt
(508) 435 3414
retail; wholesale

Woodland Barn Nurseries
Lichfield Road, Abbots Bromley
Rugeley, Staffordshire, England
    W515 3DN
A. and S. Slater
micropropagation laboratory

Woodlanders
1128 Colleton Avenue
Aiken, South Carolina 29801, U.S.A.
Robert Mackintosh
(803) 648 7522
mail order

Wright's Nursery
1285 S.E. Township Road
Canby, Oregon 97013, U.S.A.
Art Wright
(503) 266 8895
wholesale

Bibliography

Alpha. 1882. Garden flora. *The Garden* 52: 6–7.

American Forest Association. 1986. National register of big trees. *American Forests* 92(4): 21–52.

Anderson, W. C. 1975. Propagation of rhododendrons by tissue culture: Part 1. Development of a culture medium for multiplication of shoots. *International Plant Propagators' Society, Proceedings* 25: 129–135.

Barrett, L. I. 1941. War revives an old industry. *American Forests* 47: 503–506, 543.

Barton, B. S. 1802. Some accounts of the poisonous and injurious honey of North America. *Transactions of the American Philosophical Society* 5: 51–70.

Bassett, W. F. 1893. A variegated-leaved *Kalmia*. *Gardening* 1: 222.

Beal, W. J. 1867. Agency of insects in fertilizing plants. *American Naturalist* 1: 254–260.

Bean, W. J. 1897. Trees and shrubs. *Gardens* 52: 77–78.

Benson, A. B. 1937. *Peter Kalm's Travels in North America*. Wilson-Erickson, New York.

Bent, E. N. 1994. Clonal confusion. *American Nurseryman* 179(5): 52–55.

Bir, R. E. 1992. *Growing and Propagating Showy Native Woody Plants*. University of North Carolina Press, Chapel Hill and London.

Bir, R. E., and T. E. Bilderback. 1989. Growing better mountain laurel in containers. *International Plant Propagators' Society, Proceedings* 39: 442–447.

Bir, R. E., and J. Conner. 1991. *Kalmia* revisited. *American Nurseryman* (July 1): 56–63.

Bir, R. E., J. E. Shelton, V. P. Bonaminio, J. R. Baker, and R. K. Jones. 1981. Growing native ornamentals from cutbacks in western North Carolina. In *NC*

Nursery Crops Production Manual, edited by V. P. Bonaminio. North Carolina Agricultural Extension Service, Raleigh.

Botacchi, A. C. 1980. Soil aeration—don't guess. *Connecticut Greenhouse Newsletter* 101(September): 1–3.

Brand, M. 1996. Keeping ericaceous plants growing throughout the winter. *Yankee Nursery Quarterly* 5: 16–19.

Britton, E. G. 1913. Wild plants needing protection. *Journal of the New York Botanic Garden* 14: 121–123.

Burke, J. W., R. W. Doskotch, C. Ni, and J. Clardy. 1989. Kalmanol, a pharmacologically active diterpenoid with a new ring skeleton from *Kalmia latifolia* L. *Journal of the American Chemical Society* 111: 5831–5833.

Buttrick, P. L. 1924. Connecticut's state flower, the mountain laurel, a forest plant. *Marsh Botanic Garden Publication* (Yale University) 1: 1–28.

Clawson, A. B. 1933. Alpine kalmia (*Kalmia microphylla*) as a stock-poisoning plant. *U.S. Department of Agriculture Technical Bulletin* 391: 1–9.

Clayberg, C. D., and R. A. Jaynes (eds.). 1974. *Breeding Plants for Home and Garden: A Handbook* (Brooklyn Botanic Garden Record) 30: 1–76.

Copeland, H. F. 1943. A study, anatomical and taxonomic, of the genera of Rhododendroideae. *American Midland Naturalist* 30: 533–625.

Cowles, R. S. 1995. Black vine weevil biology and management. *Journal, American Rhododendron Society* 49: 83–85, 94–97.

Coyier, D. L., and M. K. Roane (eds.). 1986. *Compendium of Rhododendron and Azalea Diseases*. APS Press, St. Paul, MN.

Crane, M. B., and W. J. C. Lawrence. 1938. *The Genetics of Garden Plants*. 2nd ed. Macmillan, London.

Crawford, A. C. 1908. Mountain laurel, a poisonous plant. *U.S. Department of Agriculture Bureau of Plant Industry Bulletin* 121: 21–35.

Davis, D. D., and J. Mix. 1993. Fungi associated with leafspots of mountain laurel (*Kalmia latifolia* L.). Results of a survey. *Plant Disease Quarterly* 14: 27–29.

Davis, L. D. 1957. Flowering and alternate bearing. *Proceedings of the American Society of Horticultural Science* 70: 545–556.

Del Tredici, P. 1992. Seedlings versus tissue-cultured *Kalmia latifolia*: The case of the missing burl. *International Plant Propagators' Society, Proceedings* 42: 476–482.

Dudley, T. R. 1967. Ornamental mountain laurel and a new cultivar: *Kalmia latifolia* 'Bettina'. *American Horticultural Magazine* 46: 245–248.

Ebinger, J. E. 1974. A systematic study of the genus *Kalmia* (Ericaceae). *Rhodora* 76: 315–398.

Eddison, S. 1990. *A Patchwork Garden.* Harper & Row, New York.

———. 1992. *A Passion for Daylilies.* Henry Holt, New York.

El-Naggar, S. F., R. W. Doskotch, T. M. O'Dell, and L. Girard. 1980. Antifeedant diterpenes for the gypsy moth larvae from *Kalmia latifolia*: Isolation and characterization of ten grayanoids. *Journal of Natural Products* 43: 617–631.

Flemer, W., III. 1949. The propagation of *Kalmia latifolia* from seed. *Bulletin of the Torrey Botanical Club* 76: 12–16.

Forbes, E. B., and S. I. Bechdel. 1930. Mountain laurel and rhododendron as food for the white-tailed deer. *Ecology* 12: 323–333.

Fordham, A. J. 1979. *Kalmia latifolia* selections and their propagation. *Journal, American Rhododendron Society* 33: 30–33.

Galle, F. C. 1987. *Azaleas.* 2nd ed. Timber Press, Portland, OR.

Gibbs, R. D. 1974. *Chemotaxonomy of Flowering Plants.* McGill-Queen's University Press, Montreal.

Gray, A. 1877. Large trunks of *Kalmia latifolia. American Naturalist* 11: 175.

Hardin, J. W., and J. M. Arena. 1969. *Human Poisoning from Native and Cultivated Plants.* Duke University Press, Durham, NC.

Hawes, L., and D. Kier. 1993. *Irrigation Design: Design Flow and Operating Pressure.* Hydro-Tech, Vista, CA.

Heichel, G. H., and R. A. Jaynes. 1974. Stimulating emergence and growth of *Kalmia* genotypes with CO_2. *HortScience* 9: 60–62.

Holmes, E. M. 1884. Medical plants used by the Cree Indians, Hudson's Bay territory. *American Journal of Pharmacy* 56: 617–621.

Holmes, M. L. 1956. *Kalmia*, the American laurels. *Baileya* 4: 89–94.

Howes, F. N. 1949. Sources of poisonous honey. *Kew Bulletin* 167–171.

Hummel, R. L., C. R. Johnson, and O. M. Lindstrom. 1990. Root and shoot growth response of three container-grown *Kalmia latifolia* L. cultivars at two locations to growing medium and nirogen form. *Journal of Environmental Horticulture* 8: 10–13.

Huse, R. D., and K. L. Kelly. 1984. A contribution toward standardization of color names in horticulture. *American Rhododendron Society Publications Committee.*

Jaynes, R. A. 1968a. Interspecific crosses in *Kalmia. American Journal of Botany* 55: 1120–1125.

———. 1968b. Self incompatibility and inbreeding depression in three laurel (*Kalmia*) species. *Proceedings of the American Society of Horticultural Science* 93: 618–622.

———. 1968c. Breaking seed dormancy of *Kalmia hirsuta* with high temperatures. *Ecology* 49: 1196–1198.

————. 1969. Chromosome counts of *Kalmia* species and revaluation of *K. polifolia* var. *microphylla. Rhodora* 71: 280–284.

————. 1971a. Laurel selections from seed: True-breeding red-budded mountain laurel. *Connecticut Agricultural Experiment Station*, Circular 240.

————. 1971b. A gene controlling pigmentation in sheep laurel. *Journal of Heredity* 62: 201–203.

————. 1971c. Seed germination of six *Kalmia* species. *Journal of the American Society of Horticultural Science* 96: 668–672.

————. 1971d. The kalmias and their hybrids. *Quarterly Bulletin of the American Rhododendron Society* 25: 160–164.

————. 1971e. The selection and propagation of improved *Kalmia latifolia* cultivars. *International Plant Propagators' Society, Proceedings* 21: 366–374.

————. 1974. Inheritance of flower and foliage characteristics in mountain laurel (*Kalmia latifolia* L.). *Journal of the American Society of Horticultural Science* 99: 209–211.

————. 1975. *The Laurel Book: Rediscovery of the North American Laurels.* Hafner Press, New York.

————. 1976. Mountain laurel selections and methods of propagating them. *International Plant Propagators' Society, Proceedings* 26: 233–236.

————. 1981. Inheritance of ornamental traits in mountain laurel, *Kalmia latifolia* L. *Journal of Heredity* 72: 245–248.

————. 1982a. Germination of *Kalmia* seed after storage of up to 20 years. *HortScience* 17: 203.

————. 1982b. New mountain laurel selections and their propagation. *International Plant Propagators' Society, Proceedings* 32: 431–434.

————. 1983. Checklist of cultivated laurel, *Kalmia* spp. *Bulletin, American Association of Botanic Gardens and Arboreta* 17: 99–106.

————. 1988. *Kalmia: The Laurel Book II.* Timber Press, Portland, OR.

Johnson, E. A., and J. L. Kovner. 1956. Effects on stream flow of cutting a forest understory. *Forest Science* 2: 82–91.

Kingsbury, J. M. 1964. *Poisonous Plants of the United States and Canada.* Prentice-Hall, Englewood Cliffs, NJ.

Kinsey, J. 1985. Propagating and producing *Kalmia latifolia* conventionally. *International Plant Propagators' Society, Proceedings* 35: 626–629.

Kurmes, E. A. 1961. *The Ecology of Mountain Laurel in Southern New England.* Ph.D. dissertation, Yale University.

Kyte, L., and J. Kleyn. 1996. *Plants from Test Tubes: An Introduction to Micropropagation.* 3rd ed. Timber Press, Portland, OR.

Lacy, A. 1986. *Farther Afield*. Farrar, Straus & Giroux, New York.

Lampe, K. F. 1988. Rhododendron, mountain laurel, and mad honey. *JAMA* 259: 2009.

Leach, D. G. 1961. *Rhododendrons of the World and How to Grow Them*. Charles Scribner's Sons, New York.

Lipp, L. F. 1973. Propagating broad-leafed evergreens. In *Handbook on Broad Leaved Evergreens* (Brooklyn Botanic Garden Record) 29: 78–80.

Lloyd, G., and B. McCown. 1980. Commercially-feasible micropropagation of mountain laurel, *Kalmia latifolia*, by use of shoot tip culture. *International Plant Propagators' Society, Proceedings* 30: 421–427.

Lovell, J. H., and H. B. Lovell. 1934. The pollination of *Kalmia angustifolia*. *Rhodora* 36: 25–28.

Macdonald, B. 1986. *Practical Woody Plant Propagation for Nursery Growers*. Timber Press, Portland, OR.

Malck, A. A., F. A. Blazich, S. L. Warren, and J. E. Shelton. 1989. Influence of light and temperature on seed germination of mountain laurel. *Journal of Environmental Horticulture* 7: 161–162.

————. 1992. Initial growth of seedlings of mountain laurel as influenced by day/night temperature. *Journal of the American Society of Horticultural Science* 117: 736–739.

Mancini, S. D., and J. M. Edwards. 1979. Cytotoxic principles from the sap of *Kalmia latifolia*. *Journal of Natural Products* 42: 483–488.

Marsh, C. D., and A. B. Clawson. 1930. Mountain laurel (*Kalmia latifolia*) and sheep laurel (*Kalmia angustifolia*) as stock-poisoning plants. *U.S. Department of Agriculture Technical Bulletin* 219: 1–22.

Mastalerz, J. W. 1968. CO_2 enrichment for a small greenhouse. *Flower and Garden* November: 27, 28, 47.

Meyer, M. 1986. Semiportable laminar flow hood for tissue culture and microscope use for research and teaching. *HortScience* 21: 1064–1065.

de Montigny, L. E., and G. F. Weetman. 1990. The effects of ericaceous plants on forest productivity. In *The Silvics and Ecology of Boreal Spruces*, edited by B. D. Titus, M. B. Lavigne, P. F. Newton, and W. J. Meades. IUFRO Working Party S1.05-12, Symposium Proceedings, Newfoundland, 12–17 August. *Canadian Forest Service Information Report* N-X-271.

Moore, J. N., and J. Janick, eds. 1975. *Advances in Fruit Breeding*. Purdue University Press, West Lafayette, IN.

Muensche, W. C. 1957. *Poisonous Plants of the United States*. Rev. ed. Macmillan, New York.

Murashige, T., and F. Skoog. 1962. A revised medium for rapid growth and bio-assays with tobacco tissue cultures. *Physiologia Plantarum* 15: 473–497.

Nichols, L. P. 1955. Diseases of ornamental shrubs and vines. *Pennsylvania State University College Agricultural Extension Service*, Circular 429.

North, C. 1979. *Plant Breeding and Genetics in Horticulture*. J. Wiley & Sons, New York.

Peterson, E. B. 1965. Inhibition of black spruce primary roots by a water-soluble substance in *Kalmia angustifolia*. *Forest Science* 11: 473–479.

Pierce, L. J. 1974. An unusual intergeneric cross. *Quarterly Bulletin of the American Rhododendron Society* 28(1): 45.

Pirone, P. P. 1970. *Diseases and Pests of Ornamental Plants*. 4th ed. Ronald, New York.

Pritchard, W. R. 1956. Laurel (*Kalmia angustifolia*) poisoning of sheep. *North American Veterinarian* 37: 461–462.

Rand, E. S. 1876. *The Rhododendron and "American Plants"*. Hurd and Houghton, New York.

Rathcke, B. J., and L. A. Real. 1993. Autogamy and inbreeding depression in mountain laurel, *Kalmia latifolia* (Ericaceae). *American Journal of Botany* 80: 143–146.

Real, L. A., and B. J. Rathcke. 1991. Individual variation in nectar production and its effect on fitness in *Kalmia latifolia*. *Ecology* 72: 149–155.

Rehder, A. 1910. Notes on the forms of *Kalmia latifolia*. *Rhodora* 12: 1–3.

Sabuco, J. J. 1990. Exploring the native range. *American Nurseryman* (November 15): 28–37.

Skroch, W. A., S. L. Warren, and L. B. Gallitano. 1991. Herbicide tolerance of selected ericaceous species. *Journal of Environmental Horticulture* 9: 196–198.

Southall, R. M., and J. W. Hardin. 1974. A taxonomic revision of *Kalmia* (Ericaceae). *Journal of the Elisha Mitchell Scientific Society* 90: 1–23.

Sprague, E. 1871. *The Rhododendron and American Plants*. Little, Brown, Boston.

Stein, S. 1993. *Noah's Garden*. Houghton Mifflin, Boston.

Tallent, W. H., M. L. Riethof, and E. C. Horning. 1957. Studies on the occurrence and structure of acetylandromedol (andromedotoxin). *Journal of the American Chemical Society* 79: 4548–4554.

Ticknor, R. L. 1987. Weed control around rhododendrons. *Journal, American Rhododendron Society* 41: 10–14.

Titus, B. D., S. S. Sidhu, and A. U. Mallik. 1995. A summary of some studies on *Kalmia angustifolia* L.: A problem species in Newfoundland forestry. *Canadian Forest Service Information Report* N-X-296.

Towe, L. C. 1985. The garden of Henry Wright. *Journal, American Rhododendron Society* 39: 125.

Trehane, P. 1995. *International Code of Nomenclature for Cultivated Plants—1995.* Quarterjack Publishing, Wimborne, UK.

Trumpy, J. R. 1893. Propagating kalmias. *Gardening* 1: 222.

Valchar, G. 1993. *My Connecticut Garden.* Timber Press, Portland, OR.

Viehmeyer, G. 1974. Taming the wild ones. In *Breeding Plants for Home and Garden: A Handbook* (Brooklyn Botanic Garden Record) 30: 46–49.

Wahlenberg, W. G., and W. T. Doolittle. 1950. Reclaiming Appalachian brush lands for economic forest production. *Journal of Forestry* 48: 170–174.

Waud, R. A. 1940. The action of *Kalmia angustifolia* (lambkill). *Journal of Pharmacology and Experimental Therapeutics* 69: 103–111.

Williams, R. F., and T. E. Bilderback. 1980. Factors affecting rooting of *Rhododendron maximum* and *Kalmia latifolia* stem cuttings. *HortScience* 15: 827–828.

———. 1981. Comparison of intermittent mist and polyethylene tent propagation of *Kalmia latifolia* L. stem cuttings. *The Plant Propagator* 27: 4–6.

Wood, C. E., Jr. 1961. The genera of Ericaceae in the southeastern United States. *Journal of the Arnold Arboretum* 42: 10–80.

Wood, H. B., V. L. Stromberg, J. C. Keresztesy, and E. C. Horning. 1954. Andromedotoxin: a potent hypotensive agent from *Rhododendron maximum.* *Journal of the American Chemical Society* 76: 5689–5692.

Index